Handbook for Social Skill Development with Children and Adolescents: From Research to Practice

Richard Bulkeley PhD

Handbook for Social Skill Development with Children and Adolescents: From Research to Practice

Copyright

Richard Bulkeley

9 St Botolph Lane

Orton Longueville

Peterborough PE2 7DG

United Kingdom

Website: rbulkeley.co.uk

ISBN 9781980559924

Handbook for Social Skill Development with Children and Adolescents: From Research to Practice

Dr Richard Bulkeley, Clinical Psychologist

About the author

The author has in-depth experience of employing social skills approaches with both younger children and adolescents. This is supported by four decades of experience as a psychologist working with this age group, both in clinical and educational settings. His doctoral thesis was on social skills training with children and adolescents and he has contributed to the following two papers on his research in this area:

- Bulkeley R & Cramer D (1990). Social skills training with young adolescents. *Journal of Youth and Adolescence*, 19 (5) 451–463.

- Bulkeley R & Cramer D (1994). Social skills training with young adolescents: group and individual approaches in a school setting. *Journal of Adolescence*, 17, 521–531.

Why this book is important

There is an increasing demand for comprehensive, evidence-based, skill-focused interventions with children and young people in schools, statutory and voluntary social agencies and child mental health services. Equally there is a need to review the importance of social skills input in mainstream education. This book provides evidence-based coverage of the relevance of social skills input for a range of client groups, and considers educational issues.

Spence (2003) stated: "*Social Skills Training has become a widely-accepted component of multi-method approaches to the treatment of many emotional, behavioural and developmental disorders*" (p 84). Assistance with the development of social skills is crucial for many areas in which children and young people may be challenged or vulnerable, for example Attention Deficit Hyperactivity Disorder, Autistic Spectrum Disorder, Conduct Disorder, Social Anxiety, difficulty with peers, and offending behaviour. The book provides evidence-based coverage of the relevance of social skills input for a range of client groups, and recognises the need to review the importance of social skills input within mainstream education.

Who will be interested in this book

The book will be valuable to psychologists (including academics, qualified clinicians, trainees and assistants), and will be relevant for all other professionals working with children and adolescents. The book maintains a scholarly approach to the evidence base and therefore will be of particular interest to professional and academic trainers in fields such as clinical and educational psychology, child psychiatry, paediatrics, speech and language therapy and occupational therapy, in addition to researchers working in the field of social skills with children and adolescents from a range of perspectives.

The Evidence Base

Within each chapter there is a comprehensive review of the evidence base for a specific approach or client group.

A Range of Conditions

The applicability of a social skills approach for a wide range of conditions and problems is fully illustrated.

A Range of Approaches

The book provides comprehensive coverage of a range of approaches, illustrated by case examples. Individual approaches allow for detailed assessment and formulation, and enable skills and techniques to be tailored to the specific needs of the client. Working within a group is a very helpful experience for improving social competence, and children and young people can learn rapidly in a group context.

Those who are isolated can gain more confidence within the group context as the equivalent of a natural peer group will be provided. Those who lack self-control can learn to modify their behaviour patterns through positive reinforcement in a controlled situation. Detailed guidance for group facilitators will be provided.

Finally, the importance of parental involvement is emphasised to support both group and individual approaches.

Synopsis

Part One- Issues of theoretical background and assessment are addressed in the first two chapters. There will be coverage of individual approaches in Chapter 3 and group approaches in Chapter 4.

Part Two- Attention is focussed on intervention in different contexts (e.g. home, school, psychiatric unit, clinic and youth offender centre and care settings) in the remaining chapters.

There is coverage of approaches with a variety of client groups (e.g. socially anxious children and young people, those affected by autistic spectrum disorder or attention disorder with hyperactivity, youngsters with behaviour problems and those who break the law) illustrated by case examples.

Reference

Spence SH (2003). Social skills training with children and young people: Theory, evidence and practice. *Child and Adolescent Mental Health*, 8(2) 84–96

CONTENTS

PART ONE

EVIDENCE BASE AND APPROACHES TO INTERVENTION

Chapter 1   Theoretical Background & Evidence Base

Chapter 1 provides a guided tour of the theoretical rationale and evidence base for social skills training with children and young people. The literature is surveyed and summarised with the addition of up-to-date comment on Social Skills Development techniques and applications which may assist with a variety of specific presenting problems experienced by children and young people.

Chapter 2   Assessment: Key Issues and Evidence Base

Assessment approaches include questionnaires, role-playing, visual material, vignettes, and sociometric procedures. This chapter introduces the evidence base, with some discussion of the advantages and disadvantages of each approach.

Chapter 3   Social Skills Development with Individuals

General principles of intervention are outlined. The importance of tailoring an intervention to a child or young person's needs is emphasised. The chapter covers micro-skills (such as eye contact), assertiveness, interpersonal problem-solving and dealing with negative social cognitions, providing illustrative examples.

Chapter 4   Social Skills in Groups

This chapter addresses the key ingredients of successful group social skills programmes such as role-play, feedback, coaching, and homework setting; session plans and examples are included, and the skills required for group facilitators are delineated. Sample programmes and guidance on a psychodynamic approach are provided in appendices to this chapter.

Appendix 1

Sample series of social skills group work sessions are presented. Each session plan provides a structure for activities and an outline of objectives. Setting homework, (assignments), is important to promote generalisation. Two group programmes are presented, one with a standard approach and one with an individualised approach. The individualised approach may produce better generalisation as the focus is on setting homework which will be especially helpful for the group member concerned. A short course is also included.

Appendix 2

Some useful pointers for adopting a psychodynamic approach to social skills group work are added here.

PART TWO

CLINICAL AND EDUCATIONAL APPLICATIONS

Chapter 5   Autistic Spectrum Disorder: Assessment & Intervention

Difficulties with social communication are characteristic of children identified as belonging to this client group. Highly structured and appropriately tailored social skills approaches can assist these children in adapting to social situations and building positive relationships.

Chapter 6   Prosocial Behaviour

Throughout this chapter the importance of supplementing individual or group work with interventions in the system and social context is emphasised (e.g. with family and school); this is crucial to the learning process and to generalisation.

Section A: Younger children

Younger children who are beginning to present with patterns of 'challenging behaviour' can be helped to learn appropriate assertiveness, anger management and negotiation skills through a social skills approach. Children suffering from Attention Deficit/Hyperactivity Disorder (ADHD) may benefit from similar approaches.

Section B: Adolescents

Adolescents at risk of offending can be helped to form more appropriate social cognitions and avoid recourse to aggression

Chapter 7   Social Anxiety

This chapter explores how individuals suffering from social anxiety, including those with complex needs, may be helped by social skills development techniques to overcome stigma, generate self-confidence and operate successfully in a range of social situations.

Chapter 8   Bullying: Clinical and Systemic Interventions

This chapter addresses the issue of developing social skills programmes in schools and clinics with a focus on helping the victims of bullying. Techniques discussed will include assertiveness training, role-play and the multi-systemic approach.

Chapter 9   Interventions in Education

In this chapter, theories of social and emotional competence are reviewed and approaches to educational intervention are described and evaluated.

Chapter 10   Overview

This chapter reviews the issue of '*horses for courses*', noting which social skill approaches appear to work best for which client groups given the current evidence available from research. Key issues are identified and a practical overview of useful resources is provided. Topics covered are summarised and ways forward are suggested.

HANDBOOK FOR SOCIAL SKILLS DEVELOPMENT WITH CHILDREN AND YOUNG PEOPLE: FROM RESEARCH TO PRACTICE

PREFACE

There is an increasing demand for skill-focused interventions with children and young people within schools, statutory and voluntary social agencies, and child and adolescent mental health services. The skills we are frequently seeking to generate are in fact positive social skills. We may wish to help young people to develop friendship skills, relationship skills, avoid risky situations and inappropriate behaviour, avoid harming others and keep out of trouble. Such skills may also be helpful for youngsters with difficulties, such as Attention Deficit Hyperactivity Disorder (ADHD) Autistic Spectrum Disorder (ASD) and learning disability. This book is primarily designed for psychologists and other professionals working in the public services or independent agencies, but may also be useful to young people themselves and their families.

Social skills include the ability to express oneself clearly using both speech and 'body language', the ability to show genuine regard for others, the ability to solve problems that crop up with others, and the ability to listen and respond. Effective social skills are necessary to maintain friendships, build relationships and respond appropriately in any situation from the most intimate to the most mundane (e.g. going through the checkout in a supermarket). We are born with the potential to develop these skills but require appropriate social experience (such as being brought up in a stable and loving family context and being exposed to a range of social situations) to realise and make the most of that potential. Both adults and peers may be role models for the developing young person.

The author has a background of working in education and subsequently as a mental health professional. Outcome research has demonstrated the efficacy of social skills training and education with children and young people. In this book the evidence is provided and some of the author's own research is cited. This approach aims to provide an 'extra boost' to the social learning that all young people do all the time. It may be that some 'faulty' learning has occurred which can be corrected by skilled professional attention. This is not to say that anyone is 'to blame'. It is important to create a no-blame culture and to see social skills as not much different from other skills like playing football – we are all better at some things than others.

The author has been using this approach with children and young people within the National Health Service for three decades and more recently on an independent basis. The approach is useful both with individual young people and with groups. Children and young people can learn rapidly in a group context. Those who are isolated can gain more confidence and those who lack self-control can learn to modify their behaviour patterns.

Orientation

The aim of this book is to provide psychologists and other interested professionals (e.g. teachers, social workers, primary mental health workers, health professionals, youth workers, and psychiatrists) with evidence-based knowledge and skills which will be helpful in promoting social skills development in children and young people.

In terms of knowledge, there will be a broad coverage of theoretical issues and the evidence base. The author has sought to make this comprehensible to a range of specialists. In terms of skills, the book aims to supply detailed information on a range of useful assessment techniques and relevant interventions with social skills for children and young people. The focus is on helping children and young people with specific issues where the application of social skills will be helpful. The book offers a comprehensive overview of group and individual interventions, supported by a range of examples. Material on assessment and intervention used by the author and his colleagues is included.

Part One includes Chapters 1-4. By way of introduction, Chapter 1 provides a brief 'guided tour' of the theory and evidence base for this professional approach, concluding with an overview of the most recent research. This demonstrates the scientific grounding for the book. Chapter 2 examines the issues of assessment in some detail. Chapters 3 and 4 address general issues of intervention for practitioners from the perspective of individual and group approaches respectively. There is evidence that the group approaches introduced in Chapter 4 have excellent potential; however, practitioners may not always have resources available to set up groups, and may be able to make better use of individual approaches.

Part Two includes Chapters 5-10. Chapters 5 to 8 address methodologies for using the approach with young people experiencing various types of social difficulty, such as social anxiety, autism spectrum conditions, and bullying. Chapter 6 addresses the evidence base for social skill development as a technique for modifying challenging behaviour. Social skills development approaches may not be sufficient on their own to resolves these problems and conditions, but may well have a useful part to play in their management.

In terms of prevention, Chapter 9 looks at ways to enhance social and emotional competence within mainstream education. Chapter 10 provides a conclusion and overview.

How to use this book

Having obtained useful background from the first four chapters (Part One), readers may find it helpful to scan the contents page and turn directly to chapters in Part Two about specific areas of work or client groups in which they have a particular interest.

Readers who are mainly concerned about developing 'hands-on' and 'how-to-do-it' skills may prefer to go straight to the relevant chapter on clinical or educational intervention with a client group, or consult the appendices for specific procedures.

PART ONE

EVIDENCE BASE AND APPROACHES TO INTERVENTION

CHAPTER 1   **THEORETICAL BACKGROUND AND EVIDENCE BASE**

Introduction

The aim of this chapter is to demonstrate to the reader that social skill development (originally termed social skills training) has a rational theoretical basis, is useful and has a proven track record with children and young people.

First, the historical background will be described. This will give some indication of the different components of the theory. Specific applications with children and adolescents will then be addressed, with reference to different clinical areas. The evidence base will be briefly summarised.

Background

The story started when the researchers, Zigler and Philips (1961) found that social competence was linked to the outcome of treatment in mental disorders. In other words, patients who were more socially able had a better chance of recovery. Argyle and Kendon (1967) proposed a model of social skills application. The process was analysed as follows:

1   We make a move towards realising a social goal.
2   We perceive the effect of that move on the environment.
3   We modify our behaviour in the light of that perception.

What is important here is that social skill is a learned behaviour, like driving a car. We learn from experience. As we learn to negotiate roundabouts, so we learn to negotiate human contacts.

The 'nuts and bolts' of social communication are often called 'micro-skills' by social skills researchers and trainers. These are the basic ways in which humans communicate – both verbal (conversational skills) and non-verbal (body language). Somewhere between these two is tone of voice, together with other qualities of voice such as pitch, loudness and timbre.

Non-Verbal Skills

The non-verbal social skills include facial expression, gesture, posture (stance), eye contact and body proximity (Searle, 1975). Perhaps the most researched has been facial expression. Ekman (1971) looked at facial expression in widely differing types of society (five literate and two preliterate cultures). They developed a 'neuro-cultural theory'. In many ways, the expression of emotion or feeling by the face and other parts of the body is determined by our neurology and musculature and the role of these in communication with other members of the species (Darwin, 1872); for example, raised eyebrows may indicate 'startled', enabling the eye to 'take in' sudden new information. However, there may be cultural differences in the use of facial expression for communication. Whilst the smile is universal as an expression of friendship and pleasure, Darwin noted that in rage the lips may be retracted (most common in European culture) or protruded (as reported anecdotally in Bengali and Native Australian culture).

Social Learning Theory

Following Pavlov's experiments on classical conditioning, in which dogs were taught to salivate in response to bells, behavioural psychologists had developed theories of operant conditioning, in which animals were trained to produce certain behaviours in response to rewards (positive reinforcement). These principles (known as learning theory, and often exploring how a given stimulus might elicit a given response) were increasingly applied to human behaviour. Bandura and Walters (1977) introduced 'social learning theory' which looked at processes of modelling, imitation and self-reinforcement as ways in which human behaviour patterns could be acquired.

Under these influences, social skills training developed as an active, performance-based technique, using newly available technologies such as videotaping to enhance modelling effects and to provide learners with direct feedback on their social performance. The emphasis was on the detection of specific deficits such as faulty eye contact and on teaching more appropriate and more successful social behaviours. In the 1980s these techniques were widely applied, e.g. in mental health, disability, with offenders, in police training, and job interviews. For example, Arnold Goldstein and his colleagues developed Structured Learning Therapy, an approach to life skills training, to assist people who had been discharged from psychiatric hospitals (Goldstein et al., 1981). Developments in medication have enabled more than half of long-stay patients in psychiatric hospitals in the USA to be discharged, but these people were found to be lacking in the social skills which would enable them to cope in the community.

Assertiveness

Assertiveness training, now used in a variety of contexts, was another component of the packages that were involved. Clinicians found that it was helpful for people to learn to express themselves clearly and confidently in a social context. Carr and Binkoff (1981) provide a useful overview of theory, research and practice in relation to assertiveness training. They state: *'In the past, assertive behaviour was largely synonymous with standing up for one's rights. More recently, however, the concept of assertion has been expanded to include other forms of interpersonal behaviour especially that involving the appropriate expression of thoughts and feelings, both positive and negative. A hallmark of assertive behaviour is that it is direct and honest and equally important, that it takes into consideration the rights and feelings of others. Last, and of considerable significance, assertive behaviour involves effective communication with a view to achieving personal goals'* (p 133).

Winter and Marzillier (1983) noted that clients with social skills difficulties commonly exhibited poor conversation skills, poor appearance, a lack of appropriate assertiveness and an inability to form friendships, together with limited range of social activities, poor social sensitivity and low social self-esteem. Training was sometimes carried out within a group framework, enabling patients to learn from one another. Trower (1979) felt it was important to examine the social situations in which difficulty was experienced, given the finding of Mischel (1968), that people respond to different situations in various ways.

Friendship-Making Skills

It was also recognised that friendship-making skills could be taught (Trower, 1979). The norms which apply to friendship making were analysed.

1. Visual Interaction: External cues such as dress, appearance, manner
2. Initial Contact: A catalogue of information is exchanged
3. Affiliation: Involves self-disclosure and accommodation.

Goffman (1972) believed that supportive interchanges such as greetings and partings had a special significance. The basic structure (sequence of stages) appears to be universal across culture.

People are not always the best judges of their own social skills and Hopps (1983) recommends that the opinions of parents, teachers and peers be sought in making an evaluation of social skill in children and young people. Naturally during social skill development, it is hoped that people will become more accurate observers of their own social skills.

Action-Focused Programmes

Goldstein et al. (1981) analysed 25 social skills programmes to work out what the key components were. They considered that social skills development was based on sound theory and research evidence, and was best implemented using modern educational techniques. They defined social skills training as follows: '*Social skills training is the planned, systematic teaching of the specific behaviours needed and consciously desired by the individual in order to function in an effective and satisfying manner, over an extended period of time, in a broad array of positive, negative and neutral contexts. The specific teaching methods which constitute social skills training directly and jointly reflect psychology's modern social learning theory and education's pedagogic principles and procedures*' (p 162). They emphasised the importance of modelling, roleplay, performance feedback and homework, stating that these procedures would promote optimal learning in the training situation and effective transfer of the skills practised to real life settings. They considered it essential for the training setting to be as similar to real life as possible, to facilitate transfer. For similar reasons, they advocated the teaching of general principles.

Evaluation of Social Skills Programmes

How do we know whether the social skills approach works? Research on social skills development addresses the question of whether it is effective, and then investigates the question of what the effective ingredient might be. Two aspects of effectiveness may be distinguished. First, are the skills learned? Second, do they transfer to real life?

Our own research was carried out with mixed gender groups aged 12–13 in a school setting. In the first study (Bulkeley & Cramer, 1990) a group identified as having social skills difficulty received a 10-session social skills training package. Change was assessed on three measures: pre-treatment, post-treatment, and at three-month follow-up. Significant improvement was found on two of the measures and maintained (slightly enhanced) on follow-up.

The measures on which improvement was found included the young people's own perception of their social competence as indicated by questionnaire (self-report) and the teachers' perception of their social competence, also indicated by questionnaire. Our observation was that the parents' opinion coincided with that of the teachers. Consequently, there was some evidence that social skills had been learned and had transferred to real life.

We speculated as to what might be the effective ingredients of this package. As advocated by Goldstein et al. (1981) we had included modelling, role-play, performance feedback and homework. We provided the training in a setting close to real life. We assessed the clients carefully and attempted to help them improve the skills in which they were deficient. We taught the skills systematically, working from simple skills to more complex skills. We consciously reinforced the clients for gradually enhancing their patterns of social behaviour. In feedback on homework assignments clients were encouraged to share with peers their success in achieving change and to reflect on their failures. The comprehensive nature of the package had ensured thorough learning, thereby enhancing 'response availability' in social learning theory terms. There were three therapists who could act as models and in addition, using role-play, peers were available as models. This enhanced 'stimulus availability'. This approach builds on Pavlov's theory of conditioning which looks at the relationship between a 'stimulus' (what the organism experiences) and a 'response' (what the organism does).

Our second study (Bulkeley & Cramer, 1994) using the programme with four groups found significant improvements on two out of three measures. One of the measures showed that the students had increased their understanding of social situations. This study found that as predicted those students who had an approach including homework assignments individually tailored to their skill deficit (e.g. under-assertiveness) did better than those offered the standard programme.

Therefore, from our two studies we found that a comprehensive, carefully designed social skills geared to individual need could be effective.

Social Skills Development for Children and Young People

It is particularly important for social skills development programmes to be offered to children and young people. It is known that social difficulties early in life may be a risk factor for a range of personal problems at a later stage in the life cycle. For example, Van Hasselt and his colleagues (1979) reviewed 14 studies linking childhood social difficulties to later problems of adjustment. They stated that there was '*A considerable body of research demonstrating a relationship between children's level of social functioning and their long-term adjustment*' (p413). Studies had found that social isolation in childhood was linked to offending behaviour in adolescence, dropping out of school, bad conduct discharges from the army and mental health difficulties.

Furthermore, social problem solving and emotional recognition skills if delivered within an educational environment can enhance educational attainment, as Greenberg and his colleagues have demonstrated in their studies on the PATHS programmes (Greenberg et al., 2003). This is an indicator that social skills development can contribute to self-esteem and self-confidence thereby enhancing health and happiness.

How can social skills be described in relation to children and young people? Rinn and Markle (1979) define social skills as a repertoire of verbal and non-verbal behaviours which enable children to affect the response of others in such a way that desirable outcomes are attained and undesirable outcomes avoided without inflicting pain on others. They consider expressive skills, including expression of feeling and positive self-statements; assertive skills, such as disagreeing and denying unreasonable requests; and communication skills, such as conversing and interpersonal problem solving. Spence and Donovan (1998) defined social competence as the ability to obtain successful outcomes from interactions with others, while Bierman and Welsh (2000) conceptualised social competence as an organisational construct that reflected the child's capacity to integrate behavioural, cognitive and affective skills to adapt flexibly to diverse social contexts and demands.

Evidence Base for Social Skills Development Programmes with Children and Young People

Spence (2003) affirms that deficits in social skills and social competence play a significant role in the development and maintenance of many emotional and behavioural disorders of childhood and adolescence. Her view is that social skills development aims to increase the ability to perform key social behaviours that are important in achieving success in social situations, and employs methods such as instruction, modelling, behavioural rehearsal feedback and reinforcement, often in association with interpersonal problem-solving and social perception skills. Furthermore, she suggests that effective change in social behaviour may require interventions that reduce inhibiting and competing behaviours, such as cognitive restructuring, self- and emotional-regulation methods and contingency management (Spence, 2003).

Social skills training (SST) involves teaching specific skills (e.g. maintaining eye contact, initiating conversation) through behavioural and social learning techniques (White et al., 2007; Cooper, Griffeths & Filer, 1999). SST has been found an effective component of treatment regimes for childhood disorders such as social phobia (Spence et al., 2000) and specific learning disabilities (Kam et al., 2004). Beidel et al. (2006) report that Social Effectiveness Therapy with Children (SET-C) can result in long-term positive effects for youth suffering from social phobia. They conducted a number of in-depth studies concluding with a longitudinal study employing a control group. SET-C combines social skills training, peer generalisation experiences and individualised in vivo exposure for the treatment of social phobia.

Children and young people requiring intervention may lack assertiveness skills (Bornstein et al., 1977; Jackson & Marzillier, 1983; Sharp & Cowie, 1994; Greco &

Morris, 2001) or may need help to avoid alienating peers by overassertive or antisocial behaviour (Filipzak et al., 1980.). Young offenders may be taught social skills, but Hollin and Henderson (1984) caution that this may not necessarily lead to a reduction in offending.

Different types of approach may be best for particular age groups. Approaches to intervention with younger children may use adult or peer modelling or video presentations, whilst comprehensive group packages such as those used by Arnold Goldstein with adults are more useful with older children and young people (Beck & Forehand, 1984).

Group approaches enable peer modelling to be used in line with social learning theory; and children and young people are by nature imitative anyway. Group training packages were found helpful by La Greca and Santogrossi (1980) working with children aged 8–11 who were low on peer acceptance ratings. They used coaching, modelling and roleplay to teach smiling, greeting, joining, inviting, conversing, sharing, cooperating and complimenting skills. These clients improved their knowledge of such skills, demonstrated the skills in roleplay, and became better at starting up social interactions.

Group Social Skills Programmes for Adolescents

Sarason and Sarason (1981) found that modelling and roleplay strengthened the cognitive and social skills of high school students. Jackson and Marzillier (1983) carried out group social skills training in a youth club setting with encouraging results. Following a systematic approach to instruction, they taught eye contact, use of facial expression and voice intonation (micro-skills) in the earlier sessions and more complex processes such as conversational skills, assertive skills and dealing with teasing in later sessions. Verduyn and her colleagues (Verduyn et al., 1990) ran a group programme in a UK middle school with children aged 10–13. Inderbitzen–Pisaruk and Foster (1990) support the use of group social skills training for young people, since such an approach offers an opportunity for practice of the skills requiring development. Berner et al. (2001) reported on a multi-component social skills programme for pre-adolescent girls with few friends. A six session manualised group treatment programme was used. At post-test, the treatment group spent less time alone, more time initiating conversations and more time interacting with others than a control group.

Social Problem Solving

Another useful approach to social skills training is interpersonal problem solving. In this approach children are presented with vignettes describing common social problems and encouraged to brainstorm appropriate solutions. The method was developed in the United States (Shure & Spivack, 1982) and applied extensively in Australia by Peterson, who generated the *Stop Think Do* model associated with traffic lights (Peterson, 1992). The use of visual cues is of course very helpful to aid learning. It is appropriate to use the more inclusive term, Social Skill Development, to incorporate the more traditional social skills (SST) which have a behavioural orientation along with social problem solving approaches which have a more cognitive slant.

Social Impairments in Autism

Mundy et al (2003) identifies specific brain mechanisms which may underpin social function and may be implicated in the social impairments characteristic of autism. A body of research which will not be reported here has explored genetic components of autism. Senju et al. (2004) found experimentally that autistic children were less responsive to eye gaze as a social cue than were children with more typical patterns of development, and there is a good deal of evidence that autistic children struggle with processes of social interaction from an early age. In the light of such important suggestive evidence, treatments for autistic children incorporating a social skills component are likely to be helpful. No doubt such treatments would need to be tailored to the specific needs of autistic children and equally would need to allow for individual differences.

Recent Developments

Recently, social skills interventions have been found helpful for high-functioning children with autism. Bauminger (2002) reported on a study involving 15 clients aged 8–17 who received training in t interpersonal problem-solving, knowledge of emotion, and social interaction. The children were more likely to initiate positive social interaction with peers after treatment. They improved eye contact and were more able to share their experience with peers. They produced more relevant solutions to social situations, provided more examples of complex emotions, and were rated higher by teachers for assertion and cooperation after treatment. Nikopoulos and Keenan (2003) found that video modelling training enhanced the social initiation skills of four out of seven developmentally delayed children. It facilitated appropriate play engagement, which generalised across settings, peers and toys. Further discussion of such treatments for children with a diagnosis of autistic spectrum disorder will be found in Chapter 5.

Social Anxiety

There has been considerable interest recently in the diagnosis and treatment of social phobia and social anxiety (La Greca & Lopez, 1998; Spence et al., 2000; Kashdan & Herbert, 2001). Social anxiety is not necessarily correlated with observed social skill deficits (Cartwright et al., 2003). Therefore, it should be assessed independently. If social anxiety (or social phobia) is present, it may be treated by intensive social skills training combined with graded exposure and cognitive challenging (Spence et al., 2000). Behavioural treatment programmes for social anxiety may be conducted in school (Masia et al., 2001).

Attention Deficit Hyperactivity Disorder

As with other conditions, social skills enhancement can be a useful adjunct to interventions with children diagnosed as having Attention Deficit Hyperactivity

Disorder (ADHD). Tutty et al. (2003) reported on an eight week behavioural and social skill class (BSS) for children newly diagnosed with ADHD and their parents. Eligible families were randomly assigned to an intervention group (59) or a control group (41). BSS functioning was improved in the home setting for the intervention group, who did significantly better than the control group in some areas (e.g. more consistent discipline practice) suggesting that the main benefit was obtained via the parents.

Challenging Behaviour

Whilst social skills training can undoubtedly be helpful with anxious and withdrawn children and children who find it hard to make friends, it can also contribute to interventions with children who present challenging patterns of behaviour. Webster–Stratton et al., (2001) reported on a study in which their manualised programme, the *Incredible Years Dinosaur Social Skills and Problem Solving Curriculum*' was used to assist families of children aged 4–8 years with early onset conduct problems. Ninety-nine families were assigned either to a child training treatment group or to a waiting list control group. After treatment, the children who attended the programme showed significantly fewer behaviour problems at home, less aggression at school, more pro-social behaviour with peers, and more conflict management strategies than children in the control group. However, negative parenting styles such as maternal criticism and physical force were found to undermine improvement in child conduct difficulties. The one year follow-up indicated that most of the significant post-treatment changes were maintained. This is quite impressive evidence of lasting change.

Social skills training may also be extremely helpful in the context of family-based cognitive-behaviour therapy. There may be social skills difficulties underlying behavioural issues and parents can be encouraged to help identify and overcome such difficulties, helping youngsters to identify problematic social situations and develop appropriate anger management strategies.

Conclusion

Hopefully enough has been said to convince the reader that social skills intervention has a rational theoretical basis and has a useful track record in a variety of contexts with children and young people. It has potential for enhancing intellectual and emotional development and for the prevention, treatment or alleviation of troublesome conditions. The evidence available to date certainly suggests that in combination with other treatments, Social Skills Enhancement may be helpful to children and young people presenting with a range of difficulties. Spence (2003) affirms that '*Social Skills Training has become a widely accepted component of multi-method approaches to the treatment of many emotional, behavioural and developmental disorders*' (p 84).

References

Argyle M & Kendon A (1967). The experimental analysis of social performance. In *Advances in Experimental Social Psychology* (vol 3). New York and London: Academic Press.

Bandura A & Walters RH (1977). Social Learning Theory.

Bauminger N (2002). The facilitation of social-emotional understanding and social interaction in high-functioning children with autism: Intervention outcomes. *Journal of Autism and Developmental Disorders*, 283–298

Beck S & Forehand R (1984). Social Skills Training for Children: A methodological and clinical review of behaviour modification studies. *Behavioural Psychotherapy*, 12, 17–45

Beidel DC, Turner SM & Young BJ (2006). Social Effectiveness for Children: Five years later. *Behaviour Therapy*, 37(4) 416–425

Berner ML, Fee VE & Turner AD (2001). A multi-component social skills group training programme for pre-adolescent girls with few friends. *Child and Family Behaviour Therapy*, 23(2) 1–18

Bierman K & Welsh JA (2000). Assessing social dysfunction: The contribution of laboratory and performance-based measures. *Journal of Clinical Child Psychology*, 29, 526–539

Bornstein MR, Bellack AS & Hersen M (1977). Social skills training for unassertive children: A multiple baseline analysis. *Journal of Applied Behaviour Analysis*, 10, 183–195

Bulkeley R & Cramer D (1990). Social skills training with young adolescents. *Journal of Youth and Adolescence*, 19(5) 451–463

Bulkeley R & Cramer D (1994). Social skills training with young adolescent: group and individual approaches in a school setting. *Journal of Adolescence*, 17, 521–531

Cartwright HS, Hodges L & Porter J (2003). Social anxiety in childhood: the relationship with self and observer rated social skills. *Journal of Child Psychology and Psychiatry*, 44(5) 737–42

Carr EG & Binkoff JA (1981). Self-Control. In: AP Goldstein, EG Carr, WS Davidson & P Wehr (Eds). *In Response to Aggression: Methods of Control and Prosocial Alternatives*. New York: Pergamon

Cooper MJ, Griffeths KG & Filer J (1999). School intervention for children with and without disabilities. *Focus on Autism and Other Disabilities*, 14(2) 110–115

Ekman P (1971). Universals and Cultural Differences in facial expressions of emotion. In: J Cole (Ed.) *Nebraska Symposium on Motivation*. Lincoln: University of Nebraska Press

Filipczak J, Archer M & Friedman RM (1980). In-school social skills training; use with destructive adolescents. *Behaviour Modification*, 4, 243–263

Goffman E (1972). *Relations in Public: Microstudies of the Public Order*. Harmondsworth: Penguin

Goldstein AP, Carr EG, Davidson WS & Wehr P (1981). *In Response to Aggression: Methods of Control and Prosocial Alternatives*. New York: Pergamon

Greco LA & Morris TL (2001). Treating childhood shyness and related behaviour: Empirically evaluated approaches to promoting positive social interactions. *Clinical Child and Family Psychology Review*, 4(4) 299–318

Greenberg MT, Weissberg RP, Utne, O'Brien M, Zins JE, Fredericks L, Resnik H & Elias M J (2003). Enhancing school-based prevention and youth development through coordinated social, emotional and academic learning. *American Psychologist*, 58, 466–474

Hollin CR & Henderson M (1984). Social skills training with young offenders: False expectations and the 'Failure of treatment'. *Behavioural Psychotherapy*, 12, 331–341

Hopps H (1983). Children's social competence and skill: Current research practices and future directions. *Behaviour Therapy*, 14, 3–18

Inderbitzen–Pisaruk H & Foster SL (1990). Adolescent friendship and peer acceptance: implications for social skills training. *Clinical Psychology Review*, 10, 425–439

Jackson MF & Marzillier JS (1983). Investigation of the treatment of adolescent social difficulty in a community-based setting. *Behavioural Psychotherapy*, 11, 302–319

Kam CM, Greenberg MT & Kusche CA (2004). Sustained effects of the PATHS curriculum on the social and psychological adjustment of children in special education. *Journal of Emotional and Behavioural Disorders*, 12(2) 66–78

La Greca AM & Lopez N (1998). Social anxiety among adolescents: linkages with peer relations and friendships. *Journal of Abnormal Child Psychology*, 26(2) 83-94

La Greca AM & Santagrossi DA (1980). Social skills training with elementary school students: a behavioural group approach. *Journal of Consulting and Clinical Psychology*, 48, 220–27

Masia CL, Klein RG, Storch EA & Corda B (2001). School-based behavioural treatment for social anxiety disorder in adolescents: results of a pilot study. *Journal of the American Academy of Child and Adolescent Psychiatry*, 40(7) 780–786

Mischel W (1968). *Personality and Assessment*. New York: Wiley

Mundy P, Delgado C, Block J, Venezia M, Hogan A & Seibert J (2003). Early social communication scales (ESCS). *Coral Gables,* FL: University of Miami.

Nikopoulos CK & Keenan M (2003). Promoting social initiation in children with autism using video modelling. *Behavioural Interventions*, 18(2) 87–108

Peterson L (1992). Stop–Think–Do: A systems based pro-social skills training programme. *Guidance and Counselling*, 8(2) 24–35

Rinn RC & Markle A (1979). Modification of social skills deficits in children. In AS Bellak & M Hersen (Eds). *Research and Practice in Social Skills Training*. New York: Plenum

Sarason IG & Sarason BR (1981). Teaching cognitive and social skills to high school students. *Journal of Consulting and Clinical Psychology*, 49, 908–918

Searle JR (1975). Indirect Speech Acts. In: Cole P & Morgan JL (Eds). *Syntax and Semantics*, Vol 3: Speech Acts. New York: Seminar Press

Senju A, Tojo Y, Dairoku H & Hasegawa T (2004). Reflexive orienting in response to eye gaze and an arrow in children with and without autism. *Journal of Child Psychology and Psychiatry*, *45*(3) 445-458.

Sharp S, Cowie H & Smith PK (1994). In Sharp S & Smith PK (Eds). *Tackling Bullying in Your School: A Practical Handbook for Teachers*. London: Routledge

Shure MB & Spivack G (1982). Interpersonal problem-solving in young children; a cognitive approach to prevention. *American Journal of Community Psychology*, 10(3) 341–356

Spence SH (2003). Social skills training with children and young people: Theory, evidence and practice. *Child and Adolescent Mental Health*, 8(2) 84–96

Spence SH & Donovan C (1998). Interpersonal problems. In Graham PJ (Eds.). *Cognitive Behaviour Therapy for Children and Families*. New York: Cambridge University Press

Spence SH, Donovan C & Brechman–Toussaint M (2000). The treatment of childhood social phobia: the effectiveness of a social skills training-based, cognitive-behavioural intervention, with and without parental involvement. *Journal of Child Psychology and Psychiatry*, 41(6) 713–26

Trower P (1979). Fundamentals of interpersonal behaviour: A social-psychological perspective. In Bellack AS & Hersen M (Eds). *Social Skills Training – A Practical Handbook for Assessment and Treatment*. New York: Plenum

Tutty S, Gephart H & Wursbacher K (2003). Enhancing behavioural and social skill functioning in children newly diagnosed with attention-deficit hyperactivity in a paediatric setting. *Journal of Developmental and Behavioural Paediatrics*, 24(1) 51–7

van Hasselt VB, Hersen M & Bellak AS (1979). Social skill assessment and training for children: An evaluative review. *Behaviour Research and Therapy*, 17, 4113–4439

Verduyn CM, Lord W & Forrest GC (1990). Social skills training in schools: An evaluation study. *Journal of Adolescence*, *13*(1) 3-16.

Webster–Stratton C, Reid J & Hammond M (2001). Social skills and problem solving for children with early-onset conduct problems: who benefits? *Journal of Child Psychology and Psychiatry*, 42(7) 943–52

White SW, Keonig K & Scahill L (2007). Social skills development in children with autism spectrum disorders: A review of the intervention research. *Journal of Autism and Developmental Disorders*, 37(10) 1858–1868

Winter K & Marzillier JS (1983). Psychiatric outpatients. In Spence S & Sheppherd G (Eds). *Developments in Social Skills Training*. London: Academic Press

Zigler E & Philips L (1961). Social competence and outcome in psychiatric disorder. *Journal of Abnormal and Social Psychology*, 63, 264–271

CHAPTER 2 ASSESSMENT: KEY ISSUES AND EVIDENCE BASE

This chapter will provide an overview of the key issues and evidence base for assessment of social skills, together with details of appropriate procedures. A summary of the author's research using social skill assessment is included.

Key Issues

The following issues have been found to be relevant for clinicians in planning assessment for social skills development. A clear decision-making process in relation to these issues will ensure a sound basis for planning assessment procedures.

1. *The type of social difficulty to be assessed*

   Possible causes of concern are antisocial behaviour, rejection or neglect by peers, social anxiety, or social impairment due to an autistic spectrum condition or a learning disability. Depending on the type of social difficulty, the clinician wishes to identify and provide help, therefore the choice of assessment tool is likely to vary.

   Social skill difficulty may occur in children and young people who superficially present opposite characteristics. On one hand, there may be excessive withdrawal, anxiety and timidity; alternatively, there may be excessively impulsive behaviour which alienates others. The research evidence indicates that, to ensure provision of appropriate treatment, it may be important to distinguish between two groups of children. The first group are "neglected" by the peer group, being socially isolated and not selected by peers for companionship because they lack certain positive qualities (O'Connor, 1972; Conger & Keane, 1981); the second are "rejected" owing to behaviours actively resented and seen as antisocial (Gottman et al., 1975). These groups may be characterised as "withdrawn" and "challenging" respectively; the 'withdrawn' young people are likely to have had previous negative experiences with the peer group and therefore avoid peer situations and possibly become socially phobic (or at risk of developing social anxiety disorder). The 'challenging' young people may have difficulty both with the peer group and with adults because of their negative interactional styles. In terms of treatment using a cognitive-behavioural model, the former group needs to learn more positive interactive behaviours and to be more assertive (Bornstein et al., 1977), while the latter in addition to acquiring more positive behavioural attributes, also need to inhibit off-putting, intrusive behaviour and become less obviously aggressive (Feindler & Ecton, 1986). They may need to develop anger management skills, to reduce their arousal level and building a greater understanding of situations which trigger their angry or impulsive responses.

A clue to the type of social skill difficulty being experienced may be given using *sociometry.* Sociometry is a technique for mapping the positions of individuals within a social group. By using questionnaires for example, it is possible to identify individuals who may be isolated or rejected. Using a sociometric rating, a child or young person might be asked to rank order class members in terms of who might be preferred as a partner in a work or play activity. Children who fail to receive a positive rating (e.g. of friendship choice) are termed "neglected". Children who receive high negative ratings on such a procedure, indicating that they are actively disliked are described as "rejected" (Zettergren, 2003).

 Sociometric procedures can be undertaken easily in an educational context, and may provide valuable information about client difficulties which may inform planning. However, sociometric procedures may not be sensitive to behaviour change and may not therefore be the best outcome measure. It appears that an individual may sometimes achieve positive change in some aspect of social skill (e.g. assertiveness, friendship-making) without a change in social status occurring. By such methods, it is possible to determine what type of social skill intervention is likely to be helpful.

2. *The selection of an assessment tool (based on 1)*
   This may be a screening process, aimed at identifying the type of problem the client seems to be experiencing. Screening will ensure that only those requiring intervention will be selected for treatment. Screening by sociometry can be carried out in schools, as the author's description of his own research will demonstrate.

The criteria used to select children for social skills training tend to vary; different "yardsticks" may be used. This is partly due to the pragmatic approach which informs social skill applications; a specific age group with a developmental need is often targeted, and so the criteria for selection may be tailored to that situation. As explained in Chapter 1, individuals may have problems with social skill in a particular situation, rather than having a general problem with social skills. In a preschool programme aimed at prevention or early intervention as many as 50% of the age group in a school may be involved (O'Connor, 1972). However, more in-depth assessment can also be helpful. The purpose of the assessment needs to be considered. The assessment should help determine the specific areas in which the client would benefit from social skill development. For example, assertiveness (a positive characteristic) or social anxiety (an area possibly needing improvement) can be assessed by observation, questionnaire or other methods to be described later in this chapter. If the intervention involves assertiveness training, unassertiveness may be assessed (Bornstein et al., 1977). Multiple measures are likely to be used in selection for more elaborate programmes with older youngsters (Verduyn et al., 1990). Matching assessment to intervention is important. Tiffen and Spence (1986) gave the same social skills development programme to "rejected" and "neglected" youngsters. Neither group were significantly improved by treatment. It may therefore have been more helpful for both assessment procedure and intervention to be more "tailor-made" for these disparate client groups.

If the same assessment tool is used before and after treatment, this can provide evidence as to whether the treatment has or has not produced change. This may assist with the evaluation of outcome in the individual case, and the collated results may contribute to the assessment of the efficacy of the procedure being used. In a randomised controlled trial (RCT) clients are randomly assigned to a treatment and control (no intervention) group, and the results for the two groups are compared. RCTs are considered the most objective way of measuring treatment outcome.

3. *The type of input planned (group vs. individual).*
   If group input is planned, and it would be helpful to obtain some evidence of outcome by administering the same measure before and after the treatment package, this will affect the choice of measure. If individual input is planned, a more in-depth analysis of the social difficulties experienced by the individual may be necessary. It is of course possible to offer both types of input and indeed this can be very helpful. In this case a broad range of measures might be appropriate, depending on time and resources available.

4. *The client mix*
   If a mixed group is planned (e.g. mixing antisocial or disruptive youngsters with withdrawn youngsters, or mixing genders), the ability of a specific client to adjust to such a group will need to be assessed. Even if all clients are presenting with the same behavioural difficulty, there will be issues of balance to be considered in setting up a group. This makes it important to carry out individual assessments which will contribute towards the goal of having a balanced group which will be more likely to achieve a positive outcome.

Curran (1979) took the view that whatever the cause of social difficulty, social skills training is robust enough to be helpful with a wide range of difficulties, since in his view, interpersonal skills, once learned, may be generalised to new situations. This may well be the case, but from a clinical point of view it is important, if a group approach is used, to ensure that that the group experience provides a congenial climate within which appropriate social learning may occur.

5. *The attributes to be assessed (determined by 1)*
   Clients may be deficient in specific skills, either in competence (potential) or performance (demonstrated in specific situations). Typical attributes or skills to be assessed would be assertiveness (the ability to respond positively to challenging situations) or friendship-making skills (which could be broken down into several sub-skills, e.g. initiating conversation, demonstrating empathy, coping with stress in interpersonal relationships, maintaining friendships). Assessment measures may either be normative (based on known norms for age group, culture and gender) or behavioural (based on observed behaviour in controlled situations). The purpose of these assessment measures will be to determine the presence or absence of the salient skills or attributes. Such measures may be used both as a prelude to intervention and a means of determining outcome by comparing scores before and after intervention (see 3, above).

6. *The need for multiple assessments*

   Gresham et al. (2010) have confirmed the frequently replicated finding that the correlation of social skill measures from different sources (e.g. students' self-report, parents and teachers) tends to be mild or moderate. This is not surprising as individuals tend to operate differently in different environments. Therefore, it is important to gather information from a variety of sources.

Evidence Base: Approaches to Measurement

Van Hassalt et al. (1979) describe the following types of measure: sociometric questionnaire (assessment by classmates), teacher rating, direct interview, self-report inventories, social-cognitive tasks (e.g. role-taking, vignettes), naturalistic observation and roleplay techniques. Teacher nomination may be used in conjunction with social interaction rate (Conger & Keane, 1981). These approaches are reviewed below.

Sociometric Techniques

In relation to sociometric techniques, Merrell and Gimpel (1998) state that although sociometric procedures tend not to be standardised, their generally favourable technical properties nonetheless have been demonstrated, and these procedures should be viewed as a potentially useful method of assessing peer relationships and social skills. They describe four sociometric techniques:

- Peer nomination may involve a student naming three classmates with whom s/he might like to spend time on a designated activity,
- Picture sociometrics, is similar to peer nomination however is used with preliterate students (using photographs of classmates)
- "Guess Who" where students are asked to write down the names of a few classmates who fit a given description (e.g. "Guess who fights with other children?")
- "Class Play" students are asked to assign classmates to various roles in an imaginary play.

A high proportion of negative roles are held to indicate low social status. Merrell and Gimpel (1998) voice concerns shared by this author regarding the use of negative ranking procedures on ethical grounds.

Sociometric procedure can be useful in educational settings, for example as part of a procedure for selecting youngsters in school who would benefit from a social skills training programme.

Behavioural Observation

Merrell and Gimpel (1998) emphasise the difference between assessment and screening. They discuss behavioural observation in some depth. "Observer drift" is a problem, they state, if carrying out direct behavioural observation. The observer's perceptions may become less objective over time. "Observer reactivity" occurs when the presence of the observer alters or modifies the behaviour of the subject. Behaviour may be specific to a given situation (Kazdin, 1982). Merrell and Gimpel (1998) further define four types of observational coding procedure: event recording (measuring or recording target behaviours), interval recording (dividing a period into equal intervals), time-sample (behaviour noted as present or absent at pre-specified moments) recording, and duration and latency recording. Latency recording measures delay in response (e.g. the time taken by a shy child to respond to an overture.) Observations should be descriptive rather than evaluative. Specific behaviours should be described in terms of frequency, intensity and duration.

Behaviour Rating Systems
Merrell and Gimpel (1998) consider that behaviour rating scales resolve some of the problems of direct behaviour observation, but are themselves prone to bias of response, e.g. leniency or severity effect, and error variance e.g. source variance - the way ratings vary between different raters. To counter this, they recommend employing a range of informants, settings and rating scales.

Merrell and Gimpel (1998) review six norm-referenced, easily available behaviour rating systems which assess social competence and peer relations:

- Behavioural Assessment System for Children (BASC) is a sophisticated instrument incorporating self-report, parent and teacher scales. Many items and subscales sample social competence (Merrell and Gimpel, 1998).
- Matson Evaluation of Social Skills with Youngsters (MESSY; Matson et al., 1983) is well researched but the drawback is that the user needs to refer to averages and measures of range reported in the research findings. The procedure includes both a self-report inventory and a staff questionnaire. Items sampled include micro-skills "*I look at people when I talk to them*", overassertiveness "*I threaten people or act like a bully*", impulsivity "*I become angry easily*", and overconfidence "*I brag about myself*". The staff questionnaire also samples a range of negative behaviours (e.g. "is bossy") and positive social skills (e.g. "helps a friend who is hurt"). The MESSY could certainly be useful for identifying clients who would benefit from anger management programmes.
- Preschool and Kindergarten Behaviour Scales (PKBS)
- School Social Behaviour Scales (SSBS)
- Social Skills Rating System (SSRS)
- Walker-McConnell Scales of Social Competence and School Adjustment (SSCSA)

Interviews
Interviews are useful for obtaining detailed information about quality of social relationships, social situations and settings in which difficulties occur and for planning content of interventions (Spence, 2003). Structured or semi-structured interviews may be used; Spence (2003) proposes that a semi-structured cognitive-behavioural interview with young people, parents or teachers might include items such as the following: '*how many friends does the young person have, what is the frequency of*

contact with friends, how long do friendships last, does the young person attend social functions/activities/clubs/sports or join groups of peers, who does the young person spend time with, how does the young person get on with teachers, how does the young person get on with parents and other family members, are there any social situations in which he/she becomes anxious.' We have found it useful to develop rating scales using such items to record such interview information, incorporating items about being bullied verbally or physically. These can be repeated informally after treatment giving some indication of outcome.

Self-Report

Self-report is not seen as a very reliable social skill measure (Gresham, 1989; Spence & Liddle, 1990). Nevertheless, the self-report measure in the SSRS may have some utility. Some self-report measures may be helpful in providing insight into a young person's social relationships. For the older "rejected" young people, Feindler and Ecton (1986) provide useful guidance on assessment of anger processes. Anger management problems frequently add to social difficulty.

Assessing Social-Cognitive Competence

Social cognition is another attribute we might wish to assess and enhance by intervention. Social cognition denotes the ability to evaluate and respond to social situations. To demonstrate appropriate social cognition, an individual must have reached an appropriate level of intellectual development and social awareness. Therefore, the construct is somewhat similar to that of "emotional intelligence". Social cognition may include such skills as social perspective taking (empathy, placing oneself in another's shoes, and perception of emotion in others). The ability to display empathy for another, having correctly perceived their emotion, is an important related skill.

Assessment procedure may depend on the theoretical framework underpinning the proposed intervention. Utilising a cognitive perspective, Trower (1982) suggests that assessment be aimed at measuring "competence" which he defines as "*social knowledge and the ability to make social plans*". Yeates et al. (1991) have demonstrated a link between social-cognitive performance, behavioural adjustment and social status. The area investigated was that of interpersonal negotiation strategy and there is certainly scope for further investigation of how this skill may be usefully assessed in the future.

Social knowledge would include our ability to predict outcome. For example, if a child is bullied, can s/he predict the outcomes of different responses on his/her part, such as getting angry and upset on the one hand and responding humorously on the other? Mize and Ladd (1990) applied this cognitive approach to social learning by training children in four skills: leading peers, asking questions of peers, making comments to peers, and supporting peers. Their aim was to address potential deficits in children's knowledge, the ability to translate knowledge into skilled performance, and the ability to monitor social interaction. Their training group showed a significant increase in social skills and knowledge, but no change in sociometric status. Nevertheless, a correlation was noted between social skill and knowledge of social friendship-making strategies. (*See Vignettes, below*).

Role-play

In interview, a young person's behavioural repertoire may be tested by using role-play techniques, thus providing more objective data (Merrell & Gimpel, 1998). Bornstein et al., (1977) found role-play useful in planning behavioural treatment. The initial role-play assessment gives an idea of the social skills present in the young person's repertoire. Role-play assessment as a repeat measure provides valuable evidence of learning during treatment sessions, and may be used to measure change on specific variables (e.g. eye contact). Other measures will be required to establish whether a generalisation to real-life social situations has occurred.

Bornstein et al., (1977) used role-play to assess four unassertive children who had difficulty in standing up for their rights and in expressing anger when appropriate.

They identified four specific difficulties experienced by these youngsters; poor eye contact, paucity of speech, mumbling, and inability to make requests. They set the youngsters nine role-play tasks using prompts.

"You are part of a small group in science class. Your group is trying to come up with an idea for a project to present to the class. You start to give your idea when Amy begins to tell hers also."

The role-play was videotaped and rated for verbal and nonverbal components of assertive behaviour and for overall assertiveness. All subjects received nine sessions of training over three weeks. The role-play scenes were used as training scenes. Assertive behaviour was demonstrated (modelled) and practiced in role-play. Video recording showed an improvement as each new skill was taught. This example shows how role-play assessment can be linked to training.

Use of Video

Both in training and assessment, it can be useful to make a video recording of role-play. The video provides an objective sample of behaviour which can be evaluated according to set criteria. To control for observer bias, the video recording may be scored separately by one or more worker, using the same criteria.

Socially anxious clients may not be ready for either role-play or the use of video in the first session. It may therefore be better to postpone the use of this form of assessment to the second or third session with such clients.

Role-play Observation Checklists

To assist in live and video assessment of role-play, observation checklists may be used, focusing on factors such as the following:

Verbal Social Skills: Fluency, clarity, logic, liveliness, forcefulness, humour, overall verbal social skill

Voice Qualities: Pitch, loudness, tone, variation, expressiveness, emphasis, overall voice qualities

Non-Verbal Social Skills: Facial expression, posture, gesture, eye contact, nearness, physical orientation, overall non-verbal skills

The checklists can be constructed to enable each of these to be assessed on a 5-point scale.

Vignettes

Assessment of social knowledge or social cognition may be carried out using vignettes (Mize & Ladd, 1990). Vignettes are mini-situations in which the subject is offered a choice of responses. Mize and Ladd (1990) included a "conflict" situation in which a peer knocked down the subject's block tower, a "support" situation in which the subject observed one peer being teased by another, and a "potential entry" situation in which the subject observed two peers playing with blocks while other toys lay nearby. Children's responses were rated in terms of friendliness and assertiveness. Such material may be administered interactively or pictorially, and the content can be adapted to subjects' developmental level. These approaches are not yet standardised but can be useful in identifying areas for work or discriminating among a group of youngsters to select those in greatest need. Vignettes involve an element of role-taking or perspective-taking, as the subject must adopt the perspective of the character illustrated in the vignette.

Multimodal Assessment

It is important to obtain multiple measures of social skill (e.g. self, parent, carer, teacher) to increase reliability and validity. Gresham et al. (2010) found that cross-informant agreement for social skill ratings was mild to moderate. Beidel et al. (2006) utilised a multidimensional assessment strategy consisting of self-report, parental report, clinician ratings and direct behavioural assessment in a longitudinal study of Social Effectiveness Therapy for Children (SET-C). Webster-Stratton and Lindsay (1999) correlated children's social information processing measures with parent and teacher reports of social adjustment and with actual observations of interactions with peers and parents. Findings indicated that young children with conduct problems have deficits in their social information processing awareness or interpretation of social cues – they overestimate their own social competence and misattribute hostile intent to others. They had fewer positive problem-solving strategies and positive social skills, more negative conflict management strategies and more delayed play skills with peers than comparison children. This study highlights the importance of synthesising multiple measures in obtaining a reliable estimate of children's social skills, social cognition and social competence (Webster-Stratton & Lindsay 1999).

Research in Classical Autism

Structured interview techniques (Autism Diagnostic Observation Schedule – ADOS) have been used to demonstrate the effectiveness of social communication intervention for classical autism, targeting parental communication in a randomised design (Aldred, Green & Adams, 2004). ADOS may be used for assessment to aid diagnosis of autism, either in a clinical or a research context.

Research Examples of Assessment:

First Study

Our initial study (Bulkeley & Cramer, 1990) was presented in Chapter 1 as an example of an intervention. It is discussed again here so that an understanding of the measures used can be obtained. A comprehensive social skills programme was provided to young adolescents in a school setting. School staff were involved in selection, assessment and intervention. Selection was by teacher nomination. Staff were given prior information about the type of youngster who might benefit from the groups. Timid, isolated youngsters might be included along with more aggressive individuals actively rejected by their peers. Assessment measures were administered before treatment, after treatment and at three-month follow-up.

Assessment measures included a teacher questionnaire, a self-report questionnaire and peer sociometric nomination. Teachers were asked to rate the subjects' intellectual and academic level; to assess the frequency and main areas of peer group difficulty and difficulty in interacting with adults; to assess relative frequency of difficulties in interaction with peers and adults; to rate overall severity; and to identify the settings and situations in which difficulties were experienced.

The self-report measure used was the "List of Social Situation Problems" (Spence & Liddle, 1990). This is a 60-item questionnaire. Difficulties with both peers and adults are included and areas such as social anxiety and difficulty with authority are covered. In peer sociometric nomination, subjects were asked to name a classmate whom they would choose as partner or companion in each of four activities.

The outcome was that significant improvements were demonstrated on the teacher questionnaire and self-report questionnaire, but there was no measurable change on the peer sociometric questionnaire. The changes that did occur were maintained at follow-up. This brief account of the use of social skills measures used in the study demonstrates the value of employing a range of assessment measures both in accurate selection of clients for intervention and in checking the efficacy of treatment.

Second Study

In our second study (Bulkeley & Cramer, 1994) a programme of group social skills training for 26 adolescents aged 12-13 years ran over two years with each client receiving 10 weeks consecutive training. Selection was based on three screening measures: teacher nomination, self-report questionnaire (short form), and sociometric questionnaire. Teachers were asked to nominate "overassertive" and "socially isolated" young people. Examples of behaviour were given, which would qualify young people for inclusion in each category. Just four questions from the Social Problem Checklist (Spence & Liddle, 1990) were used for the screening. In the sociometric questionnaire, a variant of the "Roster and Rating" method was used (Van Hassalt, 1979). Young people were presented with an alphabetised list of classmates and asked to rank order the five with whom they would most like to share an activity (using rank ordering increases accuracy). By pooling the results of this screening using predetermined criteria and cut-off points, approximately 15% of each year group was selected.

Assessment was carried out before and after treatment using three measures: the full Social Problem Checklist (Spence & Liddle 1990), the sociometric questionnaire, and a role-taking test, based on the subjects' ability to respond appropriately to pictorially presented social situations (considered as both a perspective-taking test and a test of social knowledge). The outcome was that significant improvement was shown on both the role-taking test and the Social Problem Checklist. Some improvement was shown on the sociometric questionnaire but this did not reach statistical significance.

Again, this study demonstrates the value of employing a variety of measures. From both studies, self-report questionnaires, tests that measure social cognition and teacher questionnaires may be more sensitive measures of change than sociometric measures. There is a strong case for employing an appropriate range of measures geared to the client group and checking on positive change by a simple procedure of repeating administration on completion of treatment and at follow-up. The results can then be systematically analysed. This is good practice even if there is no plan to publish the results

References

Aldred C, Green J & Adams C (2004). A new social communication intervention for children with autism: pilot randomised controlled treatment study suggesting effectiveness. *Journal of Child Psychology and Psychiatry*, 45(8) 1420-1430

Beidel DC, Turner SM, Samuel M & Young BJ (2006). Social effectiveness therapy for children: Five years later. *Behaviour Therapy,* 12, 416-425

Bornstein MR, Bellack AS & Hersen M (1977). Social skills training for unassertive children: A multiple baseline analysis. *Journal of Applied Behaviour Analysis*, 10, 183–195

Bulkeley R & Cramer D (1990). Social skills training with young adolescents. *Journal of Youth and Adolescence,* 19(5) 451-463

Bulkeley RM & Cramer D (1994). Social skills with young adolescents: group and individual approaches in a school setting. *Journal of Adolescence,* 6(17) 1-11

Conger JC & Keane SP (1981). Social skills intervention in the treatment of isolated and withdrawn children. *Psychological Bulletin,* 90, 478-495

Curran JP (1979). Pandora's Box reopened? The assessment of social skills. *Journal of Behavioural Assessment*, 1(1) 55-71

Feindler EL & Ecton RB (1986). *Adolescent Anger Control; Cognitive-Behavioural Techniques.* New York: Pergamum

Gottman J, Gonso J & Rasssmusen B (1975). Social interaction, social competence and friendship in children. *Child Development,* 46(3) 709-718.

Gresham FM (1989). Social skills deficit as a primary learning disability. *Journal of Learning Disabilities,* 22(2) 120-124

Gresham FM, Elliott SN, Cook CR, Vance MJ & Kettler R (2010). Cross-informant agreement for ratings for social skill and problem behaviour ratings: An investigation of the Social Skills Improvement System—Rating Scales. *Psychological Assessment,* 22(1) 157-166

Kazdin AE (1982). The token economy: a decade later. *Journal of Applied Behaviour Analysis,* 15(3) 431-445

Matson ML, Rotatori AF & Helsel WJ (1983). Development of a rating scale to measure social skills in children: the Matson evaluation of social skills with youngsters. *Behaviour Research and Therapy,* 21(4) 335-340

Merrell KW & Gimpel G (1998). *Social Skills of Children and Adolescents.* Mahwah, New Jersey. Lawrence Erlbaum Associates

Mize J & Ladd GW (1990). A cognitive-social learning approach to social skills training with low-status preschool children. *Developmental Psychology,* 26(3) 388-397

O'Connor RD (1972). Relative effects of modelling, shaping and combined procedures for modification of social withdrawal. *Journal of Abnormal Psychology*, 79, 327-334

Spence SH & Liddle B (1990). Self-report measures of social competence for children; an evaluation of the Matson Evaluation of Social Skills for Youngsters and the List of Social Situation Problems. *Behavioural Assessment,* 12(3) 317-336.

Spence SH (2003). Social skills training with children and young people: theory, evidence and practice. *Child and Adolescent Mental Health*, 8(2) 84-96

Tiffen K & Spence SH (1986). Responsiveness of isolated versus rejected children to social skills training. *Journal of Child Psychology and Psychiatry*, 27(3) 343-355

Trower P (1982). Towards a generative model of social skills: a critique and synthesis. In Currran JP & Monti PM (Eds) *Social Skills Training – A Practical Handbook for Assessment and Treatment.* New York: Guildford Press.

Van Hassalt VB, Hersen M, Whitehill MB & Bellack AS (1979). Social skill assessment and training for children: An evaluative review. *Behaviour Research and Therapy*, 17(5) 413-437

Verduyn M, Lord W & Forrest GC (1990). Social skills training in schools: an evaluation study. *Journal of Adolescence*, 13(1) 3-16

Webster-Stratton LW & Lindsay DW (1999). Social competence and conduct problems in young children: issues in assessment. *Journal of Clinical Child Psychology*, 28(1) 25-43

Yeates KO, Schultz LH & Selman RL (1991). Development of interpersonal negotiating strategies in thought and action: a social-cognitive link to behavioural adjustment and social status. *Merrill-Palmer Quarterly,* 37(3) 369-403

Zettergren P (2003). School adjustment in adolescence for previously rejected, average and popular children. *British Journal of Educational Psychology*, 17(2) 207-221

CHAPTER 3   SOCIAL SKILL DEVELOPMENT WITH INDIVIDUALS

Introduction to Theory

Research has been carried out to assess aspects of social skill development with children and young people, such as problem-solving training to reduce aggression (Guerra & Slaby, 1990); friendship development (Inderbitzen-Pisaruk & Foster, 1990); individualised training (Bulkeley & Cramer, 1994); and the relationship between social information processing and social adjustment (Crick & Dodge, 1994). Wentzel and Erdley (1993) found that knowledge of appropriate and inappropriate strategies for making friends was related to cooperative behaviour and this in turn was linked to peer acceptance. The implication is that good knowledge of strategies leads to positive social behaviour, which in turn, encourages acceptance by peers.

Other important skill areas, such as social problem solving, evaluation of social context, expression of emotion, emotional literacy, assertiveness and the processing of negative cognitions are discussed in more detail below within this chapter.

Social Problem-Solving

Research on social or interpersonal problem-solving was initiated by D'Zurilla and Goldfried (1971). Using a problem-solving approach, a child or young person might "brainstorm" ways of dealing with the problem constructively, instead of retaliating in a manner likely to produce undesirable consequences. Wentzel and Erdley (1993) showed how problem-solving (based on sound knowledge of social skill strategies) helps to produce cooperative behaviour and win peer acceptance. Shure and Spivack (1980) have demonstrated that ability to generate effective solutions to social problems led to better behavioural outcomes in preschool children. Guerra and Slaby (1990) found problem-solving strategies were helpful in reducing aggression in young people. In terms of cognitive processes maintaining aggression, Guerra and Slaby (1989) found that aggressive boys had difficulty with problem definition, generation prioritisation of solutions, and evaluation of consequences; they were likely to perceive others as hostile adversaries.

Evaluation of Social Context

Combs and Slaby (1977) defined social skills as *"the ability to interact with others in a given social context in specific ways that are socially acceptable or valued and at the same time personally beneficial, mutually beneficial or beneficial primarily to others"* (page 162). The social contexts which are particularly important for young people include school, peer group, family, and wider society. Children and young people need to be aware of the social rules and norms relating to each of these contexts at a level which others would think appropriate given their stage of development. Most authorities consider that the effectiveness of behaviour in social situations depends on an understanding of the social context and an ability to produce appropriate behaviour as a consequence of understanding (Merrell & Gimpel, 2014). Clearly several processes are required to enable such successful adaptations to be made. The interaction between the individual's behaviour pattern and the social environment must be observed, evaluated, and if necessary modified. This is well explained by Crick and Dodge in their exposition of the social information processing model (Crick & Dodge, 1994). It follows that social skill development programmes must attend to these higher-order cognitive skills and processes to be successful. For this reason, social cognition is a key ingredient of such programmes.

Expression of Emotion
In Darwin's (1872) book "T*he Expression of Emotion in Man and Animals*", it was argued that the face evolved as the organ designed to give "*outward and visible signs of the internal emotional state.*" Similarly, other bodily responses, e.g. gesture and posture, are held to be signals of imminent behaviour and therefore a natural sign of the organism's emotional state. Ekman (1971) developed Darwin's thinking, taking the view that our non-verbal communications are determined partly by genetic codes and partly by cultural learning. It may be considered a fair assumption that some forms of non-verbal communication (e.g. smiling) are universal within the human species, whilst others, such as eye contact, are culturally determined (and therefore transmitted by social means) (Moran et al, 2014). Consequently, it is helpful to incorporate development of appropriate non-verbal communication (facial expression, gesture, posture) in social skill development programmes. These skills are commonly termed "body language". Together with conversational skills and tone of voice, non-verbal communication skills are sometimes referred to in social skill development programmes as "microskills".

Emotional Literacy
 Within education, theories such as emotional literacy and emotional intelligence (Wigelsworth et al, 2010) have become influential. Intuitively it makes a good deal of sense to include knowledge of emotion in a social skill development programme.

Social Information Processing
Crick and Dodge (1994) presented a new viewpoint on the relation between social information processing and social adjustment in childhood. In their opinion there is overwhelming evidence to support the link between characteristic processing styles and children's social adjustment. Crick and Dodge believe that these processes can be taught and include the following:

Encoding
Representation
Response Search
Response Decision
Enactment

This cycle is repeated and hence the model is circular. The "internal database" includes social memory; reference to this database is made at frequent points during the social information processing. This database incorporates social schemata (systematic ways of interpreting social experience or "templates"), scripts (basic social assumptions), and social knowledge.

<u>CAGDA</u>

The five stages described in the Crick and Dodge (1994) model may usefully be encapsulated in a model incorporating five steps in the social response process as follows:

Cue
Assess
Goal
Decide
Act

Use of the acronym CAGDA may enable practitioners to support clients with the appropriate processing of social information.

- In Encoding (*Cue*), specific cues in a situation are picked up and coded. The "database" (social memory) is used at this stage to provide a coding system.
- This "database" (social schemata, scripts and knowledge) is similarly used at the Representation stage (*Assess*). The child or young person is in effect thinking "*what do I make of this*" "*where do I go from here*". Of course, this process may not be conscious, or internally verbalised, but nevertheless takes place at some level. Attributions of (i) cause & effect and (ii) intentions of others will be made at this stage. Inferences will be made about the perspective of others in the situation. The outcomes of previous similar social exchanges will be reviewed.
- Response Search (*Goal*) uses the social memory database and typically involves selection of a goal, e.g. "*Stay out of trouble*", "*Get even*", "*Make friends*" or "*Get a toy*". A plan is now generated and solutions are considered; options are brainstormed to facilitate decision making about a response.
- In Response Decision (*Decide*), the response repertoire will be accessed with reference to the internal database (social memory) and a suitable response will be selected. Alternatively, a new response will be constructed utilising the experience contained in the social memory. At this stage, new options may be considered and further material from social memory may be accessed, e.g. rote patterns of response or "gut instinct". A predicted emotional response by another person may assist in assessing likely outcome. For example, behaviour that may make a boss angry is likely to be instinctively avoided by an employee. This is a final opportunity for the child to reflect on consequences before enacting the planned response.
- In Enactment (*Action*), a behavioural response is finally performed. Behavioural enactment leads to peer evaluation and response - and so the cycle continues.

In this model, social competence consists of an ability to manage this process continuously working steadily towards a more effective attainment of realistic social goals; having first formulated these goals in response to the ongoing social environment.

It will be seen that the model emphasises a reciprocal relationship between social experience and social information processing. Reactions from peers will be noted, e.g. "*Hitting that kid was easy and it really worked: she gave me back the ball*". Equally peer disapproval of aggressive behaviour may be noted and could have an influence.

There will also be a reciprocal link between self-perception and social adjustment. For example, a child experiencing peer aversion and neglect might form a negative self-perception leading to social withdrawal. This would be in effect a negative interaction cycle between self-perception and social adjustment. There might then be a case for cognitive behaviour therapy to alter the negative self-perception and provide a springboard for more positive social adjustment.

Crick and Dodge (1994) consider that there is evidence that rapid and irrational social information processing is likely to result in negative social outcomes. They term this as "automatic" or "pre-emptive" script-based processing. They report that such processing is accompanied by negative emotional arousal. For example, rejected non-aggressive boys are found to process information inadequately under such conditions.

It can therefore be argued that coaching children in verbal, reflective social information processing is likely to reduce negative outcomes. It would also be helpful to support children and young people in processing negative emotions to reduce the risk of negative social outcomes. Importantly, use of the Crick and Dodge (1994) model may be helpful in developing techniques for intervention with children and young people found to be on the autistic spectrum.

The influence of Emotion
Crick and Dodge (1994) explain how cognitive processes (thought processes) may be closely linked to emotion in the processing of social information.

- During Encoding, an increase in heart rate may have an impact on internal cues. For example, fear may be induced and an avoidant response may be generated at a later stage in the processing. Alternatively, anger may be induced and an aggressive response may be generated.
- During Representation, anger or anxiety may lead to a negative interpretation – e.g. dislike of a peer met for the first time.
- At the stage of Response Search, anger towards a peer may provide an impetus towards a retaliatory goal.
- At Response Decision, fear may suggest responses such as running away.

- During Enactment, behaviour that leads to negative outcome is likely to be rejected.

Application of the Crick and Dodge model will assist in enabling clients to process social information effectively allowing for the influence of emotion.

Schemata

Schemata are memory structures which organise information in a way that facilitates comprehension (Gerrig, 1988). They may be used when cues are interpreted.

Schemata are efficient but may lead to disregard of the immediate context. An aggressive schema may lead to the ignoring of cues suggesting play fighting. Aggressive children are likely to use unhelpful schemata. They are likely to make attributions about causes of events and the intention of peers which will lead them to retaliate. In the same way withdrawn children may make negative attributions leading to further avoidance of social contact (Bicchieri & McNally, 2015). Deciding whether oneself or a peer is responsible for knocking over a glass of milk may influence response selection and decision, in relation to interaction with that peer. Generally, aggressive behaviour is related to the attribution of hostile intentions. The way in which a child evaluates the self in terms of social competence is correlated with peer status generally, but this does not hold well with aggressive children – they tend to evaluate themselves highly but they are not evaluated highly by other children.

Children with effective social adjustment as measured by peer status tend to choose goals that are helpful to peers; children with bad social adjustment do not (e.g. they may pick retaliatory goals.

In Response Decision, the model proposes that after formulating a mental representation of the stimulus array and a goal for the situation, children access responses from long-term memory. Children will consider the content of each response together with the likely outcome and their capacity to perform the response.

Rationale for Individual Programmes

Groupwork may not be possible and it is entirely feasible to carry out a similar programme on an individual basis. What is needed is the availability of a programme which is suitable for the needs of the client for whom treatment is being planned. The client can be given tasks such as observing and recording social behaviour, social problem identification and social problem solving. It may be possible to enact simple role-plays in the session and to use video playback. As ever, rapport with the client is of crucial importance. One advantage of individual work is that there is a greater scope for individually tailored modelling, role-play and homework assignments.

Assessment

It is essential in planning individual training to carry out detailed assessment (See Chapter Two). The individual approach enables the trainer to make full use of the detailed assessment by constructing tailor-made programmes to help the client tackle specific difficulties. In particular, the trainer seeks to elicit a breakdown of the type of situations in which difficulty is encountered. This may be done by direct interview of the client, by questionnaire, and by obtaining information from teacher or parent, again preferably through questionnaire format. There are few appropriately standardised questionnaires and therefore the tutor needs to use careful and seasoned judgement in assessing the severity of the difficulty. The frequency and duration of specific difficulties can be obtained with reasonable accuracy by careful questioning though the tutor will need to form a realistic appraisal of the reliability of the source; socially unskilled youngsters may not be very accurate reporters of their own social behaviour, though they will certainly be able to give an account of their social experience provided rapport can be obtained.

Behavioural Monitoring Charts

Behavioural assessment forms can be designed, yielding information such as the following:

- Who was involved in the situation?
- What happened? Who did what?
- Why was the situation difficult for the client?
- How did the client respond to that difficulty?
- What was the outcome?
- How does the client evaluate the response?
- How does the client evaluate the outcome?

Gathering information in this way helps the client by structuring social perception, identifying problem situations, and evaluating response in terms of outcome. This method of social monitoring also sets the scene for later cognitive work (problem-solving on specific situations) and behavioural work (rehearsing and applying more effective coping strategies).

Implementing Individual Training

Agreeing Goals

Having carried out an assessment, the tutor will have some idea of the situations causing difficulty and of the client's strengths and weaknesses. It is now a suitable time to reach agreement with the client on specific goals for social skills training:

Tutor: *Now we have talked about various situations you find difficulty with* (trainer enumerates a few situations) *I wonder if you could say what are the main situations you would like to cope with better?*

Client: *I'd like to stop Sam, John and Geoffrey bullying me in break. They keep asking me for money and it's really getting to me.*

Tutor: *O.K., so you want to stop Sam, John and Geoffrey bullying you in break.*

A specific goal has now been agreed. The tutor then suggests skills which may assist in attaining the goal, e.g. learning more assertive styles of behaviour and learning to make friends. It is useful to present global (more complex) skills at this stage, as this makes more sense to the client. Micro-skills can be presented later.

Agreeing a goal provides structure for the training and gives the trainer and client a common aim to work towards. Agreeing a goal provides hope for the client and motivation to work for change.

Monitoring Behaviour and Situations
Having agreed a goal, it is useful for the client to continue monitoring behaviour and situations using the behavioural monitoring chart and supplementing this with a diary in which socially stressful incidents are recorded. If the client does not like writing, a system of codes and symbols denoting certain events can be agreed with the client. This enables the client to build up a language for reporting the socially stressful events. By recording the events, the client begins to think reflectively and proactively. The tutor positively reinforces the client for this recording.

Cognitive Preparation (Explaining the Model)
Having enabled the client to identify problem situations and a goal for change, the next step is for the tutor to explain about the social skills development model and the way in which it might be helpful for the client:

Tutor: *There are ways we learn these skills, like dealing with bullying and making friends. Sometimes, we learn them for ourselves, by trying different ways to do it and noticing what other people do. Sometimes, it's good to get help. What we could do is talk about some ideas you could try in here, and give you a chance to do some practice. Then you could try these new ideas out next time you get in one of these nasty situations, and see how you get on.*

The tutor encourages the client to believe in the possibility of behavioural change and being proactive, rather than feeling he will always be stuck in the unpleasant situations in which he finds himself. There is an important element of cognitive work here, as the client may believe that the awful situations are an inevitable consequence of his unfortunate personality, physique, appearance, stupidity etc.
Explaining about the model provides the client with a deeper understanding of how steps towards the desired goal can lead to change, enhancing motivation. The client is provided with new conceptual tools for thinking about the problem and understanding the problem situations.

Skill Acquisition
The tutor can now initiate sessions of role-play and modelling:

Tutor: *It sounds to me as if you need to be more forceful with these characters, when they have a go at you. How about trying some phrases like "Shove off mate" "Some people can't take a hint" or "I don't need this". You'd need to stand up to them, and look them in the eye, and show you mean business. Let's role-play the situation now. I'll be one of the bullies* (stands up) *and you stand here and get ready to give me one of those forceful answers.* (Client stands up, and the situation is roleplayed, with the tutor, in the role of bully, initiating the roleplay with some offensive remark).

Key situations can now be discussed, with a focus on enhancing social coping strategies. The client is reinforced for appropriate behaviours in roleplay and real life. The client is helped to understand social interactions better through taking the social perspective of others. Behavioural microskills are identified which could be causing difficulty (e.g. poor eye contact, unsure tone of voice, unclear speech). The client is praised for small but significant gains, and progressively learns by "shaping" to acquire more positive skills, and enhance his repertoire of social behaviours.

The skill acquisition stage proceeds with activities such as the following:
- Problem-solving
- Behavioural Monitoring
- Review of problem situations and strategies
- Formulation of rules for dealing with difficult situations
- Reinforcement of client for specific gains in roleplay and real life

Once the agreed goal is attained, the tutor reviews with the client whether the goal should be reformulated, or whether enough work/ progress has been made. Issues of maintenance and generalisation will need to be considered.

Building a Programme
The process of building a programme must be based on theory and on accurate individual assessment. Furthermore, it is essential for the practitioner to proceed from a clearly formed and understood theoretical perspective.

Similarly, accurate individual assessment must underpin good programme-building. The methodology of social skill assessment has been elaborated in Chapter 2.

The programme we build should address six main areas,
1. Developmental considerations
2. Social context
3. Type of social difficulty experienced
4. Situations, behaviours, and emotions
5. Additional skills needed at this juncture
6. Interventions required to meet the needs of the individual

Developmental Considerations
It is important to take individual variations in biological growth into account, bearing in mind the great variability of the age in reaching puberty.

Where biological variation is part of the issue, information should be offered to clients to enable them to see themselves from a different perspective, accept their current physical attributes, and avoid accepting or attracting the role of scapegoat. Difference in appearance from others may occur, owing to disease, genetic and ethnic factors, and may cause scapegoating. Again, information should be offered, supported by counselling and self-esteem building. It is important that clients should find positive aspects of themselves to focus on and use as a basis for their future personal development.

Where there is evidence of victimisation or bullying, the tutor or counsellor should seek ways to work locally with other agencies to reduce the incidence of such pernicious processes in schools and other organisations. Counselling should be a community process and not just a private process.

Moral development may be an issue in cases where clients are presenting antisocial behaviour patterns and delinquency. Training in ethical issues and perspective-taking should be included in programmes for such clients. Otherwise superficial social skill enhancement can simply lead to the offender avoiding the consequences of his actions.

Some social difficulties may occur partly because an emotional trauma from an early stage has not been resolved. This too is a developmental difficulty - a blockage in emotional development. For example, separation from a career in early life may lead to school refusal associated with separation anxiety. In such cases, the client needs emotional support through counselling in addition to behavioural approaches to help with the school refusal.

Social Context
In addition to looking at developmental factors, it is also important to consider social context. For example, a school refuser might have a mother who is sometimes anxious and over-protective, thereby making it hard for her youngster to become independent. Family counselling would therefore be appropriate. The school may have disciplinary procedures which are frightening to the child, or the classrooms may be unruly. The young person may be disoriented by many family moves, or struggling to cope with recent parental separation. All these factors arise from the social context, and appropriate means for coping with this context, whatever it may be, must be built into the programme to help the troubled young person. As a bare minimum, the problems arising from the context should be discussed with the young person and they should be helped to develop and maintain appropriate coping strategies (including the use of social skills). Direct action with family or school should be attempted if practicable. And again, where possible, the social skill trainer, facilitator or counsellor should at least feel concerned about the wider context in which the trouble occurs, even if, as so often, circumstances preclude any effective action for change.

Type of Difficulty Experienced

Some social difficulties associated with high anxiety may be associated with excessively severe child-rearing practices; others such as an antisocial behaviour pattern may be a failure to internalise social norms due to inconsistent handling, an impoverished environment or ways of responding to emotional stress within the family. The programme should have due regard for the type of social difficulty experienced by the client and offer different social skills to enable the client to respond in a manner which will be more advantageous from the perspective of self and others.

Situations, Behaviour, and Emotions

It is important for the client to come to understand what situations seem to be causing difficulty, what responses are currently being evoked by these situations, and how these responses can be altered. The consequences of current coping strategies should be evaluated and the possibility of developing new social strategies should be considered. Clients should also be encouraged to determine emotional components of their current pattern of response (e.g. anxiety, anger), notice how they currently respond to these emotions in social situations and consider alternative ways of responding. For example, school refusers can be helped to cope more adaptively with their anxiety and get to school, and violent offenders can learn safer ways of expressing their anger.

To summarise, an approach based on evaluating the relationship between behaviours, situations and emotions, leading to a re-formulation of coping strategies may be used to tailor the individual programme to the specific type of social difficulty experienced by the presenting client.

Skills and Techniques

Skills to be developed and techniques to be used by the trainer are listed and described below:

- <u>Microskills</u> include non-verbal communication processes, conversational skills and tone of voice. They are the "nuts and bolts" of social communication. They can be developed in role-play. For individual work, it may be useful to involve another adult or a peer when setting up role-play. The individual can be rewarded by praise for demonstrating helpful microskills in role-play. Simple role-plays should be used initially, e.g. "greeting a friend", in which the smile and "eyebrow raise" can be practised.
- <u>Joining in</u> is a skill which can be developed in role-play. Joining in an existing conversation is a slightly more challenging task than greeting, as it requires more assertive styles of behaviour. Conversational skills such as listening and asking appropriate questions can be practised along with non-verbal skills (e.g. eye contact).
- <u>Empathy</u> denotes positive but not intrusive involvement with the world and experience of the person with whom one is interacting. Empathic behaviour

would typically involve active and friendly listening, smiling and perhaps nodding, suitable turn-taking in conversation and generally having time for the other person. Eye contact would be frequent but not so intense as to register strong emotion. Empathy skills can be practised in a role-play involving friends discussing their respective interests.

- Assertiveness is a useful skill in a variety of social situations, e.g. taking a defective item back to a shop, complaining about poor service or dealing with "criticisms" from adults or peers. Assertiveness may be a type of social response on a continuum between aggressiveness and inaction. The type of behaviour depends on the situation and the criterion is that a reasonable goal should be achieved with the minimum of offence to others. In a situation requiring assertiveness, microskills and empathy may be used to good effect. Role-play with feedback from a third party will assist in the development of appropriate assertive behaviours.

- Negotiation occurs when an individual works with another to reach a joint solution in a situation of potentially conflicting interests. Joining in, empathy and assertiveness skills are all important. The goal will have a mutually acceptable outcome, followed by closure.

- Friendship making involves the use of a range of skills to develop and maintain friendship. Microskills and joining skills are important for initiating contact and maintaining social interaction. Empathy enables the friendship to deepen. Assertiveness protects the individual from exploitation within the relationship. Negotiation facilitates the pursuit of mutually satisfactory goals.

- Interpersonal problem solving refers to the process of dealing with problems that crop up in social interaction. The problem is analysed, the various options are brainstormed and the most appropriate solution is selected. Initially problem solving is used with specific situations; at a later stage the skill is generalised.

- Dealing with negative cognitions may cause low self-esteem and unrealistically negative self-perception may be unhelpful in social situations. Lack of confidence as a result of low self-esteem may impair social skill performance in children and young people. There may be an expectation of negative judgements by others. The resulting anxiety may lead the individual to avoid social situations making it difficult to establish a pattern of social interaction. It is therefore important to shift the pattern of negative thinking.

- Interpretation of Social Context: The individual will need to make correct evaluations of social context, to decide on appropriate ways to respond, making valid assessments of social situations and planning effective performance. See CAGDA, for guidance on support with social information processing.

Techniques for Training
Techniques will vary according to the age and abilities of the individual concerned. It is important to liaise with families, school and other agencies to obtain support with the development programme. Specific help with implementation may be requested

and feedback obtained. The following will be found useful:

- Review of problem situations: Analysis of the individual's response to specific situations will be carried out as part of the assessment. The implications of social context will be discussed.
- Target setting: Strategies for specific situations will be developed, using the interpersonal problem solving model. Desired goals for change will be agreed.
- Role-play: In the context of social skill development, role-play is sometimes termed "behavioural rehearsal". It gives the individual a chance to have a "trial run" at challenging situations in a supportive context. Feedback helps the individual to modify responses in the desired direction. A peer or second adult may be recruited to make the role-play more lifelike. Trainees need to be introduced to role-play gradually so that confidence can be built up. Trainers need the necessary skills in order to develop role-play.
- Coaching: The tutor can help the client to develop progressively more complex skills, in a programme geared towards individual need.
- Homework setting: After a role-play session, real-life tasks can be set to enable specific skills to be practised. Situations that are likely to occur in real life can be anticipated. Use of non-verbal skills, tone of voice and conversational skills (e.g. language and useful phrases) can be rehearsed at this stage.
- Follow-up on homework/behavioural monitoring: Follow-up gives the individual an opportunity to report back on real life experiments in social situations. The tutor can obtain subjective feedback on social skill performance.
- Review of problem situations and strategies: The tutor may observe social behaviour (e.g. microskills) in the training session, and perhaps observe directly some of the real-life practice which has been planned, if feasible.
- Formulation of rules for dealing with difficult situations: This process is sometimes called "generalisation". It requires a certain level of cognitive ability. The individual may be encouraged to develop personal rules for dealing with specific challenging situations, brainstorming strategies, using role-play for behavioural rehearsal and carrying out real life trials. At the stage of follow-up on real life trials, the individual may be encouraged to develop personal rules for what is likely to work classes of challenging situation (e.g. experiencing criticisms). These rules can then be reviewed, and if necessary revised, in subsequent "homework feedback" sessions. This process will enable the individual to habitualise the act of reviewing social process internally and developing increasing social competence.
- Reinforcement of client for specific gains in role-play and real life: In the coaching role, the tutor may praise social skill development demonstrated in role-play and real life, making specific comments both on microskills and more complex aspects of responding (e.g. assertive behaviour, problem solving and formulation of rules).
- Indirect interventions: It is important to liaise with families, school and other agencies to obtain support with the development programme. Specific help

with implementation may be requested and feedback obtained.

Cognitive Behaviour Therapy
Cognitive behaviour therapy offers an array of techniques for dealing with social phobia, anxiety and depression. If emotional factors are seriously inhibiting the development of social skills, the use of such techniques should be considered.

Case Examples

Abbie, aged 12

Background
Abbie was seen by an independent multidisciplinary agency to help with social skill development. She had received special educational treatment in ordinary primary school but had experienced difficulties on transfer to secondary school at age 11. Initially she had been placed in a class for children with severe disability and learning difficulties in the secondary school, but was then transferred to a class for children with more moderate learning difficulties. Within this context, she found relations with the peer group stressful.

Diagnosis
Following prenatal brain injury, Abbie was diagnosed with autism, attention deficit hyperactivity disorder and uneven cognitive development. On verbal-cognitive tasks her scores were within average limits, but she experienced spatial difficulties and had trouble with perceptual reasoning. She was visually impaired, dyspraxic and had speech and language difficulties. She suffered from epilepsy and obesity. The obesity may have been due to an under-functioning thyroid gland.

Family Context
Abbie lives with her mother and older brother. Abbie's parents separated when she was 5, and she has no contact with her biological father. Her maternal grandmother lived locally at the time of initial assessment and helped a good deal with family care. Other relatives live in the area but contact with these is limited.

Educational Context
Abbie's case had been referred to a tribunal for a review of her special educational needs. There was an issue between the family and the school regarding the type of teaching group which would be most appropriate for Abbie – "mainstream" or "special". The integrated treatment service in the meantime had set up an arrangement to observe Abbie in school to assist with her special needs.

Support Systems
The main support system was immediate family. Input was provided by a range of specialist disciplines including Speech and Language Therapy, Occupational Therapy, Physiotherapy and Clinical Psychology. The family participated in varied out-of-school activities including music tuition and horse riding.

Social Experience

After transfer to secondary education in the previous September, Abbie attended school in a different area of the city, therefore she did not have a group of children from her own primary school moving with her to secondary school. As the family moved for her to attend this school, Abbie did not have links with neighbouring children in her new area. Hence, she started attending the secondary school at something of a social disadvantage.

Clinical Assessment

1. Cognitive assessment was carried out using a reputable structured technique. In terms of conceptual understanding, Abbie's performance was superior on the verbal side as opposed to the non-verbal. Scores were comparatively low for spatial ability involving the replication of patterns using coloured blocks and for Perceptual Reasoning using pictures. Her scores were significantly better for Verbal Reasoning and Verbal Comprehension. On a test of vocabulary, she experienced difficulty in providing definitions. This would suggest some impairment of verbal fluency.

2. Her Working Memory for sequences of digits and numbers was better than her Verbal Comprehension and Perceptual Reasoning. This suggested that her executive function was relatively less impaired for this type of task where visual and motor skills are not required. Her processing speed on pencil and paper tasks involving symbols was fairly slow, but suggested some impairment of her visual and motor processes rather than limited reasoning ability. It seemed that when tasks required both visual input and motor execution, she experienced difficulty. This was hardly surprising, as she was known to be disadvantaged both in terms of visual perception and of movement.

3. Her Reading Age, assessed using a standardised assessment procedure, was around 8 years as is her spelling age. This was not surprising given her various cognitive impairments.

4. In terms of Social Skills, Abbie appeared to have difficulty relating to children of her own age. She became easily upset when criticised by adults. At times, she found it difficult to express her needs to adults. When she did so, it was sometimes in a somewhat immature manner. Abbie also had difficulty in relating to the world of others and understanding their point of view, in expressing herself non-verbally, through facial expression and gesture, and in understanding the non-verbal communications of others.

5. In terms of emotional difficulties, she tended to become anxious and depressed because of her educational and social difficulties; she could be withdrawn at times. She stated that she would appreciate being in a class where she had more stimulation. At times, she had felt vulnerable at her current school. She tended to flap her hands when her emotions were aroused.

6. In order for Abbie to be able to see both the whiteboard on the right and the interactive board on the left, it was best for her to sit at the front of the class in the middle desk. It was hard for her to decode joined-up or small writing.

7. The three students who *"talked quite a lot in class"* were named.
8. Difficult situations with her own age-group could include people talking too much and a boy with whom she became friendly before he moved to a different class. This boy tended to have tantrums and blame her for things.
9. Abbie described a difficult situation with an adult, when the adult gets on with other girls and laughs at their jokes, but does not laugh at Abbie's jokes.
10. Making friends was harder in school than at home. Break times gave a good opportunity.
11. Abbie felt that she could stand up for herself quite well to stop herself being bullied. The thing that worried her at school was that a student named X swore and was nasty to other students and Abbie was a bit afraid of him saying nasty things to her.
12. Abbie became upset when people said bad things about her mum. Abbie tended to become distracted when other students were disruptive and would sometimes join in the disruption. Abbie tended to become upset if staff told her off or reminded her of things in a sharp tone of voice. If she got quite distressed, she might yell back, otherwise she tended to stay quiet.

Treatment Plan

Regarding her social communication difficulties, the psychologist planned to work closely with a colleague (a speech & language therapist), who had relevant expertise in this area. The aim was to use role-play to develop Abbie's skills in areas such as active listening, greeting, exchanging information, negotiation and dealing with challenging behaviour presented by others. Abbie would also receive counselling about using these skills in real life situations. It was hoped that by using such methods, it would be possible to build up her self-confidence and self-esteem and reduce her emotional difficulties. She would also be offered assistance with stress management techniques including relaxation. The family would be advised about how to support her with the social skill development and stress management programmes. It was hoped that school staff might assist Abbie in promoting her self-confidence, social skills, language skills and ability to express her needs in an appropriate manner.

Intervention

Abbie was seen for 11 sessions. Role-play, computerised intervention and individualized counselling were the main techniques used. Regular review of problem situations led to the development of strategies, targets, and the generation of rules for dealing with social difficulties.

Preparation for Role-Play

Role-play was difficult for Abbie to deal with at first. In order to desensitize her brief role-plays were introduced initially and she was reinforced for participation. She "turned a corner" when she found she could enjoy assertive responding in role-play.

*   Role-play 1 involved joining in conversation and asking a question. Abbie performed well in role.

- Role-play 2 involved joining in a computer activity with a peer in free time at school. Abbie asked good questions.

Assertiveness

Abbie was engaged in a role-play in which the threatening student X said *"Why are you looking at me?"*. She found this difficult to deal with. An assertive response was modelled and she was encouraged to keep her voice down.

Joining in

A role-play on "joining in" was initiated; two other girls are having a successful conversation with a member of staff. Abbie found it difficult to join in. "Joining in" behaviour was demonstrated to neutralise Abbie's anxiety.

This was construed as a problem-solving situation. Abbie needed to think in terms of social behaviour; whether she needed to do things differently to be more successful in the social situation. Alternatively, this might be a social situation which she didn't need to get involved in as it didn't matter very much to her. Abbie should think about the options and make choices.

Engaging with Peers

Abbie was encouraged in role-play to engage with a very assertive loud-voiced female peer in a computer session. She smiled and asked a question but found it difficult to persist.

Abbie was helped to generate more questions. She was asked to make a list of more interests so that she could generate focused questions and join in that way. She also began to list computer sites which she could demonstrate to others and thereby get them interested.

This approach enabled Abbie to build on her strengths and to become less focused on herself and more focused on others, allowing her to develop empathy.

Friendship Building

Abbie was advised to get involved in activities that would be interesting to other students, particularly on the computer, to avoid getting involved in disruptive activities.

Abbie was supported interactively on computer, to develop skills in friendship building. She was encouraged to develop appropriate questions, focusing on the world of others. In this way, Abbie's natural sociability was developed.

Target Setting

The specific targets for Abbie were
- To practise "joining in" skills
- To use all opportunities in school to do this

- To keep her voice down
- To avoid getting sucked into disruptive behaviour
  - To practise calm, assertive responding when someone gives her a criticism
  - To develop internal problem-solving skills
  - To make positive statements to herself when she feels upset

Assertive Response to Criticism

Various styles of responding to "put-downs" were discussed and illustrated by visual material. (NB criticism may be experienced with adults or peers).

1. Aggressive/confrontational
2. Assertive, "cool"
3. Ignoring, non-committal
4. Report to member of staff

} The importance of eye contact was emphasised

Coaching was inaugurated to practise these styles. Abbie was supported in developing and rehearsing specific responses to specific types of "put-down" situation. Abbie's mother was provided with visual prompts to support Abbie's social learning about assertiveness.

Assertive Response to Authority

The visual prompts were used to generate different verbal and non-verbal responses when being told off by teachers. Abbie was coached using this material. Facial expression and tone of voice were discussed. It appeared that the use of eyebrows and a sigh with a soft voice were effective. These were also the least likely actions to cause a negative response from teaching staff.

Abbie stated that she preferred the assertive/cool response, indicating that she remembered the phrases from these cards quite well. Abbie seemed to cope well with the different role-plays, gaining in confidence and in her ability to use the different responses. Abbie accepted direct feedback about her tone of voice and facial expression and made a second attempt at some responses.

Outcome

At session 11, it was noted that Abbie had made a positive start at a new school and was displaying more confidence in role-play and real life social situations. For example, she could demonstrate negotiation skills with a peer in role-play, even though these had not been specifically taught- hence this was a sign of generalization. It appeared that continuing observation and the provision of booster sessions would be sufficient to enable her to maintain the gains she had made.

Discussion

The individual sessions were used to tailor approaches geared to Abbie's needs and prepare suitable materials. Computer activities were used to reinforce role-play and help with motivation. Positive rapport was established, which enabled Abbie to provide accurate information about difficulties occurring in the social context, so that careful plans could be made to provide input to deal with these situations.

Faith, aged 7

Faith was referred by the School Nursing Sister. She was experiencing night terrors and screaming in her sleep. She was described as having poor memory and making repetitive clicking, clapping and vocal noises. There were some symptoms suggesting Tourette's Disorder but this was not diagnosed. She had previously been given assistance with speech however there were still concerns that her speech was often inappropriate for the situation. Her social skills were poor and she had difficulties making friends.

The McCarthy Scales of Children's Abilities was used to assess her cognitive functioning. Her ability was found to be in the average range. However, a discrepancy between perceptual/ performance functioning and verbal functioning was noted. Her verbal abilities were more limited than her non-verbal abilities. The Wechsler Objective Reading Dimensions (WORD; Wechsler, 1993) was used to assess her literacy skills. She scored in the average range for her age. The school was advised of the findings of the assessment.

It is likely that Faith's relatively limited verbal skills contributed to her difficulties with social skills which in turn made it hard for her to make friends. This could have contributed to her emotional disturbance and night terrors.

In addition to her speech difficulty, mild cognitive impairment could have been present which could have affected her understanding of social situations and her skills in dealing with and understanding more complex emotions.

Note: Had intervention been requested for Faith; a similar approach to that used with Abbie would have been helpful. As Faith was a younger child an approach using Social Stories might have been tried. Both young people might well respond to activities designed for more able children on the autistic spectrum.

References

Bauminger N, Edelsztein HS & Morash J (2005). Social information processing and emotional understanding in children with Learning Difficulties. *Journal of Learning Disabilities*, 38, (1) 45-63.

Bulkeley R & Cramer D (1994). Social skills training with young adolescents: group and individual approaches in a school setting. *Journal of Adolescence*, 17, 521-531.

Crick NR & Dodge KA (1994). A review and reformulation of social information-processing mechanisms in children and adolescents. *Psychological Bulletin*, 115, (1) 74-101.

Combs ML & Slaby DP (1977). Social skills training with children. In Lahey BB et al (eds) *Advances in Clinical Child Psychology.* New York: Plenum

Darwin C (1872). *The Expression of the Emotions in Man and Animals.* London: John Murray.

D'Zurilla TJ & Goldfried MR (1971). Problem-solving and behaviour modification. *Journal of Abnormal Psychology,* 78, 107-126.

Ekman P (1971). Universals and cultural differences in facial expressions of emotion. In J Cole (Ed) *Nebraska Symposium on Motivation.* Lincoln: University of Nebraska Press.

Guerra NG & Slaby RG (1989). Evaluative factors in social problem solving by aggressive boys. *Journal of Abnormal Child Psychology,* 17, (3) 277-289.

Guerra NG & Slaby RG (1990). Cognitive mediators of aggression in adolescent offenders: II Intervention. *Developmental Psychology,* 26, (2) 297-277.

Moran, R. T., Abramson, N. R., & Moran, S. V. (2014). *Managing cultural differences.* Routledge.

Inderbitzen-Pisaruk H & Foster SL (1990). Adolescent friendships and peer acceptance: implications for social skills training. *Clinical Psychology Review,* 10, (4) 425-440.

Shure MB & Spivack G (1980). Interpersonal problem-solving as a mediator of behavioural adjustment in preschool and kindergarten children. *Journal of Applied Developmental Psychology,* 1, 29-44.

Wentzel CR & Erdley CA (1993). Strategies for making friends: Relations to social behaviour and peer acceptance in early adolescence. *Developmental Psychology, 29,* (5) 819-826.

Wigelsworth M Humphrey N Afroditi K & Landrum A (2010). A review of key issues in the measurement of children's social and emotional skills. *Educational Psychology in Practice: Theory Research and Practice in Educational Psychology,* 26, (2) 173-186.

Merrell, K. W., & Gimpel, G. (2014). *Social skills of children and adolescents: Conceptualization, assessment, treatment.* Psychology Press.

Wechsler, D. (1993). Wechsler Objective Reading Dimensions. London: The Psychological Corporation

CHAPTER 4   IMPLEMENTING GROUP PROGRAMMES

This chapter provides a theoretical formulation, practical guidance and case examples in terms of group process, evaluation and outcomes for individual members. Appendix 1 provides sample programmes and Appendix 2 offers some useful tips on psychodynamic perspectives.

Theoretical Foundation

It has been found that children who are at risk of emotional and behavioural difficulties are more likely to have social skills deficits than other children (Lo et al, 2002). Cowen et al (1973) found that the presence of social deficits in children was a strong predictor of future mental health problems, delinquency, substance misuse, school dropout and academic underachievement. It has been found that social skills groups are often an effective intervention for a wide range of difficulties, e.g. depression (Sommers et al, 2000), social anxiety (Whittenberg, 1995), low self-esteem (Deffenbacher et al, 1996), aggression (Kamps et al, 2000; Pepler et al, 1991) and impulsivity (Kamps et al, 2000). Other research (Bulkeley and Cramer, 1990; 1994) strongly suggests that teaching social skills through the medium of groupwork is helpful.

Rationale

Working in groups is a natural way to enhance social performance. The group provides a safe environment for experimenting with social skills and the therapists can control the situation and ensure that suitable skills are practised. Clients have the opportunity to build up their skills by incremental stages and receive suitable feedback both from therapists and peers for their increasingly successful social efforts. Groupwork is an art as much as a science, and as such can only be acquired by appropriately supervised experience.

Group work may also assist with the following areas:
- Building a sense of interdependence within the group which reduces the sense of isolation and promotes a mutual acknowledgement of needs.
- Sharing developmental concerns, thereby reducing insecurity and promoting a secure sense of identity.
- The provision of help and support with ongoing interpersonal difficulties.

Group training provides a natural peer group, within which new styles of social behaviour can be safely tried out. Group training programmes draw on a "core" model, but may be "tailored" to the needs of the individual clients involved.

A group can be defined as "closed" (having the same composition for a set number of sessions); "open "(clients come and go and the emphasis is more on joint learning, mutual support and learning from the group process); or "slow open" (the entry of new members is controlled to limit the disruption to the group experience which might be caused by excessive changes in group membership.) Closed and slow open groups are best for social skill training. It is advisable that there be a relatively fixed structure and content so that the adolescents have the experience of progressing together through similar stages of work.

Objectives
In running social skills groups, we have the following general objectives:
- To develop self-expression and self-esteem
- To enable members to enhance their social skills, also increasing their knowledge of appropriate social strategies, laying the foundations for more satisfying social experiences in the future
- To enable individual members to become more aware of social norms and more responsive to others
- To maintain boundaries – setting the scene for the group, ensuring the group follows the set programme, encouraging respectful and positive interaction – using the group process as far as possible to achieve this goal e.g. helping group to generate its own rules at the first session

The skills to be developed (for clients) and the techniques (for trainers) are as described in Chapter 3. Therefore, it is likely that extensive use of role-play will be involved. The group will provide an ideal environment for practising active listening skills.

Role-play
Role-play can be used helpfully in social skill development groups in several ways:
- To practise skills required in specific social situations and receive feedback and positive reinforcement, thereby building greater skill and confidence in dealing with those situations. For example, a child or adolescent who experiences bullying role-plays a situation in which he deals assertively with the bullies, who soon give up and move on
- To provide an opportunity to develop empathy and perspective taking abilities. For example, a child or adolescent may take part in a role-play in which he is encouraged to display listening skills and help someone else solve a problem; a child or adolescent after being in a role-play in which difficulty is experienced with someone in authority, then plays the person in authority (a parent or teacher) - this technique is known as "role reversal".

- To provide an opportunity to learn social processes by observation. For example, after role-playing a situation in which an adolescent "loses his cool" with a teacher, the group can discuss the consequences of his action, and how the situation could be handled differently.
- To role-play facilitates emotional expression, heightens involvement in the group process, and creates immediacy by making the situation happen "right there" in the room.

Identification of emotion (discrimination of emotional states in self and others) may be enhanced by role-play, flipchart work, games and exercises. A useful initial approach is to generate lists of feelings and encourage the group to mime these feelings using appropriate posture, gesture and facial expression. Empathy training can be carried out by modelling and role-play using video.

Setting Up a Group
Group work with children and adolescents requires structure, a strong sense of direction, and clear ground rules. It is necessary to negotiate both with the children and adolescents themselves and with carers in order to ensure attendance. It is important firstly to have a clear notion of the aims of the group and the type or types of social difficulty being addressed, and secondly, to carry out detailed assessment and to build client motivation prior to group attendance.

Contact with Potential Referrers
Group programmes must start from an adequate and informed referral base and therefore it is essential to establish good contact with potential referrers providing (a) succinct and convincing written hand-outs about what is on offer, (b) your contact details and (c) referral forms.

Selecting Clients
Having obtained sufficient referrals of clients (allowing for some to be eliminated during individual assessment) and (b) carried out assessments, clients should be allocated to groups using the criteria for group formation mentioned above.

Group Composition
Eight is recommended as a maximum number of clients for a social skills group. Children or young people with autistic spectrum disorder may require smaller groups. It is helpful to ensure some compatibility of group members, and to avoid a situation where one individual stands out as different. Therefore, groups should either be balanced for gender or single sex. Matching clients with similar social difficulties to each other may also be helpful, though a mix of personalities is desirable; in a group of withdrawn young people, the therapists may have to work hard to create a spark of enthusiasm!

Developmental level, as well as chronological age, is important when matching clients to for groups. Clients should be matched for developmental level. Age may not always be the best guide, as the age of reaching puberty varies considerably and puberty brings with it important psychological changes together with the obvious development of sexual characteristics. However, caution is necessary, as it is known that physical maturation is not the only determinant of sexual behaviour, and the social status of young people is to some degree conferred by the year group to which they belong within the school. Clients may be out of their depth if they are expected to work with a group of young people who are at different developmental level to themselves.

Motivating Clients

Clients and their carers should be given full explanations of what the group will involve and offered reassurance and support for any anxieties they may express. The motivation of clients and carers should be fired by the infectiousness of the trainer's enthusiasm, by careful explanation of what is on offer supported by written hand-outs, by demystification and de-stigmatisation. Emphasise that we all experience social difficulties and it is "cool" to be open about it and get some help. It may be more acceptable for clients to attend groups in school than at a clinic, as there may be a greater connotation of stigma attached to attendance at a clinic.

Forming an Overview

As with individual programmes, group programmes are planned and individually tailored to client needs. Social skill tutors form an overview of a group's needs at the start of a series of sessions and plan an appropriate programme drawing on the resources and materials which are available (e.g. published programmes, their own record of past programmes and the like). Detailed examples of group programmes are given in Appendix 1.

Choosing a Focus

Trainers decide on a focus and objective for the sessions (e.g. help clients to improve anger management, reduce experiences of bullying or reduce sense of social isolation), negotiate these goals with clients, and declare their aims to carers. In the process of setting up a group, the presence of need as indicated by referrals will trigger the focus. Goals and objectives will be negotiated with clients and parents/carers as appropriate in the individual assessment phase, before the group starts. The example at the end of this chapter will clarify the process.

Involving Carers

Adequate information should be given to parents, foster parents and/or any others who may be involved in a caring role. Carers should be fully informed about the aims of the programme and offered the opportunity to attend meetings to discuss the objectives of the group training in detail and receive feedback on the work that has been done. Conducting these sessions will help to raise the awareness of carers to social skill difficulties. Carers should be given every encouragement to support clients actively in meeting their objectives. Carers can be offered their own "Stop Think Do" group –using the analogy of traffic lights- to enable them to improve their social interaction with the young clients.

Running Groups: Ambience, Confidentiality, Venue

It is important to create positive expectations and to involve the group at an early stage in rule setting. Clients can be given a sense of ownership of the group by participation in preparation of lists of ideas on flipcharts, which are then displayed in the room. Trainers do not abdicate responsibility, but create opportunities for the youngsters to exercise it. It is important to deal in a prompt and friendly way with any situation in which the attention of the group is diverted from work. The approach to such situations should be one of reminding clients of responsibility towards the group rather than blaming and shaming.

To create an atmosphere of trust it is helpful to stress the confidential nature of the group and remind the clients of their own obligations in this respect. As clients may choose to enact role-plays about processes within their own families, it is advisable to stress that feedback to carers will be general and not specific.

Confidentiality issues may be somewhat complex. The young person may be attending other sessions for personal help and there may be a need for some sharing of information. There may be a need for a statutory response to information suggesting that others are at risk. The issues need to be thought through in advance and discussed carefully with group members at the start of the group.

The venue should be of reasonable size, convenient of access and reasonably comfortable. Clients should feel able to attend discreetly without incurring stigmatisation. Social skill training groups can be run in a variety of settings, e.g. hospitals, clinics, schools, social service departments, probation services or children's homes. What is needed is a comfortable room with chairs, beanbags and space for role-play. It is useful if the room can be near the base of the staff involved to facilitate the provision of drinks, biscuits, flipchart, and pens together with the other materials required for the various games and activities involved. It is helpful if resources for video recording and playback are available.

Explanation/Skill Acquisition

Group work includes explanation of concepts followed by skill acquisition. The explanation of concepts is designed to prepare clients for the skill acquisition phase and gives an indication of the nature of social skills training in general, the specific skills to be acquired and the way in which this learning will take place. Skill acquisition is facilitated by role-play which provides a focus of attention on the situation in which the new skills are to be practised. Coaching and feedback are used to prompt and reinforce the use of skills in the role-play situation and clients are subsequently trained to reinforce themselves for practising the skills in real life.

The phase of skill acquisition includes:
- Generating problem situations
- Generating relevant skills

- Practising those skills in role-play and real life
- Generating social problem-solving techniques
- Reinforcement, observation and feedback

Structure and Content of Sessions

Groups may be run as courses of ten sessions of an hour and a quarter each (*See Appendix 1 for sample programmes*). Alternatively, four sessions may be run and then a space allowed for the skills to be applied in real life before following up with booster sessions. This has the advantage of preventing dependency on the groups. Research suggests that social skill training has a ripple effect, with improvements continuing to occur for some time even when sessions are not being attended. This is to be expected since clients will be empowered to try out new behaviours and gradually increase their repertoire of skill.

A helpful format for a social skill group might follow the following structure:
- Check-in
- Warm-up
- Brainstorming
- Role-play
- Assignment Setting (in some meetings)
- Game

Each session begins with a check in, enabling the young people to report positive and negative events which have occurred during the day. If these events highlight social skill difficulties, they may suggest material for a role-play at a later stage in the session.

 A warm-up is a quick behavioural exercise which promotes interaction and activates the youngsters (e.g. the Name Game which involves clients throwing the ball to each other saying their own name, the name of the person to whom they are throwing the ball, or the name of the person who threw them the ball. By engaging the clients in a task of increasing difficulty the names can be learned by repetition and this will result in an increasing sense of acceptance by group members.

Brainstorming uses active means to focus attention on the main ideas which will be the subject of the session, including the role-play. Using whiteboard and flipchart, the group is asked to brainstorm situations which might create difficulty (e.g. experiences of bullying) and to generate list of coping skills for dealing with that situation. Prompts are given if necessary.

Role-play is the key part of the session. The role-play is planned in advance by the trainers and simple "props" may be used. Tables and chairs in the room serve to "set the scene". The basic structure and content of the role-play is predetermined, but the details of the verbal and non-verbal interaction are "live" and therefore offer samples of clients' behaviour pattern which can give a clue to their usual style. The role-play may be managed in two ways.

- Modelling and Behavioural Rehearsal
  The tutors model good and bad coping skills, which naturally leads to a discussion. The clients are then asked in turn to practise the skills which are presented, and given feedback. The technique of "shaping" is used to improve performance gradually by coaching, giving positive encouragement and constructive feedback. The group should be actively involved in this process, as feedback from peers is very powerful. The role-play can be recorded on video providing additional opportunities for self-observation and feedback. Clients are subsequently encouraged to try the skills in real life and report back on progress.
- Increasing Emotional Involvement in Role-play
  In the alternative version, clients are asked to focus attention on the situation which causes most difficulty from among the list that has been generated. They are asked to make a statement of their feelings on flipchart paper and draw the feeling using an appropriate colour. Each client is then asked to develop the situation into a role-play using others from the group. The client reports on feelings elicited during the role-play including physical aspects of arousal. The client is then encouraged to perform the role-play again using different strategies. Feedback and modelling are provided to enhance the client's skill.

This approach has the advantage of promoting emotional involvement and heightening arousal which intensifies the quality of the learning experience. The situation is recreated in the room more vividly. The client receives additional training in the labelling and identification of emotion which is an important part of social skill.

The role-play part of the session may take longer using this approach and it may not be possible for each client to enact a personal role-play during each session. However, the clients can learn from observation of the role-play of others, and will have opportunities to participate in the role-plays and give feedback.

Use of Video
Video and playback of the role-play provides direct feedback on the skill acquisition, greatly enhancing the learning and motivation of the group.

Assignment Setting
After the role-play, clients are asked to practise a specific skill which has been learned during the session and report back. In working with adults, these assignments are often called "homework", but this term may have negative connotations with adolescents, if they are not highly involved in their work at school!

The final activity is a game, which rounds off the session. The game should offer social experience and training in an enjoyable form, building group cohesion and ending the session on a pleasant note.

Detailed examples of session formats and exercises are given in Appendix 1/2 of this chapter.

Recording, Session Evaluation and Planning

Recording
Maintaining full and accurate records enables tutors to monitor the progress of their work and enables details of client change to be logged and fed back to referrers and, where appropriate, carers. Records are maintained of each session, and as a minimum include:

a) The structure and objectives of each session; whether the structure was followed, and whether the objectives were met

b) The names of those attending

c) The process of each session; the response of clients to the interventions, the apparent success or otherwise of the interventions, the interactions between clients, the interaction between clients and tutors, the general atmosphere of the session and any other relevant comment on the group process

d) Some detail on the thoughts, feelings and behaviour of individual clients; their motivation, level of involvement and commitment to work

Evaluation of Client Skill Development
The following procedures may also be useful:

a) Members' definition of their difficulties; self-rating of these at intervals

b) Facilitator rating of individual member's difficulties, repeated at intervals

c) Qualitative accounts of process and content based on observations by the facilitators

d) (At end of group). Statements may be made by individual group members of their experience of the process, the content, and the gains which they have made as a result of group attendance

e) Qualitative statements by others (e.g. carers, teaching staff) regarding changes which they have observed

f) Rating scales completed by others (e.g. carers, teaching staff)

The formal measures described in Chapter 2 and Appendices 1 and 2 can be used to select clients for groups and to evaluate the client's status before the intervention, after the intervention, and at follow-up.

Evaluation of Session: Formal Tasks
Tutors assess whether each of the formal objectives of the previous session were in fact achieved. A session record can be reviewed, or if this is not available, the original session plan can be used to guide the memory of the trainers.

Evaluation of Session: Social Process

Secondly, tutors review the response of the group and the responses of the individual members. The technique for evaluating social process session by session may be summarised in the following checklist of key areas: COMMITMENT, COHESION, CONFLICT, BOUNDARIES, PROBLEMS, PLANNING: *How committed were they to the learning process? Was there a feeling of positive interaction within the group? Were boundaries maintained? Are there any interpersonal difficulties requiring attention? Does this process of review highlight any problem areas, and if so how are they to be tackled?*

Planning the Next Session

The formal structure and objectives for the next session are agreed between the tutors. If a specific programme is being followed, the broad structure may already be laid down, but some last-minute adjustments may be necessary at this stage in the light of the last session and the discussion of social process. The finalised plan for the next session can then be drawn up.

Planning Long-term Follow-up

After debriefing at the end of a group programme, tutors may assess the impact of the group programme and make plans for continuing to care for group members, deciding what further input they may require. Feedback can be given to referrers at this stage.

Evaluation of Programme

The tutors may now make note of the lessons to be learned for use in future groups, e.g. by considering which activities worked well and which badly. It may be useful to carry out action research at this stage by sending out questionnaires to clients and parents. Alternatively, structured questions can be prepared for use with clients and carers in individual review sessions.

Maintenance and Generalisation

Maintenance and generalisation are processes which help the training to be effective. Maintenance refers to the effects of the development programme remaining constant over time and not fading out and being forgotten after the end of the group. Generalisation refers to the process whereby gains occurring during the course can be generalised, i.e. the skills acquired can be developed to deal with a variety of new situations and are therefore of lasting benefit.

Maintenance

Maintenance can be achieved by staggering sessions to allow skills to build up during the gap by encouraging clients to practise skills in real life and reward themselves for so doing. Providing follow-up booster sessions will also allow clients to problem-solve about areas in which they are still encountering difficulty. Clients can be encouraged to build up social support systems (e.g. parents and friends) which will help them with maintenance. A discussion of support systems in the closing and booster sessions helps to enhance maintenance. Close involvement between tutors and parents or carers at this stage will naturally also support maintenance.

Generalisation

These approaches to maintenance will also help with generalisation. Trower (1984) has suggested that the best way to help clients cope with social situations is to help them in their ability to generate skills, rather than simply to help them cope with specific situations. This is the essence of the cognitive-behavioural approach as opposed to the purely behavioural. Problem-solving (cognitive) routines are built into the social skill development method presented in this book. Clients are helped to adopt a resourceful, adaptive problem-solving style to any problem which they may encounter in social situations and relationships. As they apply this problem-solving approach in real life, young people will experience natural reinforcement through success and begin to extend the approach to other areas of their social life. Consequently, the social skill training process has a "ripple effect".

Follow-up

By arranging six-month follow-up individual sessions, it is possible to monitor the processes of maintenance and generalisation. Structured questionnaires may be used to gather information in a systematic manner. The assessment procedures detailed in Chapter 2 can be re-used as evaluation measures.

Co-Working

It is helpful for a group to be run by a pair of facilitators, ideally of different gender. Roles need to be clearly defined and a good deal of time and effort needs to go into the planning of each session to ensure good structure. It is useful for tutors to run social skills groups in pairs as more energy is then available to sustain the momentum and enhance the learning process. From a cognitive point of view "*two heads are better than one*" in planning and running the sessions. Emotionally and behaviourally the tutors can support each other. A third member may participate for training purposes and this third member may prove particularly helpful as recorder and additional role player.

Facilitator Roles

It is useful to conceptualise that there are four key roles for leaders of small groups:

a) Information Giver (the "expert")
b) Facilitator (one who helps others to contribute)
c) Coordinator (who pulls ideas together)
d) Morale builder (makes encouraging remarks)

Description of Roles

These roles will be briefly described as they may be deployed within the context of social skill development.

a) *Information Giving*

In the initial stages of the group, the tutors are the information givers. However, the clients are experts on a number of important matters, such as their own internal process, the local social norms within the peer groups to which they relate, and the characteristics of the social situations which they encounter. Therefore, the responsibility of the tutors is to provide a structure where the client can increasingly take responsibility for feeding in and processing social information in a way that enhances social performance. Hopefully, the group will provide a model for the processing of social information which will be internalised and used constructively by the client in dealing with future social situations. In other words, the processing of social information will be learned by the client as a procedure and retained for future use.

Example: A child or adolescent who is being bullied can learn to observe the social norms of the peer group and find out which behaviours are least likely to trigger aggression in peers. These behaviours can then be practised in role-play and strengthened by reinforcement both within the group (by praise and recognition from tutor and peers) and in real life (through the experience of more satisfying consequences).

b) *Facilitation*

The tutors initially are facilitators. However, there are social skills involved in facilitation - listening skills, perspective taking, and help with problem solving. It is the responsibility of the tutor to create structured situations so that these skills can be developed and practised within the group. It is also important to demonstrate and affirm that these skills are as important a part of leadership as is assertion, power and control.

Example: The tutor sets up exercises in which clients, in pairs, take turns to describe a problem and offer help.

c) *Co-ordination*

It is the task of the tutor to coordinate- to "pull things together". However, the client also must learn to "pull together" various procedures, e.g. observing and analysing social situations, evaluating the feelings and behavioural response of self and others, planning and implementing change.

d) *Morale-building/Motivation*

By clearly explaining the purpose of group and individual programmes, tutors can allay clients' anxieties, create a sense of ownership and enhance motivation. Motivation is also maintained by directly involving clients in the process of generating ideas, recording material on flipchart paper, role-play practice of behaviour in relevant situations, observation of the work of others in role-play and direct feedback to others. Motivation can be increased by direct positive reinforcement from tutors for specific gains and ultimately by training in self-reinforcement.

Guidance for Tutors/Therapists

<u>Tutor Skills and Qualifications</u>

Tutors require suitable qualifications from the mental health or helping professions, and specific knowledge and experience of social skill development. This should include experience of assessment as well as training. Non-specific skills in counselling (e.g. active listening skill) and general experience of children and adolescents are also important.

Skills in Group Management

Tutors need:

- To be able to operate as confident and competent group leaders and have skill in planning and structuring groups and in eliciting and maintaining client motivation
- To be enthusiastic and demonstrate commitment to social skill development
- To set clear boundaries, both in terms of time and establishing behavioural norms
- to give group members a sense of ownership, e.g. by involving them in the creation of flipchart material which documents the content of brainstorming sessions
- To maintain rapport with clients showing sensitivity to their developmental needs
- To be aware of the social situations of clients within the group (e.g. the nature of their family and school experience and any areas of social stress) and notice what information is brought into the group about these matters
- To cultivate a flair for fostering positive social interaction between group members, both in structured role-play and in responding to opportunities which arise naturally in the life of the group
- To have reasonable social skills but to present a "coping" rather than a "perfect" model
- To develop a style which suits their personalities-it is important to be warm, positive and assertive and to provide appropriate structure and boundaries, whilst at the same time facilitating participation and involvement on the part of the clients.

Role Allocation

The tutors may choose to divide their function systematically, e.g. by taking it in turns to introduce activities. They may prefer to allow this to develop spontaneously, each being ready to initiate the prepared activity. In either case, tutors need to be ready to back each other up. If one tutor is initiating an activity, the other can be keeping an eye on the time, thinking about the next activity, providing reinforcement to group members, and helping members to stay on task. Tutors need to ensure that they do not both start to speak at the same time. This provides a valuable model of turn-taking for the clients. As always, tutors need to *practise what they preach*.

In general, it takes time for tutors to learn to work together and therefore it is advisable to aim for a more formal division of responsibilities at the start of a new partnership.

De-briefing

It is helpful for tutors to have space to "debrief" (talk and share their feelings) shortly after a session, whilst memories and impressions are still fresh.

Managing Conflict in the Co-Working Relationship

The planning sessions provide a natural opportunity to debrief, enabling tutors to review their roles and deal with any clashes or confusion. It is essential to be honest, open, sensitive and courteous in dealing with any difference of opinion. By keeping the air clear in this way, trainers ensure that they present the group with an appropriate model of openness, warmth, trust and caring. It is also useful to allow space at the end of the group for a natural debriefing process to occur.

Reviewing the Record

Making a record of the session and following this up with a review of the record by the tutor is another excellent way to debrief.

Supervision

If trainers are sufficiently skilled and experienced it should be possible to carry out the above process without formal supervision. However, it is good practice for tutors to take every opportunity to report to appropriate colleagues on what they do and to obtain advice and feedback.

Formal Supervision

Formal supervision should be used when it is felt necessary to ensure that a high-quality package of social skill development is delivered. Formal supervision should be provided by a highly skilled practitioner possessing a good deal of experience with the model. The supervisor may observe the group through a one-way screen, receive a verbal report and/or written record of the group, listen to an audiotape or view a videotape. Additionally, or alternatively the supervisor may be present for the planning/debrief sessions.

Peer Supervision

If a highly skilled practitioner is not available, "peer supervision" may be used to ensure that basic standards are met, e.g. that boundaries are maintained, suitable plans are made, planned structures are adhered to and objectives are achieved. Peer supervision involves enlisting the aid of a colleague who is not involved in the programme to use one or more of the above techniques to monitor the process.

Trouble Shooting

A list of problems and suggested solutions is given below.
   a) *Loss of motivation as group progresses*
   Solution: Ensure that the group feels that active progress is being made, and is relevant to their needs as they experience them.
   b) *Anxiety levels are too high*
   Solution: Make the group safe, reduce or clarify demands, provide support and reassurance, maintain structure.

c) *Anxiety levels are not high enough* - the group is too comfortable and "sleepy"

Solution: Generate motivation. Remind clients of their goals and the need to change.

Introduce new activities. Stimulate the group.

d) *A powerful group member tries to dominate*

Solution: Maintain boundaries. Activate other members. Provide a constructive and appropriate leadership role for the member seeking dominance. Seek to understand and help any insecurities lying beneath the surface in the dominant member.

e) *A group member is unacceptably disruptive*

Solution: Challenge. Ask other group members how they feel about the disruption. Is the disruption a message about interpersonal difficulties which could be helped by the group activities? Encourage the disruptive group member to express feelings more appropriately. Empathise with the group member, try to understand what is going on, be ready to negotiate within reason. If all else fails and there is no improvement after a warning, exclude. It is important for co-workers to be very careful, honest and objective with one another in their debriefing about disruptive group members.

f) *Drop-out; group attendance falls off*

Solution: Check whether members have improved and no longer need the group; whether there is dissatisfaction which is not being expressed; whether there is a need for a more novel or stimulating approach. Follow up clients in a friendly, non-threatening manner.

g) *The needs of individual members are not met*

Solution: Bear individual needs in mind when planning each session. In de-briefing, attend carefully to written observations on the verbal and non-verbal communications of each member, seeking to understand how the group has been for them.

Case Example

Social Skill Group Development Programme

This group is not presented as a "success story" but as a working example of the issues which tend to come up in running groups in practical terms in the field.

Two social skills groups were run for young people in the 7-11 age range in a town in UK in 2003. The groups were run by two co-workers supported by an observer as part of the child and adolescent mental health service. The programme was updated by the facilitators having regard to relevant research. Spence (1995) Parent and Child Social Skills Questionnaires were completed before and after the programme. Social skills homework was set at each session.

A third group was run with young people aged 6-7 years.

The Groups

A number of children seen by the Child and Adolescent Mental Health Service (CAMHS) displayed social skills deficits and it was felt that they would benefit from a social skills group.

Rationale

The social skills group programme was based on an earlier programme that had already been used in the service. The facilitators went through the package that existed and updated it according to current literature. Spence (1995) was mainly used to gain ideas for homework. It was felt that the content of the group needed to be age appropriate and needed to be more activity based. It has been found that activity-based groups are more effective for clients with learning difficulties (Lo et al, 2002) and it was felt that, considering developmental factors, this approach would also be more appropriate for younger children. The materials used for the assertiveness session were taken from Hough and Hartley (2000).

Ideas were difficult to gain from the literature because research generally looked at adolescent social skills groups only. Social skills development groups with the younger age group were generally run in schools looking at psycho-educating teachers and, focusing on modelling and positive reinforcement from teachers (Francis, 2003 Kamps et al, 2002; Sommers et al, 2000). Social skills development in the USA is part of the school curriculum and therefore, their approach is very different to that in England and this influences material that is available. The USA is also more proactive in setting up "buddy" or mentor systems and attempting to alleviate bullying (Kamps et al, 1998). Kamps et al (2002) opine that social skills instruction in general education is an important prevention strategy. However, this has implications for the available literature on effective techniques in teaching social skills.

Within the programme, a behavioural approach was used to promote appropriate behaviour in the group and to encourage the completion of homework. A social learning theory approach was mainly used to try and encourage generalisation of the skills learnt to the home and school setting.

Group Members

Participants were patients already in the CAMHS service whose referrer felt they had social skills difficulties and would benefit from a social skills group. The case-holder referred that patient to the group.

Once they had been referred, the facilitators completed an assessment on each participant individually approximately 1 month before the group started. It was then decided whether the individual was accepted in to the group taking in to account the following criteria:

- Age and development of the child (7 – 11 years old)

- Specific social skills deficits highlighted by themselves and their parents
- Motivation to change
- Fit well with the mix of the children that would be attending the group, as decided by the facilitators.

Group 1 accepted 6 members from 8 referred participants. Everyone accepted their places; three were female. The age of group members ranged from 7 years 9 months to 11 years 6 months. The mean age of the group members was 9 years and 11 months.

Group 2 accepted 8 members from 12 referred participants. 6 accepted their places; all were male. The age of the group members ranged from 8 years 0 months to 11 years 0 months. The mean age of the group members was 8 years 10 months.

Each group began with six group members making a total of 12 participants. In the first group, one child was asked to leave after the third session because it was felt she was being too disruptive and was not learning anything from the group. In the second group, two group members dropped out leaving a group of 4 people. The two group members that dropped out were both Looked After Children in care while the group was running.

Therefore, in total, nine members attended the 2 groups throughout and were used in the evaluation of the group package. Seven were male and two were female. The ages ranged from 8 years 0 months to 11 years 6 months. The mean age of participants was 9 years 2 months.

Method
An individual assessment appointment was set up approximately one month before the group started for all referred individuals. The appointment consisted of the following:
- An informal interview with parents/caregivers and referred person.
- To explain to the referred child and caregiver what to expect from the group
- Completion of the following questionnaires:

  a) Spence (1995) Social Skills Questionnaire (self-report) for referred child

  b) Spence (1995) social skills questionnaire (parent report) for caregiver

  c) A scenario questionnaire put together by the lead facilitator for the referred child

The group was then run following the programme that had been developed. This included a parent's session before the group started and then 6 weekly session of 1¼ hours for the group members. While the group was running, a record of attendance was kept.

An individual feedback appointment was then arranged at the end of the group, which was approximately 1 month after the group finished. The facilitators wrote a brief report for each individual to feedback at the appointment. Also, an informal interview took place to record if the parents had noticed any differences and if the child had been practising appropriate social skills. All the questionnaires that were filled in at the assessment appointment were completed again.

The flow chart which follows demonstrates a complete methodology of the process.

Flowchart of method

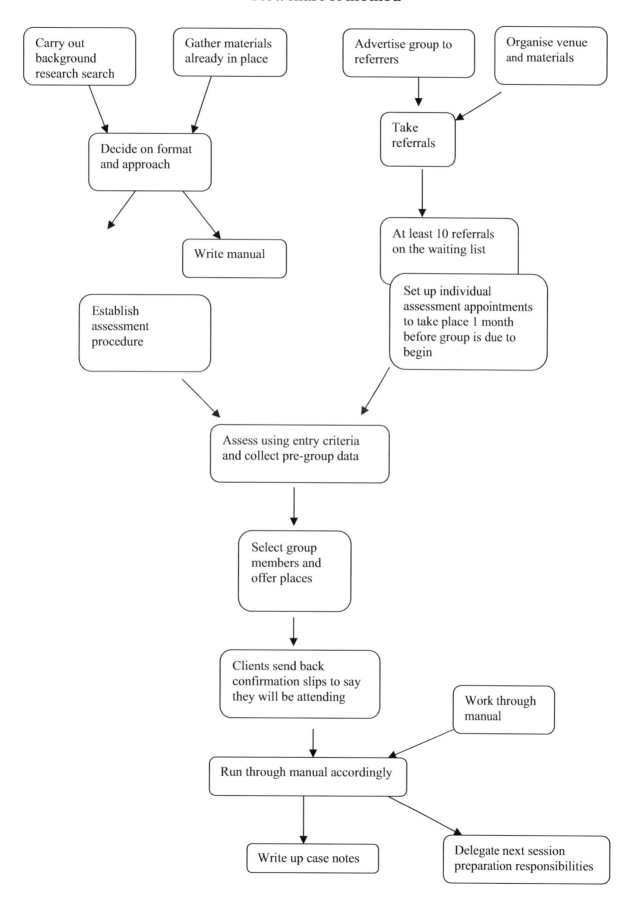

Outcome

Enhancement of Social Skills

Overall, the results of the self-report questionnaire indicated an improvement in social skills, and the scenarios questionnaire demonstrated an improvement in social knowledge. However, the parent's questionnaire indicated an overall decline in social skills. The results on the questionnaire did not reflect what parents were saying in the feedback session. Most parents were very positive about the group and felt that the group had benefited their child in some way. E.g. *"He is a lot more confident now and does not get as nervous about things", "He will avoid conflict and fights, he has never done that before"*. Two parents filled in the questionnaire on the same occasion for the same child and the difference between their scores was 20; it is likely therefore that the questionnaire does not have a good inter-rated reliability and the scores were very subjective.

Attendance

78% of the group members attended all six of the sessions. One group member attended 5 out of the 6 sessions. They missed the session because of a serious illness in the family. The last group member attended 4 out of 6 sessions. He missed one session because he went on holiday. He missed the other session because parents had forgotten about the group. Therefore, the objective for 100% attendance of all group members was not met. Illness and prearranged events that were mentioned in the assessment appointments were exception criteria with the objectives. However, we did not prepare for parents forgetting about the group.

Attendance was a big factor in creating group cohesiveness and it was obviously more difficult for the member who missed two sessions to fit in with the rest of the group.

The parent's session before the group began was a lot less well attended. 5 out of the 9 parents attended the parent session. There was a positive correlation between session attendance and subsequent parental report of improvement, as the graph below demonstrates.

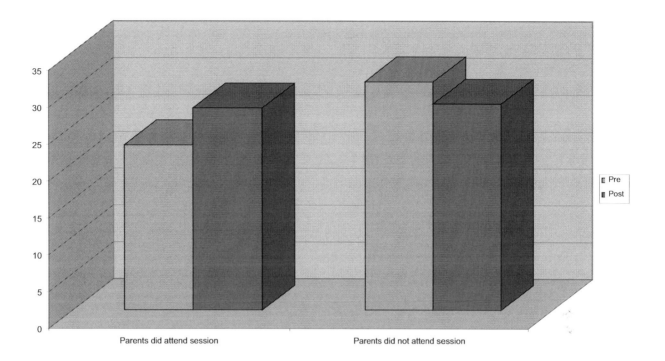

Mean scores of the Spence (1995) Social Skills Suestionnaire for parents. Comparing group members whose parents did attend the parents session versus those who did not.

Homework

Although a formal record of homework was not completed, there was allocated time each week for the group members to speak about their homework. Members of Group 1 often did not complete homework with the exception of 1 person (who completed hers every week). Members of Group 2 often had completed their homework and were able to discuss it. On this information, the objective that 50% completed all homework was met.

The homework usually consisted of writing things down on to a worksheet. One group member in the second group could not write and therefore was unable to complete the sheets. It was found that quite often the group members could talk about trying to do their homework but were not confident completing the worksheets e.g., *"My spelling isn't very good", "I don't like writing"* and, *"I'm not good at writing things".*

Discussion

It was felt that the group package did benefit, in some way, all group members who attended. The main difficulty that was found with the group was that skills that were learnt in the sessions were not always generalised to outside of the room and to other settings. This audit has highlighted several difficulties with the programme and the process, which will be discussed below.

The Assessment Process
The Spence (1995) Self-Report Questionnaire was too difficult for some children to understand and it was felt that both Spence questionnaires did not adequately reflect the social behaviour of the child.

Although informal interview style often made the child and parent feel more at ease, it was considered too unstructured and the details of answers were often not recorded. Moote et al (1999) suggests that assessments need to be accurate and determine exactly the social skills deficits of an individual. They concluded that facilitators need to focus more on the qualitative information in assessing clients' suitability for a group and when evaluating the group.
No contact was made with schools at any point throughout the group process and therefore, no information was gained from the school environment. One parent felt that it would have been beneficial to have contact with school. It was felt that this might give a more accurate overall understanding of the individual.

The facilitators for the second group also kept in mind the mix of group members and group dynamics while accepting people in to the group. It was felt that this positively affected group cohesiveness and allowed the package to run a lot more smoothly compared to the first group.

The Group Practicalities
Often the facilitators were rushing through the group content and were not able to complete everything set down in the package. It was felt that the session needed to be longer to fit in the content and there needed to be more sessions. Moote et al (1999) clarified that, currently, optimal treatment length in social skills training is unclear and further investigation in this area is needed.
Kamps and Kay (2002) suggested that a group should have 3–4 good peer models for every person who has anti-social behaviours. They would recommend against grouping people with anti-social behaviours together because it has been shown to sometimes increase problem behaviour.

Group Content
- The group content was comprehensive and covered the main topics in social skills. Bullying and responding to bullies was a topic that was not covered in the group content, which was felt to be an important issue with most group members. Kamps and Kay (2002) suggested that teaching social skills to victims is often not enough where bullying behaviour is prevalent within the school. They suggested "bully-proofing" the school and making the child "bully-proof" and a programme has been set up to achieve this
- More incentives were needed to complete homework and to generalise skills to outside the group
- More involvement of the parents was needed to aid generalisation of the skills learnt, especially as the results showed that that those parents who came to the

76

parents' session saw an improvement in their child's social skills. Those who did not attend the parent's session saw an overall decline in their child's social skills as indicated in the Spence Parent Questionnaire before and after the group. This supports Kamps and Kay's (2002) view that the main reason a social skills group fails is because of negative role modelling or limited reinforcement

- Research also suggests that school liaison and input further aids generalisation of social skills in the child. Lo et al (2002) found moderate reductions in antisocial behaviours during a pull-out social skills group and the positive changes either further declined or were maintained after classroom social skills instruction commenced. MacDonald et al (2003) concluded that facilitating the generalisation of skills required intense liaison with both parents and teachers

- It was felt that the package was too prescriptive at times and rather too inflexible. Kamps and Kay (2002) suggested that best approach would be to assess clients' needs and then chose the group content required from a "menu" of topics. This creates more flexibility that would better meet the individual needs of the clients

- The worksheets for homework often involved reading or writing something, which group members often disliked. Also, group members often were not confident with reading or writing and one member openly could not read

Feedback Sessions

Often parents and professionals found the reports very helpful and the format was very easy to follow. The recommendations at the end of the report were particularly helpful for many parents and professionals. However, it was felt that the feedback sessions were too unstructured; specific questions were not necessarily asked and detailed notes were not taken of these sessions

Planning for the Future

The following plans were made for future assessments:

a) To continue using the scenarios questionnaire

b) To include a social anxiety questionnaire and consider a general screening questionnaire for mental health problems to see if the package helped people with specific difficulties

c) To discontinue using the Spence social skills questionnaires as it is felt that they do not offer anything more to the assessment process

d) To have a specific list of questions for facilitators to ask. This would make the assessment session more structured and details of answers would be recorded, while keeping the session relaxed and informal

e) To involve schools in the assessment process. Permission to contact schools would be gained at the individual assessment session. Then a questionnaire will be posted to the school and a facilitator will conduct a telephone interview with the most appropriate teacher

f) To have a mixture of clients who have different skills and weaknesses to try and alleviate the problem that sometimes occurs when placing anti-social people together in a group

Group Practicalities and Content

The following decisions were made:

A session on bullying would be added to the content and the assertiveness content would run over 2 sessions instead of 1.

Two core facilitators would run all the groups. It was thought that this would work better than one core therapist with a different second person each time the group ran. This would help the facilitators to work as a team.

The parent session would be made mandatory and a greater emphasis on parent's attendance would be placed in the individual assessment sessions. Parents would also be involved in the last session which helped the young people to generalise their skills using role-play.

The facilitators would fill in a sheet and keep a record of what was discussed at the end of each session. The questions on the sheet would help create discussion and reflection.

The content would remain the same. Having a theme for each session worked well.

A behavioural chart would be used to record whether each group member had completed homework.

A reward would be given each week to those who have completed their homework as an added incentive.

Ideas for homework activities that do not include writing would be considered.

<u>Updated Flowchart of Method</u>

Planning Group

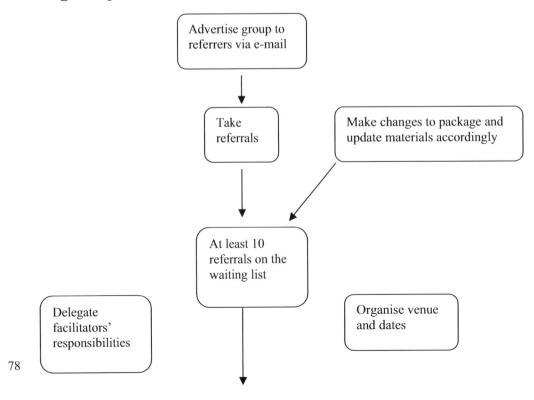

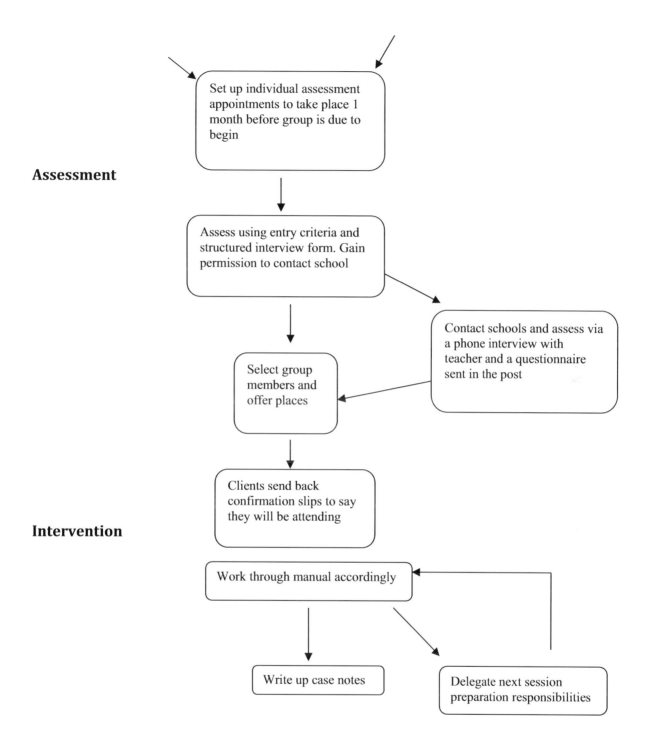

Assessment

Set up individual assessment appointments to take place 1 month before group is due to begin

Assess using entry criteria and structured interview form. Gain permission to contact school

Contact schools and assess via a phone interview with teacher and a questionnaire sent in the post

Select group members and offer places

Intervention

Clients send back confirmation slips to say they will be attending

Work through manual accordingly

Write up case notes

Delegate next session preparation responsibilities

Follow- up

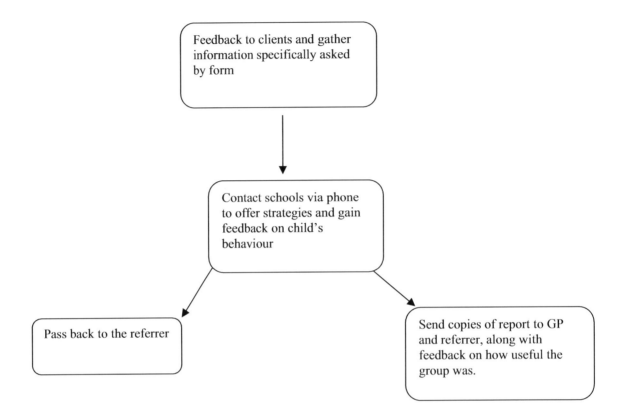

Feedback to clients and gather information specifically asked by form

Contact schools via phone to offer strategies and gain feedback on child's behaviour

Pass back to the referrer

Send copies of report to GP and referrer, along with feedback on how useful the group was.

Case Examples

Individual Outcomes of Group Participation
These three case examples are taken from our records of a social skill programme carried out in school.

June, aged 13

Assessment Information
On a sociometric procedure, June was found to be socially isolated. The teachers categorised her as "unassertive". On the self-report questionnaire (Spence, 1980) she identified 28 "unassertive" items (a high score) and five "antisocial" items. It was found useful to break down the items on the Spence Problem Situation Questionnaire in this way.

June is the youngest of five children and the only girl. Her mother is asthmatic and suffers from migraine attacks. June suffers from eczema.

June's parents agreed that she was socially isolated and unresponsive. They felt she avoided contact with peers at school, and did not get on well with school staff. They reported that June was frequently involved in disputes at home, particularly with her siblings. Outside school, she had poor relations with peers.

Treatment Outcome
After completing a ten-session social skills course, June said that she enjoyed the group and would have liked to continue. The reason she enjoyed it, she said, was because she never felt left out as she had felt in other groups.

She reported a general improvement in her social life, and said that she had more friends than she had previously. In dancing classes at the school, she had always been the one left out, without a partner. Now she could make sure that she got a partner. "*I just go and grab one now*".

The tutor reported that June had made substantial gains. Regarding self-expressive skills, she had done particularly well in expressing her opinion, made gains in expressing feelings, accepting compliments and making positive statements about herself. She had also improved in making positive statements about others, praising others and expressing her own point of view to others. Her communication skills were better, especially her conversational skills. After a course of ten sessions, the tutor felt that June could cope well in the future without requiring further social skill sessions.

Comment
Since her mother found it difficult for physical and possibly psychological reasons to adopt an active role within the family, and June had no sisters; June may have been somewhat lacking in female role models to help her in her social development at home. Being the only girl, June perhaps found it hard to relate to her peers within in the family and this difficulty may have been reproduced outside the family owing to lack of experience and confidence. The social skills group provided June with an active young female adult role model, and a mixed group of peers within which June could practise and acquire new skills which would enable her to make friends and reduce her social isolation.

Ian, aged 13

Assessment Information
The sociometric procedure identified Ian as isolated. The teachers categorised him as unassertive. The Bristol Social Adjustment Guide (Bell & Cohen, 1981) showed him to be "under-reacting". On the self-report measure, he identified 25 "unassertive" items (a high score) and 7 "antisocial" items (including "lose my temper easily"). Ian considered himself "shy" at the time of the referral.

His biological father left his mother when he was still a baby. His two young brothers are children of his mother's remarriage, which subsequently dissolved. His mother moved into the area with her new partner, towards whom Ian has positive feelings.

The family agreed that Ian was socially isolated and unresponsive and had difficulty in initiating and maintaining contact with other youngsters, both in and out of school. He tended to get involved in disputes with siblings. Parents reported severe difficulties in terms of eye contact, "fiddling" during social interaction and lack of fluency in speech.

Treatment Outcome

Ian reported that he felt uncomfortable during the first few group sessions, but subsequently began to relax and enjoy the groups. He afterwards reported that the groups helped him to feel less shy. He described being able to go into a shop without feeling uneasy.

Psychometric assessment showed a slight improvement in Ian's scores. His self-rating of behaviour in certain situations showed an improvement, as did the family's rating. The tutors reported improvement in skills of self-expression and assertiveness, *"expression of opinion", "positive statements about self"* and *"disagreeing with others"*. Communication skills had also shown improvement.

It was felt that Ian would benefit from some "booster" sessions to bring his social skills to an appropriate level. Ian himself expressed the need for these sessions.

Comment

Clearly, there were several precursors to Ian's social skill difficulty, including family stress, sibling rivalry and a move to a new area. It is possible to speculate that the family background created conditions favouring sibling rivalry, with Ian perhaps feeling pushed out by younger siblings supported by their natural father. Sibling difficulty can frequently pave the way for peer difficulty, as unresolved conflicts and "unfinished business" are transferred outside the family. Possibly Ian's initial stepfather (subsequently apparently rejected by mother) was a suitable role model for Ian in his social development. Moving to a new area could be an additional stressor, adding to the social difficulties, consequently demanding skills which Ian did not yet possess.

Prior to the group, Ian was assessed as having difficulties in a wide range of measures of social skill. After the group, improvements were noted by family, peers, therapists and Ian himself. This case neatly demonstrates the importance of matching assessment with treatment.

Sharon, aged 13

Assessment Information

Sharon had trouble in controlling her temper. She had an older sister, who, she said, was beautiful and wanted to be a model. Sharon's remark about all of this was that "*It really cheesed her off*". She talked about not wanting to take a boyfriend home because she knew he would prefer her older sister. Both Sharon and her sister had many arguments with their Dad whom they found overbearing. Their mother suffered from an illness which led to her regularly falling and bruising herself (possibly epilepsy, but a full history was not taken) and therefore the girls felt unable to argue with their mother.

On the self-report questionnaire, Sharon identified 14 "antisocial" items (a relatively high score), including "*You find you don't have many friends*". Her profile score on the Bristol Social Adjustment Guide suggested hostility to others. The family agreed with the view of school staff that Sharon was *overassertive, creating tension and alienating others, e.g. dominating discussions, never listening, having a short fuse and being physically aggressive*". Disputes were frequent and severe particularly with her sister. Her relations with school staff were poor and she frequently engaged in disputes with peers in and outside school. In terms of micro-skills, a severe "fidgeting" problem was identified, together with moderate difficulties in eye contact and posture.

Treatment Outcome

Sharon reported that the Social Skills Group was a positive experience. She felt accepted and comfortable within the group. She said that the group had helped her with keeping her temper and with making friends. She was given positive feedback on her performance within the group and encouraged to continue working on these skills. She could report how she had been able to apply the suggestions for change offered to her within the group. It was felt that she would be able to maintain her improvement without further sessions.

Her self-reported behaviour rating showed improvement. The tutor reported that she made substantial improvement in the following items: expression of feeling, expression of opinion, accepting compliments, positive statements about others, conversational skills and avoiding disputes.

Comment

Sharon's ignorance of the nature of her mother's illness suggests that her family may have been lacking in communication skills. There may also have been specific difficulties around the expression of anger.

To acquire skills in expressing anger appropriately, children and young people need a positive model at home of natural anger being expressed effectively (Martin & Bush, 2000). It sounds likely that her mother's illness was used as a defence in the family, so that her father's anger "leaked out" on his daughters and they naturally retaliated, but were not able to achieve conflict resolution. It is likely that, in this family, positive skills in assertion were not modelled, acquired or reinforced. The parents, it seems, were not able to work as a team to set boundaries and therefore Sharon's aggression was not contained. Sharon's rivalry with her sister may have exacerbated the problem and deprived her of another natural ally. The teachers were too distant to act as role models, but the tutors could establish a positive bond with Sharon within the "safe" atmosphere of the group and influence her positively in the selection of more appropriate social strategies. The group helped her to understand her difficulties and work out new ways of solving social problems. She was also able to experience, within the group, what it was like to have a positive and friendly relationship with peers and what skills were necessary to maintain such a relationship.

John, aged 13

Assessment Information

John said he was referred to the group because "*I am weird*". He said he needed to be weird because his friends expected it of him. When asked when he would be able to drop this weird bit of himself, his reply was "*when I leave school*". He talked about the possibility of his family moving to a different area and said that if he moved to another school he might be able to drop the "weird" bit. John was the youngest of a family of five children and the tutor had the feeling that he had to compete hard in this large family to get his needs met. John talked sensibly and appeared to have a good understanding of his difficulties and how they might be detrimental to his future.

John reported having a fight on the morning of the assessment. He said that his cat had died and he was quite sure it had been poisoned by someone. He felt both angry and upset about this and did not know how to handle these feelings. He knew that the boy he attacked had not harmed his cat, and could understand that his angry feelings about the cat had "leaked out" on this boy who was only guilty of teasing him mildly.

Sociometric assessment suggested that John was being rejected by his peers. The teachers nominated him as "overassertive". On the self-report questionnaire, he identified 6 "antisocial" items and 13 "unassertive" items. The Bristol Social Adjustment Guide (Bell & Cohen, 1981) suggested a similar, mixed pattern of social difficulties.

John's family were aware of his difficulties in making and maintaining friendships and in controlling his behaviour. There were frequent arguments at home with all family members. Parents thought that John had difficulty relating to school staff and was teased or bullied by peers at times. He was judged to have severe difficulty with eye contact and moderate difficulty with facial expression, fidgeting and fluency of speech.

Treatment Outcome

John was considered by the tutor to have improved in expression of feeling and opinions, praising others, disagreeing with others and conversational skills. His self-rating of social behaviour showed an improvement. John had a positive experience of the group, though his angry outbursts continued to cause concern at the school. It was thought that John needed more sessions with a particular focus on anger management.

Comment

Background information is limited but it appears that John was currently getting little support at home with his emotional difficulties and had to compete with his siblings for attention. John needed a good deal of emotional support as he was very uncertain of himself and was experiencing severe difficulty in managing his anger. His inner uncertainty led him to adopt a "weird" style of behaviour to win recognition from the peer group. John did benefit from the group, but needed a more comprehensive package of support to free him from his emotional crisis and his difficulties in anger management.

Summary

Four individual cases have been presented. In each case, the response to group training has been documented. Whilst not constituting an evidence base, these examples give an idea of how clients may benefit from social skill group development programmes.

References

Bell, B., & Cohen, R. (1981). The Bristol Social Adjustment Guide: Comparison between the offspring of alcoholic and non-alcoholic mothers. *British Journal of Clinical Psychology*, *20*(2), 93-95.

Bulkeley, R., & Cramer, D. (1990). Social skills training with young adolescents. *Journal of Youth and Adolescence*, *19*(5), 451-463.

Bulkeley, R., & Cramer, D. (1994). Social skills training with young adolescents: Group and individual approaches in a school setting. *journal of Adolescence*, *17*(6), 521-531.

Cartledge, G & Milburn, JF (1992). *Teaching Social Skills to Children, Innovative Approaches*, 2nd Edition. NY: Pergamon Press.

Cowen, EL, Pederson, A, Babigan, H, Izzo, LD & Trost, MA, (1973). Long-term Follow-up of Early Detected Vulnerable Children. *Journal of Consulting & Clinical Psychology*, 41, 438-446.

Deffenbacher, JL, Lynch, RS, Oetting, ER & Kemper, CC, (1996). Anger reduction in Early Adolescents. *Journal of Counselling Psychology*, 43, 149-157.

Francis, T (2003). Social Skills Programme. http://www.educational-psychologist.co.uk

Hough, J & Hartley M (2000). *Anger Management*. UK: The Chalkface Project Ltd.

Kamps, DM & Kay, P (2002). Preventing Problems Through Social Skills Instruction. In, Alogozzine, B. & Kay P. *Preventing Problem Behaviours: A Handbook of Successful Prevention Strategies*. Corwin Press: Council for Exceptional Children.

Kamps, DM, Lopez, AG, Kemmerer, K., Potucek, J & Harrell, LG (1998). What Do the Peers Think? Social Validity of Peer-Mediated Programs. *Education and Treatment of Children*, 21(2) 107-134.

Kamps, DM, Tankersley, M & Ellis, C (2000). Social Skills Intervention for Young At-Risk Students: A 2 Year Follow-up Study. *Behaviour Disorders*, 25(4) 310 – 324.

Lo, Y, Loe, SA & Cartledge, G (2002). The Effects of Social Skills Instruction on the Social Behaviours of Students at Risk for Emotional or Behavioural Disorders. *Behavioural Disorders*, 27(4) 371 – 385.

MacDonald, E, Chowdhury, U, Dabney, J, Wolpert, M & Stein, SM (2003). A social skills group for children. The importance of liaison work with parents and teachers. *Emotional and Behavioural Difficulties*, 8(1) 43-52.

Martin, C. A., & Bush, A. J. (2000). Do role models influence teenagers' purchase intentions and behavior?. *Journal of consumer marketing*, *17*(5), 441-453.

Moote, GT, Smyth, NJ & Wodarski, JS (1999). Social Skills Training with Youth in School Settings: A Review. *Research in Social Work*, 9(4) 427 – 465.

Pepler, DJ, King, G & Byrd W (1991). A social-cognitively based social skills training program for aggressive children. In, Pepler, DJ & Rubin, K (Eds). *The Development and Treatment of Childhood Aggression: Earlcourt Symposium of Childhood Aggression.* USA: Erlbaum Associates.

Sommers, FR, Barrett-Hakanson, T, Clarke, C & Sommers-Flanagan, J (2000). A Psychoeducational School-Based Coping and Social Skills Group for Depressed Students. *Journal for Specialists in Group Work*, 25(2) 170-190.

Spence, S (1980). *Social Skills Training with Children and Adolescents: A Counsellors Manual.* Windsor: NFER-Nelson.

Spence, SH (1995). *Social Skills Training. Enhancing Social Competence with Children and Adolescents.* UK: NFER-Nelson Publishing Company Ltd.

Trower, P (1984). *Radical Approaches to Social Skills Training.* London: Croom Helm.

Whittenberg, TL (1995). A Comparison of the Effects of Self-control versus Social Skills Training with Socially Anxious Children. *Dissertation Abstracts International Section A: Humanities & Social Sciences*, 55(7-A) 1884. USA: University Microfilms International.

Appendix 1

Group Social Skill Development Programmes
The programmes given below are designed for group work. Practitioners working with individual clients may adapt the roleplay tasks for specific exercises. Practitioners working with groups should feel free to adapt the programmes in accordance with their clients' specific needs.

Research and experience alike indicate that the best way to deliver social skills development to older children and adolescents is through a multi-faceted programme. Examples of such programmes are given in this chapter.

Social Skills Programme One: Individualised Approach (Ten Sessions)
(It should be noted that this course is designed as a group social skill development programme for young people offering maximum facility to cater for individual needs within a group context).

The programme has been found useful in an educational setting. Youngsters with different types of social difficulty were mixed (e.g. impulsive, unassertive) when the programme was first used. The package is recommended for heterogeneous groups of clients, who have somewhat different issues to work on. It allows maximum flexibility for clients to work on personal goals and develop their own programmes.

The individualized approach makes it more viable to cater for a heterogeneous group.

Introduction
The group training is given in a comfortable room with ample space for role-play and video on hand. Sessions last for one hour and 15mins and were held weekly. The total treatment package consists of ten sessions. Sessions generally begin with "warm-ups" or "icebreakers" which are designed to dispel inhibitions and free up clients to participate in role-play; an essential part of the treatment. The warm-ups provide valuable training in communication skills, listening skills, turn-taking, respect for others, perspective-taking and the learning of social rules. The role-play generally follows and after feedback and task-setting, a game concludes the session.

Refreshments (a drink and a biscuit) are generally offered at some point during the group.

Rationale
In the initial session, a rationale for learning social skills is presented. It is stated that we all need social skills and often acquire these naturally; however, because these skills are so important, sometimes it is helpful to spend some time on thinking about them and understanding them.

Skill Acquisition - Phase One

The course starts off by focusing on micro-skills -these are the "nuts and bolts" or "small change" of social communication. For example, in the role-play "greet a friend across the street", the sequence is broken up into discrete social events, e.g. eye contact, verbal greeting, adopt suitable position, begin conversation, respond to other, maintain conversation, use non-verbal cues to maintain contact, end conversation, leave friend with suitable gesture. By this method, the clients are introduced to the subtle interplay of verbal and non-verbal messages which makes up communication.

Skill Acquisition - Phase Two

In later sessions, the focus switches to social situations which may be of particular relevance to clients, e.g. making friends, dealing with bullying, standing up for yourself, joining a new group, dealing with authority. Such situations and the skills necessary for dealing with them are role-played and then analysed in some detail. In this way, clients are enabled to learn new skills through practice, participation, observation and discussion.

In the role-plays, immediate feedback on performance is given both by trainers and peers. This helps clients to modify and improve their performance within the context of a situation they know to be safe. By positive reinforcement, the clients' more effective verbal and non-verbal responses are strengthened. Reinforcement by peers is particularly encouraged.

Skill Acquisition- Phase Three

As sessions progress, "real life" assignments (homework) are set for clients, in order to stimulate them to practice new styles of behaviour. Appropriate real life tasks are discussed with each client, and clients are subsequently asked for feedback on the tasks which have been set. Experience of success in these tasks provides reinforcement for new styles of behaviour. Through reporting and feedback, clients learn to reinforce themselves for more appropriate patterns of behaviour.

Skill Acquisition - Phase Four

Clients are encouraged to monitor their new patterns of behaviour and apply them across a wide range of situations, noticing their effectiveness. In this way, the new behaviours are strengthened and confirmed, so that they will continue after the group ends.

Cognitive Process

In addition to acquiring behavioural skills, clients also acquire cognitive skills. Here, Trower's theory that social skills are the ability to generate appropriate social responses (Trower, 1984) provides the rationale. The cognitive skills acquired during the treatment package include the following:

1. Identification of challenging social situations
2. Recognition of skills required to respond appropriately to challenge

3. Assessment of available skills in repertoire to meet the demands of the situation
4. Assessment of whether a new skill might be developed building on existing skills
5. Problem-solving, based on the above considerations, leading to the selection of an appropriate response.
6. Enactment of the selected response, followed by evaluation, positive self-reinforcement and review

It is not suggested that clients will subject every social problem to analysis in this kind of depth; but having been trained in the process, they will become calmer, more controlled and more effective in their everyday lives and their dealing with others.

Structure of Sessions
Each session is planned in detail, having regard to the progress made by individuals, specific needs for assessment and training, and the stage reached by the group. The aim in each session is to provide a pleasurable group experience and to enable the group members to assist each other by (a) participating in role-play & (b) offering feedback and reinforcement.

Objectives
1. To offer clients support in assessing social situations in which they find difficulty
2. To enable clients to develop skill by observing others in role-play situations
3. To enable clients to acquire new social skills by using role-play, positive feedback and reinforcement and by proceeding through the stages of skill acquisition
4. To provide individualised behaviour programmes, i.e. planning of a series of targets for each individual, within the context of group treatment

Session One

Objectives of Session
- *To establish rules and rituals*
- *To build confidence and cohesion*
- *To initiate clients into the notion of social skill training and give them some idea of how the group will proceed.*

Name Game
Using a soft ball thrown between group members, people learn each other's names.

Introduction
In pairs, clients learn specified facts about each other (e.g. name of school, name of siblings, hobbies) and then share this information with the group, introducing their partners.

Purpose of Group
The notion of social skills, and how people can be trained in them, is briefly explained.

Contract
The various rules and "rituals" of the group, covering such matters as attendance, punctuality, confidentiality and taking "time out" are established. Clients are empowered to contribute suggestions and the agreed rules are written out on flipchart paper.

Blind Partners
As a trust building exercise, pairs take turns for a "blind" partner to be conducted round the room.

True Story
Partners take turns to tell each other about a significant episode in their lives.

Eye Wink Murder
A "fun" game is used to discharge tension at the end of the group. The murderer must wink at selected victims, victims must respond by "dying" and the rest must try and guess the murderer.

_1_

Session Two

Objectives
- *To develop non-verbal communication skills*
- *To introduce the use of role-play*
- *To encourage clients to develop negotiation skills*
- *To help clients to develop skills in dealing with victimisation*
- *To help develop turn-taking and verbal skills*
- *To provide an opportunity for clients to evaluate their social difficulties*

Pass the Cat
The group passes an imaginary object (such as a cat) from hand to hand. Take turns to think of a new object.

Role-play: Coping with Being Teased
Clients in turn are briefly exposed to a teasing episode in role-play, and are complimented on positive responses.

Role-play: Negotiation
Clients in pairs briefly negotiate a choice of activity (e.g. football, movie)

Luckily, Unluckily
Going around the group, a story is created with each contributing a sentence. The sentences start alternately, "Luckily" or "Unluckily" so that the story takes positive and negative twists. Again, a game rounds off the session.

Session Three

Objectives
- *To help develop communication skills (verbal and non-verbal)*
- *To help develop skills in responding to social rejection*
- *To provide further opportunities for self-evaluation of social difficulty*

Eye Wink Murder
A game, here used as a "warm-up" offers practice of eye contact. A group member is secretly identified as the Murderer. Targeted victims must "die" if winked at. The rest must guess the Murderer who must confess if challenged.

Passing the Message
"Chinese Whispers": A message is passed round the group in whispers, and the initial message is compared with the final message.

Role-play: Being Left Out
Clients are briefly exposed to a "being left out" situation in a role-play with peers. Clients are praised for positive responses and asked to identify their feelings and any social difficulties they experience. The facilitators complete evaluation forms (rating skills from 1-5) on the verbal, non-verbal and assertive skills demonstrated during the role-play. These are used to guide subsequent client self-evaluation.

Role-play: Asking Permission
Clients are asked to enact a role-play in which they must ask permission for something from a teacher. This provides an opportunity for further self-evaluation. Again, the facilitators complete forms, noting tone of voice used, etc.

Luckily/ Unluckily
(See Session Two)

Session Four

Objectives
- *To introduce Phase Two of Skill Acquisition (role-play practice of specific skills)*
- *To help clients to focus down on skills to work on*
- *To enable them to begin to work on these selected skills*
- *Further practice of eye contact and verbal communication skills*

Introduction
Introduce notion of identifying and working on specific skills

Discussion of Goals
Increase motivation by linking increase in skill to attainable personal goals (e.g. friendship making). Facilitators list goals on flipchart paper.

Identification of Targets
By examining the list individual target skills on flipchart paper, ask each client to nominate one skill to work on, (e.g. introducing yourself, paying a compliment, standing up for yourself, negotiation).

Eye Contact Greeting
Explain social function of eye contact greeting, (eye contact plus brief eyebrow raise). Each client goes around the room greeting each other in this way.

Role-play
Set up opportunities for each client to briefly practice the skill which has been selected.

Luckily/Unluckily
Round off with a game. (See Session Two)

Session Five

Objectives
- *To strengthen motivation*
- *To continue to help clients set goals and short-term targets*
- *To provide further opportunities for behavioural practice*
- *To provide feedback and positive reinforcement*
- *To help clients develop a vocabulary of emotion*

Introduce Session

Record each client's progress on flipchart paper (a token system may be used to earn points for a reward if trainers wish to do this)

Review each client's progress, help clients to decide on suitable roleplay

Sculpture of Emotion
Emotion words are brainstormed ("happy" "sad" "angry") and the group take turns to mime these emotions, paying attention to posture, gesture, and facial expression. "Freezing" the emotion helps to focus down on detail. Video may be useful here.

Role-play: Talking with a Stranger
Clients are encouraged to "open up" in the role-play by starting up a conversation with someone they do not know (e.g. a person they sit next to on the bus, or someone they meet on holiday). Jokes, conversational ploys and taking an interest in the other person can be considered and the facilitators can model the roleplay. Change the situation so the clients must think a little rather than replicating the model.

Process Feedback
Clients are encouraged to compliment each other on steps made during the session. The role of clients in giving direct, positive feedback to each other is emphasised.

Game

Eye Wink Murder (See Session Three)

Session Six

Objectives
- *To help clients monitor progress*
- *To enhance non-verbal communication skills*
- *To help clients build an assertive style of behaviour*
- *To enable clients to set themselves a challenging task*
- *To encourage clients to give each other positive feedback*

<u>Review</u>
Discuss progress in role-plays and give positive encouragement. Ask clients to set goals for today.

<u>Looking Meditation</u>
Clients practice maintaining eye contact in pairs.

<u>Saying No</u>
In pairs, clients practice saying *No* when asked a favour. Assertiveness is developed, as clients must stand their ground while recognising another's needs.

<u>Role-Play: Dealing with a Difficult Situation</u>
Clients are encouraged to make their task harder by picking a social situation which they will experience as difficult (e.g. being bullied). By bringing their difficulty to the group, they will obtain support. Peers help brainstorm coping strategies before each roleplay.

<u>Peer Appraisal</u>
Again, clients are invited to make positive evaluations of their own work and the work of others, both in terms of content (e.g. skills practiced in role-play) and process (e.g. having the courage to pick a difficult situation).

Session Seven

Objectives
- *To introduce Skill Acquisition Stage Three (real life practice)*
- *To set up individual assignments*
- *To offer modelling, roleplay and feedback to support the assignments*
- *To continue to develop social skill through the group process*

Introduce Concept of Real Life Practice
Explain value of repetition in habit formation

Individual Task Setting
Assist in the assignment of individual tasks (e.g. meet a friend for a specific activity). Client must undertake to "break new ground" in social terms.

Modelling
Tasks are modelled by facilitators or peers.

Role-play Practice
Individuals role-play own tasks, involving peers or facilitators as they wish in the role-play.

Feedback
Positive feedback is offered by facilitators and peers.

Assignment Setting
Agreed assignments are written on small cards for members to take away, specifying what, with whom and the like.

Feedback on Group Process
Positive feedback to individual members for contribution to session (system of tokens may be used).

Luckily/Unluckily
See Session Two (or use a different game for ending if preferred).

Session Eight

Objectives
- *To convey an expectation that tasks will be carried out in real life*
- *To enhance motivation for doing this*
- *To offer an opportunity to report on last week's assignments*
- *To provide positive feedback for achievements*
- *To allow clients to practice their tasks in roleplay*

Warm-Up: Eye Contact Meditation
See Session Six

Assignment Feedback
Obtain feedback on assignments, in as much detail as possible. Compliment clients on achievements, and offer opportunity to discuss missed opportunities.

Reinforcement
Reinforce clients with stars on charts or verbal praise.

Task Setting
Encourage clients to set themselves further tasks, slightly more difficult from before. Record these on cards for clients to take away (e.g. respond assertively in a bullying or near-bullying situation which they frequently experience as victim. Specify how they will respond)

Role-play
Encourage clients once again to practice these real-life tasks in role-play, with full peer participation. Empower them to plan ways of dealing with any anxiety they may experience and help them to develop problem-solving skills.

Game: Eye Wink Murder
See Session Three.

Session Nine

Objectives
- *To review final assignments with clients, and reinforce progress*
- *To offer help to clients who have not yet completed assignments*
- *To initiate Phase Four of Skill Acquisition (Generalisation)*
- *To encourage clients to generalise their skills to new situations*
- *To help clients develop social problem-solving skills*

Warm-up: Yes/No
In pairs, one person says *Yes* and the other says *No*. This cycle is repeated for half a minute, and the changes in tone are noted.

Assignment Review
Final assignments are reviewed and individual clients are given feedback in turn, using stars on the flipchart. Help is given to those clients who have not yet completed their assignments.

Group Roleplay: Dealing with Teasing
Each client copes in turn with being teased by the group, having previously discussed coping strategies.

Problem Solving Role-play: Help a Friend
Problem solving skills are discussed and put up on flipchart paper (brainstorm options, select one, think how it would work). Working in pairs, clients role-play bringing a problem to a friend for help. The problem-solving skills are then practiced in the role-play.

One New Skill, One New Situation
Going around the group, ask each client for one skill they have newly learned, and one new situation to which they might apply it. For example, negotiation has been used to make friends; it could also be used to reduce conflict. Ensure the new situation is carefully described

Session Ten
Objectives
- *To help each client review systematically the targets and goals that have been attained and the work remaining to be done*
- *To provide positive reinforcement for these achievements*
- *To provide feedback to each client on skills requiring further development*
- *To enable each client to formulate plans for future maintenance and generalisation of their skills*
- *To facilitate individual role-play on key areas requiring work in preparation for the future*
- *To compliment the group on the work they have done together*
- *To round off the group and deal with "ending" issues*

Review of Work
Each group member is encouraged to review achievements and make a statement about goals for the future.

One Good Thing
Each group member is encouraged to make a positive "I" statement about one skill they have developed and will "take away" from the group.

Three Good Ideas
Each group member is encouraged to state three skills which they have developed on the course and will continue to practice.

One New Thing
Each group member is asked to state one new skill they will seek to develop, or one new situation they will seek to cope with.

One Old Problem
Each group member is asked to nominate one continuing issue and formulate a plan for coping.

Role-play
Offer individuals a chance to role-play any skill they choose; or select a role-play which seems to have wide relevance for group members.

Paying a Compliment
Ask group members to pay a compliment, saying something they appreciate about the person next to them.

From *Handbook for Social Skills Development with Children and Adolescents: From Research to Practice* by Richard Bulkeley. Copyright 2018, Independently Published. Permission to photocopy this Session Plan is granted to purchasers of this book for personal use only (see copyright page for details).

Knots

End with a Group Knot. Join hands and one person weaves in and out of the group, making a knot. Two people stay out and have to untangle the knot.

Programme Two: Standard Social Skills Development Programme (Ten Sessions).

This programme is suitable for a homogeneous group, who can be offered similar instructions in Stages Three and Four of the Skill Acquisition Process. There is a stronger focus on the building of micro-skills and more complex behavioural routines in Stages One and Two.

Introduction

The general approach to the training sessions is similar to that described in Treatment Programme One. At each session, a specific aspect of social interaction is considered. In the early sessions, there is a focus on the verbal and non-verbal micro-skills used in social interaction. This enables clients to develop a conceptual structure and a "dictionary" of social skills. In the later sessions, there is a focus on "real life" situations. Coaching, group discussion, modeling, role-play and real-life assignment setting are used. Assignment setting (Stage Three) is given increased emphasis during the last four sessions.

The formal structure of each session is similar to that used in Programme One. After a warm-up activity, there is a brief conceptual explanation of the area to be worked on followed by extended skill practice/role-play. Schematically, the format may be represented as follows:

1. Get the group together
2. Warm-up
3. Main Work (conceptual explanation/skills practice/discussion/role-play/homework setting)
4. Closure (e.g. favourite game).

Objectives

1. To create an atmosphere of trust
2. To provide an experience of positive social interaction within a controlled situation
3. To provide experiences which will help clients to deal with everyday social situations
4. To use the techniques of modeling, role-play practice, feedback and positive reinforcement
5. To assist clients in taking the perspective of others, whilst being positive about their own feelings
6. To assist clients in learning to cope with difficult social situations and the anxieties which such situations trigger
7. To assist clients in generalising the skills learned and perfected in the group to other situations
8. To encourage clients to undertake real -life practice of the skills learned in the group

Skills to be Practised: Role-plays

Skills to be practiced within this programme, using role-play for behavioural rehearsal, may be drawn from the following list:

Coping with teasing
Negotiating
Being left out
Asking permission from an adult
Joining a group
Coping with bullying
Talking to a stranger
Being wrongly accused
Arranging to meet friends
Helping others to solve problems
Maintaining conversation
Standing up for your rights
Introducing yourself
Paying a compliment
Giving directions
Apologising
Understanding the feelings of others

Dealing with someone else's anger
Dealing with fear
Avoiding trouble with others
Dealing with contradictory measures
Getting ready for a difficult conversation
Answering a complaint
Setting a goal
Gathering information
Dealing with group pressure
Standing up for a friend
Dealing with embarrassment
Concentration on a task
Making a complaint
Keeping out of fights
Using self-control

Facilitators should feel free to adapt the package to include topics from the above list for role-play if they will be of particular value to the group.

Games and Warmups

The following games and warm-ups may be used within this programme. Some will be familiar to the reader from Treatment Programme One and others will be explained in the text.

Name Game
Pass the Cat
Luckily/Unluckily
Eye-wink Murder
Passing the Message
Sculpture of Emotion
Expression of Emotion
Looking Meditation
Saying No
True Story
Reflecting
Knots
Blind Partners
In the Manner of the Word

Leaning Out Circle
Yes/No

Session One

Objectives
- *To explain the purpose of the group*
- *To establish rules*
- *To introduce group members*
- *To create cohesiveness*
- *To initiate lively and stimulating social interaction within the group*
- *To introduce mime, drawing attention to hand movements*
- *To provide a positive social experience*
- *To enhance motivation*
- *To encourage the social sharing of experience*
- *To create a bond between group members and facilitators*
- *To set the scene and create boundaries*

Name Game
The group members sit in a circle. One member says his name. The next member repeats that person's name and then says his own. This continues around the circle so that the seventh person must say the names of the six previous people. When the circle is completed, start in a new place and go the other way around, but this time each person puts a descriptive adjective in front of his name and repeats the other names and adjectives, e.g. "*Lazy Joe, Tough Tom, Quiet Joanne*".

Pass the Cat
The group sits on the floor in a circle. Someone mimes holding a cat and then passes the imaginary cat to the person on one side of him, and so on round the circle. Continue with other objects, e.g. chewing gum, snake, length of elastic, bucket of slime.

True Story (Version Two)
Split group into pairs. Person A describes a true incident from his experience. Person B repeats this with Person A's inflection and emphasis. Person A then tells the story again but in a different role, e.g. an absent-minded old lady. Encourage partners to discuss the task afterwards and to give each other positive feedback.

Set the Scene
Explain the objectives of the group. Explain social skills and how the group will offer help. Discuss ground rules which might be helpful and encourage participation in this discussion. Address issues such as attendance, confidentiality, mutual respect and procedures for dealing with the experience of personal stress in the group (e.g. taking time out). Write out the resultant rules on flipchart paper and bring these back to each group.

Session Two

Objectives
- *To build group cohesiveness and sense of familiarity*
- *To build verbal and non-verbal micro-skills and emphasise their importance*
- *To help clients build a vocabulary of emotion*
- *To initiate role-play -the key method of behavioural practice - and reinforce clients for acting either as participants or observers*
- *To build an understanding of the mechanics of social interaction in a simple interchange*
- *To introduce the notion of analysing a piece of social interaction into its components*

The Name Game
See Session One

Looking Meditation
Maintain non-threatening eye contact for one minute in pairs. Ask clients to sit facing each other about one and a half metres apart. Advise clients to shift gaze a little if they start to giggle.

Expression and Recognition of Emotion
Elicit from group a list of emotion words that are meaningful for them, e.g. sorrow, happiness, fear, amusement, surprise. Facilitators model some of the words in a sculpt or "frozen" posture, using both face and body cues. All group members "mirror" the posture and facial expression - and then try to guess the word. Group members initiate new sculpts and the same procedure is followed for each. Draw attention to the various cues that are used to convey the emotion -facial, gesture and posture. Give positive feedback for clear, direct cues and suggest improvements where appropriate.

<u>Friend Across the Street</u>
By this time, leaders will have identified at least one lively pair which will be prepared to volunteer for a simple role-play, with a little encouragement. Leaders should model the role-play first. *"You see a school friend/aunt/teacher on the other side of a quiet street. Although you are busy you know you must go and greet them, otherwise they will take offence"*. In advance, elicit from the group the stages of the greeting process and write them up on flipchart paper - for example:

- Eye contact at a distance
- Acknowledge eye contact with gesture (raise eyebrows)
- Brief Verbal Greeting (Hi!)
- Approach without eye contact
- Re-establish eye contact with friendly facial expression
- Conventional question and answer reciprocated (How are you,)
- Take up conversational posture
- Start conversation, linking yourself with the other's world
- Respond positively to remarks and questions of the other
- After a while, take your leave, giving a reason, say goodbye, and look forward to the next meeting

Ask each group member to observe and comment on a stage in the process. Encourage direct and positive feedback on performance during the roleplay.

<u>Luckily/Unluckily</u>
See Programme One, Session Two.

Session Three

Objectives
- *Help clients to increase their competence rapidly in a range of micro-skills*
- *Help clients develop sensitivity to tone of voice*
- *Help clients develop accurate signaling of emotion by tone of voice*
- *Help clients recognise emotion expressed in tone of voice*
- *Help clients to increase awareness of eye contact*
- *Help clients to increase awareness of physical proximity*
- *Continue to foster cohesion and trust within the group*
- *By maintaining rapid tempo, increase client's confidence in participation in roleplay and other exercises*

Introductory Exercise
Use a variant of the Name Game (e.g. throwing a ball) or "Our Day" in which each member has one minute to describe the events of the day. In "Our Day", give positive feedback for genuine, appropriate expression of feeling.

Sound Circle Echo
The group sits in a circle. A word is chosen such as *"Hello", "Please"* or *"Mum"*. One member starts off, using a particular volume, tone, or pitch. The next member tries to repeat the word using the same intonation, and so on round the group. The group then try to guess the mood being conveyed (this activity may be used in conjunction with the emotion words from the last session). The group should then be asked to find words that describe the tone of voice that was used, e.g. "excited" but what about the tone expressed excitement? Encourage the use of onomatopoeic words like "whiney".

Ask different group members to start the circle off, using new words, new tones or whatever.

Questioning Numbers
Now numbers are used as "pretend" words in a similar way. Person A puts a question with one number, using an interrogative tone; Person B replies with another number in a different tone (angry, fearful) and Person B's tone is guessed. Continue in this way round the group.

Eye Contact Greeting
The group sits in a fairly spread out circle. Individuals make eye contact with someone across the room and both acknowledge this by raising an eyebrow or nodding. Continue for some minutes. Discuss how pleasant it is to have one's greeting acknowledged.

Physical Proximity Role-play

Facilitators briefly model positions for conversation, confrontation and cooperation, matching the positions with suitable statements. The congruence between physical position and mutual feeling is emphasised.

Eye Contact Murder

The murderer, selected by drawing a secret card, must choose a victim and wink; the victim must then "die", obviously and horribly! The group must detect the murderer. One guess each is allowed. The murderer can continue to pick off victims, if not detected.

Session Four

Objectives
- *Assist in development of active listening, facilitating and empathising*
- *Promote skill and fluency in verbal self-expression*
- *Provide further experience of roleplay and similar tasks*
- *Encourage mutual positive reinforcement*

Leaning Out Circle
The group holds hands and lean backwards. In this way, each individual is supported by the group.

Nonsense Rubbish
A nonsense word exchange game. Person A says "*Nonsense, Nonsense*", Person B says "*Nonsense, Nonsense, Rubbish, Rubbish*". Person A says "*Rubbish, Rubbish, Fine, Fine*" (or whatever); and so, it goes on. Each nonsense word can be repeated more than twice.

Verbal Mirroring
Facilitators model the task. Person A relates an experience, pausing after each sentence; Person B repeats the last part of each sentence, then asking a question. Person A continues. The group then practice in pairs.

Verbal Reflecting
As with mirroring: this time, Person B shows appreciation of how Person A must have felt after each sentence.

In the Manner of the Word
One person leaves the room and the group chooses an adjective (e.g. "fussy" or use a "feeling" word from the previous exercise). The person comes back in and has to guess the word by asking the group members to perform various actions, related to the word.

Session Five

Objectives
- *Begin Phase Two of Skill Acquisition*
- *Help clients to build skills in assertiveness*
- *Initiate notion of more complex skills in interaction*
- *Observe those micro-skills which are well established and offer positive reinforcement*
- *Begin to focus on "real life" activities*
- *Encourage group to work together on "real life" issues*

Warm-up: Ask a Favour/ Say No
Going around the group, Person A asks Person B for a favour; Person B must say *No*, but show some recognition of Person A's needs. Give feedback to Person A for tone of voice and Person B for tone of voice and empathy content.

Role-play; Joining a Group
An outsider has to join an established group. Group and facilitators brainstorm in advance possible real-life school/leisure situations. Facilitators have back-up idea in case of need. Positively reinforce micro skills which are used, e.g. paying a compliment, introducing yourself, active listening (previously practiced as verbal mirroring and reflecting).

Role-play: Standing Up for your Rights
An aggrieved individual takes a defective article back to a shop. Again, positively reinforce relevant micro-skills, e.g. clear verbal expression, sticking to your point (or broken record), keeping calm, good eye contact and posture, making a plan. Write micro-skills used on flip-chart paper to display.

Game: Baked Beans
One person stands in the middle and asks questions round the group. Whatever question is asked, the answer must be "*Baked Beans*" which must be said without laughing or smiling.

Session Six

Objectives
- *Continue to help clients develop assertive skills across a range of everyday situations with peers and adults*
- *Continue to help clients develop skill in observing and monitoring social interaction*
- *To foster a positive working atmosphere with a high level of rapport within the group*
- *To encourage group to offer positive direct feedback on role play practice by individuals*
- *To encourage group to share recent experiences which may highlight areas for skill development*

Our Day
It is useful, at this juncture, to introduce the practice of going around and encouraging group members to share their day's experiences. Ask for a clear positive or negative evaluation with good expression of feeling, e.g. "*I had a really nasty experience of bullying today*". Clients can then be offered the opportunity to use role-play to develop coping skills at a later stage in the session.

Yes/No
This assertiveness warm-up is performed in pairs. Standing face to face, Person A says *Yes*, Person B says *No*; then change over. The exchange acquires momentum as the participants try different intonation strategies and respond reciprocally. The implicit mental set created by the situation is one of confrontation. Assign a group member to report on the facial changes that occur during the encounter and how these relate to changes in vocal tone and intensity.

Role-play: Dealing with Bullying
Brainstorm possible real-life situations of bullying familiar to the group and elicit various coping skills. Write these on a flipchart.

This role-play can be managed in a number of ways. One is to have one of the facilitators enact the bully and the group members in turn to try out various coping skills in the victim role. Positive feedback is then given, encouraging the group members to contribute direct feedback on performance. Sum up the skills demonstrated and enumerate the advantages of each. Allow each member to debrief and say what skill they will try out in future in a victim situation.

Keep the role-play short and focused and be mindful of the specific skills being practiced.

<u>Role-play: Being Wrongly Accused</u>
This role-play enables young people to acquire skills in dealing with confrontations with adult authority, always a tricky matter because of the power wielded by adults. The aim is to be polite and respectful whilst, at the same time, expressing one's point of view clearly and reasonably. Important micro-skills are planning, keeping calm and clear verbal expression.

<u>Eye Wink Murder</u>
See Session Three

Session Seven

Objectives
- *Begin Phase Three of Skill Acquisition*
- *Introduce notion of real-life assignments*
- *Encourage clients to develop their skills in everyday life*
- *Support the planning of real-life work with relevant role-play practice*
- *Encourage group members to support each other in planning real- life work*

Our Day
See Session Six

Eye Contact Greeting
See Session Three

Introduce Concept of Real-Life Assignments
Explain purpose of assignments. Encourage clients to consider possible areas for work.

Role-play
Encourage group to set up brief role-plays on "negotiating" (friends decide what to do), "paying a compliment", "understanding the feelings of others" and "keeping out of trouble". Work on any ideas which might have come up from "Our Day".

From the role-plays, develop possible individual assignments.

Planning of Assignments
Individual assignments, developed from the role-plays and the clients themselves, are written out on flipchart paper for reference within the group and on cards by the clients as reminders for themselves through the week. Cards must specify What, With Whom, When and How to React.

Change the Action
One person leaves the room. The group agrees a Leader and begins a repetitive movement sequence (e.g. hand clap) which the leader may switch. The person comes in, stands in the middle and has to identify the leader. This is an excellent test of observational skills.

From *Handbook for Social Skills Development with Children and Adolescents: From Research to Practice* by Richard Bulkeley. Copyright 2018, Independently Published. Permission to photocopy this Session Plan is granted to purchasers of this book for personal use only (see copyright page for details).

Session Eight

Objectives
- *Help clients to develop communication skills*
- *Help clients to practice positive assertion*
- *Help clients to practice conversation skills*
- *Help clients to deal with difficult feelings*
- *Help clients to deal with difficult situations*
- *Encourage clients to report on achievement on planned tasks*
- *Encourage clients to offer each other positive feedback for completion of real-life assignments*

Warm-up: Passing the Message
See Programme One, Session Three.

Assignment Feedback
Offer opportunities for clients to report on their achievements planned last week. Provide positive reinforcement for each event. Discuss any problems encountered, involving whole group in a problem-solving approach.

Role-play
Set up role-plays on "dealing with embarrassment", "talking to a stranger", "offering help to a friend" or other topics which appear relevant from the main list or are suggested by group members. Discuss micro skills used and provide positive reinforcement.

Assignment Setting
Encourage clients to undertake further real-life assignments to practice skills in areas of their choice. Facilitators and group members may be able to offer suggestions as a result of their observation of the client. Assignments may also be used to practice skills developed during the afternoon's role-play.

Game: Fruit Salad
Each group member chooses a fruit. A person in the middle of the group calls out the names of various fruit and the people who chose those names have to change places. The person in the middle has to slip into one of the places, leaving someone else in the middle. Calling out, *Fruit Salad*" means everyone has to change places.

Session Nine

Objectives
- *Maintenance of Micro-skills (Stage One in Skill Acquisition)*
- *Further development of Complex or Macro-skills through Role-play Practice (Stage Two)*
- *Further opportunities to practice skills in real life (Stage Three)*

Questioning Numbers
See Session Three

Assignment Feedback
See Session Eight

Role-play
Select two or three role-plays from the main list. Emphasise skills which will help areas where a number of clients are working. Encourage clients to support each other in offering positive reinforcement.

Game: Change the Action
See Session Seven

Session Ten

Objectives
- *Prepare group for ending*
- *Highlight individual and collective gains*
- *Encourage application of skills to new areas and new situations*
- *Encourage continuing analytical approach*
- *Encourage clients to find friends to support their personal work on social skills*

Our Day
See Session Six

Assignment Feedback
(As in previous sessions)

Future Plans
Discuss ending of group, suggesting further individual assignments.

Evaluation
Encourage each client to summarise main skills learned.

Moving Ahead
Encourage each group member to think of one new situation in which they will apply their social skills.

Pay a Compliment
Go around the group. Person A compliments Person B for a skill that Person B has learned in the group.

Eye Wink Murder

See Session Three

Goodbye
Allow space for group members to say goodbye to each other how they want.

Social Skill Programme Three (Short Course)

This short course of four sessions may be used as an introductory series of group sessions enabling clients to be assessed for possible further input.

Session One

Objectives
- *Set scene and introduce group members to each other and to facilitators*
- *Begin to train in micro-skills (basic communication skills)*
- *Build a vocabulary of the emotions*
- *Build spontaneity and confidence in verbal self-expression*
- *Help clients to develop non-verbal communication skills (e.g. eye contact)*
- *Introduce notion of skill practice and development*

Introductions
Pairs share name, school, favourite hobby. Each member then introduces partner to group, with prompting if necessary.

Purpose of Group
Define social skills. Explain they can be acquired naturally but enhanced by training. The focus will be on skills that will help with friendship making and dealing with bullying.

Ground Rules
Write up rules which seem appropriate on flipchart. Invite contributions from group and negotiate agreement. Include rule on confidentiality plus some discussion on what this means.

Eye Contact with Compliment
Facilitators model paying a verbal compliment with eye contact. Go around group with each member thinking of a compliment for the next person. Reinforce appropriate compliments and good firm friendly eye contact.

Luckily/ Unluckily
See Programme 1, Session 2

Eye Wink Murder
See Programme 1, Session 3

Expression of Emotion
Generate a list of emotions. Each member simulates emotion in "frozen" mode, selecting appropriate facial, postural and gestural patterns. The group replicates simulation and guess the emotion.

Or:

Walk round the room to music suggesting various moods. Facilitator suggests a feeling and group demonstrates that feeling. Members think of situations when they experienced the various feelings elicited during the exercise and debrief afterwards on the situations which came to mind.

Real Life Assignment
Practice eye contact plus compliment in one situation in real life. Clients can report back next week.

Session Two

Objectives
- *Help clients develop empathy skills and listening skills*
- *Help clients develop verbal spontaneity*
- *Help client identify and use assertion skills*
- *Offer clients opportunity to practice assertion skills in real life*
- *Help clients learn to control behaviour in a social situation*
- *Continue to build cohesiveness of group*

Our Day
Each client says how the experience of the day has been.

Assignment Feedback
Enable clients to comment on how they got on with the task suggested last week (eye contact plus compliment).

Positive Event Recording/Active Listening
Invite pairs to work in turn. Person A reports pleasant experience, Person B shows appreciation, by reflecting (repeating phrases), showing understanding of feeling and making utterances such as *"Mmm", "Wow", "Did you?"* and the like when appropriate. Each should have a turn as Persons A and then B.

Luckily/Unluckily
See Programme 1, Session 2.

Assertive Skills
Explain the concept of assertiveness simply but carefully (standing up for yourself without fighting, putting your own point of view, or however you prefer to define it)
Elicit, or list a set of assertive skills (invite group member to write on flipchart paper), e.g. express your feelings clearly (making an "I" statement), give back-up reasons, use listening skills (such as those just learned), recognise feelings of other (as just practiced), make a sensible plan, put it into practice. Clients can use" broken record" (insistent repetition) if necessary (but this technique can trigger high levels of tension if used excessively with a parent.).

Role-play (Assertiveness)
Role-play taking a defective article back to a shop, using the skills listed. Facilitators model a good and a bad way of playing the role and elicit comments from the group. Group members play the role in turn and practice the skills. Positive feedback is given for the specific skills used.

Assignment Setting
Group members are invited to create situations in real life where assertive skills may be practiced, and report back on their achievements.

Baked Beans

In the final game, which ends the session; a person in the middle generates questions such as "*What do you have your bath in?*" and each group member when addressed must reply "*Baked Beans*" without smiling or laughing. Whoever smiles or laughs when saying "*Baked Beans*" must go in the middle to continue the game.

Session Three

Objectives
- *To enhance skill acquisition by encouraging real life practice*
- *To practice assertive, communication and listening skills*
- *To integrate these in a friendship making task*
- *To continue to build group cohesion and maintain a working atmosphere*

Our Day
See Session Two

Follow-up on Task
Discuss a real-life situation in which assertiveness was demonstrated, using one verbal and one non-verbal skill.

Warm-ups
-Eye contact greeting (exchanging eye contact with other group members)
-Accusing/Responding (Go around the group: Person A accuses Person B of something, Person B must respond assertively. Facilitators write the assertive skills on flipchart, e.g. broken record, give a good reason.)
- Negative event recording/ reflecting. (Person A recounts unpleasant experience, Person B listens actively. Clients should use the list of communication and listening skills on flipchart. Facilitators should prompt use of skills and praise for specific correct uses).

Role-play
(Facilitators models friendship making". A new student arrives at your school; introduce yourself, make friends and show him round.

The group provides feedback on role-play, praising specific use of assertive and communication skills. Discuss other skills used (e.g. introducing oneself).

Set Task
 Use one assertive skill and one communication skill with a friend and report back. Ask group members which skills they will choose to practice and in which situation.

Game
"Fruit Salad". See Programme two, Session Eight

Session Four

Objectives
- *Continue to develop skill acquisition through role-play and real-life practice*
- *Continue to work on assertive skills*
- *Help clients identify and develop skills to deal with bullying*
- *Help clients to select a skill to take away for themselves and develop*
- *Help clients to cope with ending of this batch of sessions*

Our Day

Follow-up on Task
Practice assertive/communication skills with friend

Future Plans
Inform clients of help or resources that will be available after this batch of sessions.

Warm-ups

Name Game plus Adjective
Encourage each client to think of an adjective to go in front of their name and get the group to rehearse the list of names preceded by adjectives; John says "*Happy John*", Jane says "*Good Jane, Happy John*", and so round the group, with the last member rehearsing the whole string.

Yes/No
Person A says "*Yes*", Person B says "*No*", Person A says "*Yes*", Person B says "*No*" and so on. Stand face to face in pairs with maximum eye contact. Notice the shifts in tone and loudness as well as facial expression. Different strategies should be tried and responded to in the implicit confrontation. Then swap over. Get the whole group to do this exercise simultaneously, having modelled the exercise first; then break and discuss.

Ask a Favour/Say No
Person A asks a favour from Person B, Person B has to say "*No*" firmly but politely, respecting Person A's needs and feelings ("I appreciate.... *but No.*")

Three-Word Story
Go around group developing story. Each member contributes just three words at a time.

Brainstorming
Bullying situations - Who is likely to do what to whom?
Consider possible responses/skills - e.g. walk away, tell teacher, challenge assertively but calmly

Role-play

Facilitators model good and bad responses to bullying. Then discuss.
Individual behavioural rehearsal in turn. Set scene as appropriate for each client.
A facilitator or group member takes the role of bully in each case.

Feedback, commenting on specific positive factors, and possible alternative skills which could be used.

Long-term Task Setting

Specific

Get each client to specify one skill to work on dealing with bullying

General

Encourage clients to practise assertive and communication skills (giving brief examples); to observe expression of feeling, be sensitive to feelings of others, and practise using feeling words (by making "*I feel.......*" statements to themselves and others).

One skill to take away

Emphasising the ending of this batch of sessions, encourage clients to name one general skill they will make a point of developing and practising. Ask them in what situations they will use this skill.

End Game

Guess the Leader

One person goes out and a leader is selected to "change the action". The person comes in and sees the group performing the action. The leader keeps changing the action and the group follows, until the leader is guessed. Then the leader goes out and so on.

Summary

Appendix 1 has presented two ten-session social skill development programmes, one for heterogeneous and one for homogeneous groups, and a short four-session package. Readers are encouraged to develop their own programmes building on the principles and examples outlined in this book.

Reference

Trower, P (1984). *Radical approaches to social skills training.* London: Croom Helm.

Appendix 2
Psychodynamic approaches to groupwork with adolescents

A developmental approach
Dwivedi (1993) points out that small groups form part of the natural social experience of school age children and adolescents. Therefore, adolescents should adapt readily to therapeutic groupwork.

A therapeutic group may have its own developmental phases, replicating human development. In the early stages the group may be dependent like an infant; at a later stage the members may come to feel more competent and independent of the therapist.

Boundaries
According to systems theory (von Bertalanffy, 1968) a system is composed of component parts and their interaction. The psychological functioning of a group can be seen as a system of dynamically interacting components. The boundary of the group, which binds together the individual members and their interactions, is both psychological and physical, since the group get together at one point in space and time - hence, the closed door of the room symbolises the boundary. There are boundaries, too, between individual group members - these, hopefully, become increasingly permeable, as members learn to give and accept feedback to one another. The ending of the group symbolises the final closure of the time boundary, which must end all human relationships - by working constructively on the emotions aroused by ending, group members can join in a final, mutually beneficial, maturing process.

Psychodynamic concepts
Certain psychodynamic concepts are helpful in outlining the role which can be helpfully adopted by the group leader (Dwivedi, 1993). In "Communicative matching "the group leader shares in new found interests of group members, mirroring the parent whose small child wanders off to explore the world. (e.g. the adolescent reports a new social activity, the therapist takes an interest.)

Transitional objects
At times, group members may appear with objects that comfort them - e.g. a Game boy, a Walkman. In psychodynamic terms, these may be seen as "transitional objects" (roughly speaking, parent substitutes; transitional objects are identified with in the phase between merging with the mother and being separate from the mother (Winnicott, 1974). It is important therefore for the therapist to respect the emotional significance of these personal objects, whilst maintaining the group boundary. Finally, the group itself and its equipment become "transitional objects" for the members.

Auxiliary ego
Group leaders and fellow members provide group members with coping strategies to deal with difficult problems and with emotional support. These supportive strategies and approaches become internalised by the group member ("auxiliary ego"). Hence, personal growth is enhanced and the sense of self becomes firmer.

Regression

At times within the group process the phenomenon of emotional regression may be noticed. These may be understood in terms of Object Relations Theory (Trist, 1985). Trist observed that Fight/Flight, Pairing and Dependency are often manifested on such occasions. These are signs of insecurity in the group, and the therapist must help the group to identify the root cause and respond in a more constructive manner e.g. a new topic is broached which the group members feel uncomfortable with. The therapist must seek to make the situation safe, introduce the new topic sensitively, or save it for another occasion.

Examples of Regression:
- The therapist notices that clients' A and B are interacting closely with each other
- The therapist notices an atmosphere of hostility within the group
- The therapist notices a tendency for the group to look to the leaders for support

Defence mechanisms

These processes are postulated within the psychodynamic approach to influence our unconscious thoughts and feelings. They may be noticed at the individual level and the group level. In either case, the therapist needs to draw the process into awareness and encourage the individual or group to adopt more effective strategies to deal with the underlying problems which are invariably present.

These processes include splitting, denial, projection, introjection, and projective identification.

Definitions are given below.

Splitting: Seeing people, particularly significant others, as wholly good or wholly bad, e.g. an adolescent may feel totally rejecting towards parents and the police

Projection: Attributing one's own undesirable characteristics to others, e.g. an adolescent who feels intellectually inferior will tease another for being "thick".

Denial: Refusal to accept one's feelings, e.g. an adolescent feels inwardly insecure about lack of sexual experience, but covers this with bravado.

Introjection: Taking in ideas and feelings from others, e.g. an insecure adolescent goes around with a gang of bullies, and feels "big" as a result of assimilating their beliefs and pleasure in aggression.

Projective Identification; Projecting one's feelings and ideas into others and seeking to make them like oneself, e.g. An adolescent sexual abuser may falsely attribute his own sexual desires to his victim, seeking to make the victim into a willing partner.

References

Dwivedi, KN (1993) Part 1: Theoretical and practical issues. In K.N. Dwivedi (Ed.) *Group work with children and adolescents: A handbook.* London: Kingsley.

Trist, E (1985). 'Working with Bion in the 1940s: the Group Decade' In M Pines (Ed.) *Bion and Group Psychotherapy.* New York: George Brazilian.

Von Breakoff, L (1968). *General Systems Theory: Foundation, Development, Application.* New York: George Brazilian.

Winnicott, DW (1974). *Playing and reality.* Harmondsworth, U.K: Penguin.

PART 2

CLINICAL AND EDUCATIONAL APPLICATIONS

CHAPTER 5   AUTISTIC SPECTRUM DISORDER: TECHNIQUES FOR ASSESSMENT AND INTERVENTION

A number of useful techniques are suggested by the research material for this client group; others are already employed in clinical practice. This chapter provides an overview of both with examples of clinical use.

5.1 Assessment Procedures

Use of Rating Scales

The Social Skills Improvement System (SSIS; Gresham & Elliott, 2008) is well validated by a number of studies, but is not specifically designed for children with autistic spectrum disorder (ASD).

The SSIS provides rating scales based on questionnaires completed by students, teachers and parents. The rating scales provide an overview of social skills and problem behaviours and include an assessment of autistic spectrum issues for young people aged 4-18. This approach is best used with older children who have some language. The rating scales may be used to generate plans for intervention which may then be monitored by further assessments down the line.
This material is best used by a clinical or educational psychologist, or practitioner trained in psychometric approaches.

Clinical Example: The Social Skills Improvement System (SSIS; Gresham & Elliot, 2008) has been useful in developing Personal Social Skills Programmes for two young people with Asperger's Syndrome (a female aged 13 and a male aged 15). Specific needs were identified enabling individual therapy to be carried out along in collaboration school, parents and care staff.

Assessment of Cognitive, Linguistic and Communication Skills

Using tools such as the McCarthy Scales (McCarthy, 1972) and the Bayley Screening Assessment (Bayley, 2005), a profile of cognitive, linguistic and communication skills can be established. Procedures for providing input at critical developmental levels can then be put in place in a range of contexts such as school and home. Behavioural approaches can be used to enhance motivation for learning. If the client engages in useful learning at an appropriate level, many problem behaviours may disappear. The knock-on effects may be useful for social communication.

This approach may be used with less able students including those with no language, as well as with younger children. It may be used outside the specified age range to establish the overall developmental level of a student who has limited language or cognitive function. These assessments are well validated and standardised.

Clinical Example: The Bayley Screening Test (Third Edition) helpful in identifying the developmental level of children with ASD who do not have language. Their performance on nonverbal items can give a clue as to the level of social communication which they may be able to master, given appropriate instruction and encouragement. It is helpful to work closely with Speech and Language Therapists, Occupational Therapists and educators and obtain their observations to form an overview. It is important to note the cognitive ability of the young person to master the use of signs to communicate.

From a clinical point of view, it is useful to note how the students perform in terms of developmental level even though the test is designed for typically developing children and therefore the ASD students may be outside the age norms. Children of approximately average ability may be assessed intellectually using the standard Wechsler procedures (Wechsler, 2016).

Assessment of Social Communication
A useful procedure for assessing social communication has been developed by the Newsom Centre. This combines standardised assessment procedures with observation of the client in a range of situations and observing closely the client's response to social interaction. Observations are made of expressive and receptive language together with non-verbal communication. *What's Wrong?* cards, Emotion cards, and *What would you do?* cards are used to evaluate the response to social situations. These qualitative observations enable a profile of the child's social communication skills to be constructed. Children are assessed with a peer on some of these procedures which provides further useful information. This approach may be used with young children but some language is required.

Clinical Example: An assessment of social communication was conducted for a female aged 15 with Asperger's Syndrome by obtaining her report of problem situations at school and evaluating her response. This helped in identifying social situations which she found difficult and the skills which she needed to develop in order to cope with these situations more successfully. This approach was used in conjunction with the SSIS assessment which involved the parent and teacher views, enabling a valid overview to be obtained. A suitable programme was then set up for individual therapy (personalised skill building). This incorporated microskills and dealing with difficult situations such as bullying.

Clinical Example: DM, aged 17 had no language. He was socially responsive to adults and did not withdraw, but was boisterous and overactive. He was usually able to control himself when given an appropriate command word and was responsive to a firm and confident tone of voice. Informal assessment of social reciprocity, social withdrawal/avoidance and detrimental social behaviours; the identified difficulty was Self-control rather than Social Reciprocity.

Assessment of Recognition of Emotion

Difficulty in recognition of emotion is a salient feature of autism as has been shown by research on face recognition (Dawson et al 2005). Brain injury research (Tonks et al, 2007a) suggests that certain cortical and sub-cortical areas, namely the hypothalamus, amygdala, hippocampus and orbitofrontal cortex, are centrally involved in the recognition of emotion. These areas are closely linked to each other by neural pathways. It appears likely that children and young people with autism suffer from neurological impairment in these areas. Tonks et al (2007b) have found that emotion recognition abilities can be measured, using such method as the Florida Affect Battery and the Mind in the Eyes Test. The Florida Affect Battery (Bowers et al, 1999) has been found useful in measuring performance deficits in brain-injured adults. It was designed to assess the perception of facial and prosodic affect using 10 different subtests. The Mind in The Eyes Test was developed by Baron-Cohen et al (2001) to establish that a sample of fifteen children with Asperger Syndrome could not determine emotional intent from eye configuration. The Mind in the Eyes Test comprised 28 photographs of the eye region of the face. Children were asked to pick which of four words best described what the person in the photo was thinking or feeling.

5.2 Intervention Approaches

Parent Training/Early Bird

There is useful research evidence for the efficacy of Parent Training in helping children with ASD (McConachie et al, 2005). Research also highlights the importance of early intervention for children with ASD (Dawson et al, 2004).

Clinical Example: A boy of 18 months old was referred to a Child Development Unit and Autism was diagnosed. His parents researched information from the internet, read books such as "The Dragons of Autism" and attended the Early Bird Programme with other parents. They became aware of the possible underlying reasons for his behaviour, e.g. during feeding, there might have been an issue about sensation and they realised that the screaming was due to a failure in communication.

Cognitive Behaviour Therapy

Kim et al (2000) found that children who had received a diagnosis of high functioning autism or Asperger Syndrome when they were between 4 and 6 years of age were more likely to suffer from anxiety and depression than typically developing children when assessed between the ages of 9 and 14 years.

Sofranoff et al (2005) conducted a cognitive behavioural intervention for anxiety in children with Asperger Syndrome, in which children and parents met with therapists for six weekly two-hour sessions. The children demonstrated improved performance in generating strategies to deal with a hypothetical anxiety-causing scenario, whilst parental feedback indicated that children were more open to talking about their anxieties and showed more insight into interpersonal situations following the intervention.

Sofranoff et al (2006) carried out a randomised controlled trial of a cognitive behavioural intervention for anger management in children diagnosed with Asperger Syndrome. The children, aged 10-14 years, participated in a six-week intervention involving weekly sessions. Parents reported a significant decrease in episodes of anger following the intervention, along with a significant increase in their own confidence in managing anger in their child. Qualitative information from parents and teachers suggested some generalisation of strategies learned to home and school settings.

White et al (2010) reported on the development of a manualised cognitive-behavioural intervention to treat anxiety and social deficits in teen-agers with high-functioning autism. Treatment incorporated individual work and social skills group work together with parental education and involvement. The group therapy was designed to provide an opportunity to practise specific social skills and anxiety management strategies with peers. It assisted in overcoming information processing weaknesses associated with ASD and provided a positive group experience. Preliminary feasibility data was promising.

More & Davis (2010) noted that anxiety disorders were found to be highly comorbid with autistic spectrum disorders. They examined the efficacy of cognitive behaviour therapy as a treatment for children with ASD and noted the usefulness of four main modification trends – disorder specific hierarchies, use of more concrete visual tactics, incorporation of child specific interests and parental involvement These enhanced CBT treatment programs for anxiety in children with ASD.

The above research focuses on children with Asperger Syndrome and high functioning autism and there is a need to explore CBT approaches with less cognitively able children with ASD. It will be noted that CBT is used to address a range of social, emotional and interpersonal problems (e.g. anger and anxiety).

Clinical Example: Cognitive behaviour therapy was used to enhance self-esteem in a teenage girl in a school context, assisting her in coping with negative reactions from others

Social Stories
Social Stories (Gray, 2010) enable children and young people to learn social rules and learn how to cope with stressful situations. Parents and carers can learn the method and generate suitable stories. Social stories explain why we do the things that we do and clarify for autistic children what we expect them to do. Children can be taught what to do in new situations, e.g. going on holiday.

The approach is widely used by practitioners. Evidence for the efficacy of social stories is beginning to emerge; Mancil et al (2009) used a single subject design to compare a social story presented in two formats to three elementary-age students with autism. Results showed a decrease in problem behaviours for each participant. Outcomes were slightly better for a computer-assisted approach than a paper format. Results were maintained in the training setting and were generalised to another setting with a single verbal prompt.

It seems likely that whilst social stories are beneficial in reducing many disruptive behaviours, they may not reliably influence social and communicative behaviour. Social stories may also be used to reduce anxiety (O'Connor, 2009; Beard & Amir, 2008). The approach is perhaps best used in conjunction with other strategies to achieve improvement in social communication

Clinical Example: JC, a boy aged four with ASD, attended school without difficulty until there was a change in the assigned Special Needs teacher. He was helped to cope with this change using a Social Story.

'Talkabout'

'Talkabout' provides a set of learning materials which can be used by psychologists and other professionals to help children and young people generate social skills. 'Talkabout' is provided by Alex Kelly who specialises in social skills and communication counselling (Kelly, 1982). Research support is limited but in the author's experience the material has been found useful with clients. The approach may be most useful with older clients who have some language. Material is available at different levels and is helpful with the development of social skills. For young clients with ASD, the material on self-awareness and self-esteem may be useful.

Clinical Example: Talkabout was used by the author to develop self-esteem in a thirteen year-old-boy in care with communication difficulties. The self-esteem exercises are a preparation for social skills work. They can be used with ASD children to build up a sense of their own identity

Picture Exchange

The Picture Exchange Communication System (PECS; Charlop-Christy et al, 2002) trains children to communicate their needs using pictures. ASD clients learn to respond to and discriminate visual stimuli relating to their needs, progressing from simple tasks to more complex. The structured communication and hands-on approach, with picture cards being passed to and fro, serves to keep the ASD clients engaged. Therefore, useful learning occurs along with useful experience of one-to-one social interaction. This approach is useful for younger children with little or no language.

Clinical Example: Picture Exchange was used to facilitate communication with a 17 year old male with ASD who could sign but had no language. More typically it is used with younger children with ASD who have little or no language.

Role-Play

Role-play is a significant ingredient of social skill development (see preceding chapters) as it enables new behaviours to be rehearsed and immediately reinforced or modified. Video feedback is also useful.

Role-play will be particularly useful in enabling clients to remedy significant social deficits on an individual basis. A group situation provides a context for the role-play to be enacted. Ideally peers without ASD would be useful within the group to act as models. However, the peer mediation could also be conducted independently (Kasari et al, 2012).

Role-play using peers similar in age as models enables behavioural rehearsal to occur, increasing the range of appropriate social responses available within a client's repertoire. The role-play can be accompanied by coaching in the choice of responses which would be appropriate in each situation. Skills practised might include the use of eye contact and maintaining appropriate distance.

Role-play can be used for training in eye contact, social distance and communication. Coping with social situations can be practised using CAGDA (see Chapter 3). Role-play may be stimulated using cartoons and may assist with learning to improve social perspective taking using some of the standard situations mentioned in the research on that topic. Role-play may utilise scripts and signs. Role-play may be used to rehearse social stories (Gray, 2010). Repeated role-play has the effect of desensitising a young person to difficult peer situations.

Group role-play may be used to enhance children's cognitive and linguistic skills. This approach is helpful for more able students with some language. Role-play is found useful in practice depending on the skill of the practitioner and the ability of the child or young person with ASD to appreciate the value of practising a social skill in a make-believe situation.

Clinical Example: Role-play was used in the context of individual therapy with a female with Asperger's Syndrome aged 15. Situations found difficult were role-played in order to assess and modify behaviour. Initially, it was helpful to desensitise her to role play in conjunction with a colleague, using computer techniques. Subsequently, it was used to help her to cope with difficult peer situations.

Clinical Example: An elaborate role-play game was used by an educational team to involve a child with ASD in perspective taking and use of appropriate language.

Clinical Example: A speech and drama therapist used visual materials, three Russian dolls and theatrical costumes to stimulate language in Jack, a wheel-chair bound youth who had suffered a brain injury in a road traffic accident eight years previously. A narrative was developed from session to session, and in character Jack could become very assertive, using non-verbal communicative gesture such as pointing.

Stress Reduction
Stress reduction may be carried out by analysing stress factors resulting from communication difficulties. It may be important to observe how rapport is established in a learning situation, enabling shared attention to be experienced. Given the communication difficulties experienced in ASD, there can be little doubt that resolving these is a key area for stress reduction.

It may be useful to explore the effect of sensory experience on stress and reduce stress using sensory integration methods (Bogdashina, 2003). Sensory integration approaches, such as TalkTools are widely used with ASD children and young people to reduce stress.

Behavioural methods such as cognitive behaviour therapy may be used to enhance management of emotion and self-control. "Mindfulness" training and relaxation techniques may also be helpful (Zoogman et al, 2015). Applied Behaviour Analysis (ABA; John, 2014) may be used to uncover the sources of anxiety which underlie unhelpful behaviours. The anxiety can then be relieved reducing stress. Attention to sensory needs, such as noise sensitivity, touch, touch avoidance, or firm pressure may also help to soothe students with ASD. The use of music and song in the contexts of education and therapy may serve to soothe students with ASD and reduce stress.

Interaction between stress reduction and positive communication may be self-perpetuating and generate a positive cycle. Therefore, stress reduction has a particularly important part to play in the development of social and communication skills with this client group.

Clinical Example: A female with ASD persistently kept her eyes shut in school. This appeared to be a method of coping with stress. The behaviour was ignored and she was encouraged to participate and reinforced for positive responses. In the end, she opened her eyes.

Teaching Theory of Mind: Training in Emotion Recognition
Baron Cohen and his colleagues (1985) have produced several materials to assist with the teaching of "Theory of Mind". This is defined as the ability to empathise and understand that others have separate thoughts and emotions, Clients' difficulties may be related to the failure to pick up the right emotional cues and difficulty in integrating the information owing to impaired central processing. 'Mind Reading', an interactive guide to emotions is available on DVD for working with such difficulties.

Clinical Example: Thomas the Tank Engine books were used to stimulate language and social perspective-taking in a four-year-old boy with ASD. The boy would allow his parents to read books to him about Thomas and he started to speak. He began to sit and play with the toy engines and would replay scenes from the television programmes. By this method, he was taught "Theory of Mind" in that he began to attribute intentions and feelings to Thomas. Significantly, the development of speech was noted in tandem with this process.

Clinical Example: A female (13) was encouraged to take her teacher's perspective to reduce her non-compliant behaviour in school. She was encouraged to look at her teacher's face to see that the teacher was not smiling when behaviour was inappropriate.

Clinical Example: Twenty pictures depicting various emotions together with flashcards providing verbal labels were used with a thirteen year old boy with ASD to enhance emotion recognition. Using the same pictures a game of Emotion Bingo was then played with the child and carer. The child was encouraged to name emotions which he experienced in keeping his diary with aid of his key worker on a nightly basis. (Emotion Bingo is a game which teaches facial expression and the names of emotions).

Clinical Example: In a session with a female client with Asperger's (15) a game was played in which therapist and young person mimed emotions in turn which then had to be guessed by the other person.

Training in Social Information Processing
Using the theoretical model proposed by Crick and Dodge (1994; see Chapter 3) in combination with techniques such as role-play or vignettes; the stages of interpretation and response can be practised and trained, using the CAGDA acronym to breakdown the process. Training in social information processing may be supported by training in perspective taking. Neurological impairments of the social processing mechanisms in the brain (Insel & Fernald, 2004) make it difficult for children with ASD to operate in this sphere.

Applied Behaviour Analysis (ABA)
This is a method of using intensive behavioural training methods which can be extremely helpful with autistic children. The method has been used extensively in the context of parent training with younger children (John, 2014). Applied Behaviour Analysis examines reinforcement patterns – including social reinforcement – in order to initiate helpful behaviour change. This approach may be best used in conjunction with a developmental approach.

Clinical Example: HL (male, 17 with ASD and no language) presented a pattern of behaviours which placed himself at risk by eating a range of inappropriate objects (pica). A plan was made to monitor detrimental behaviours, in terms of frequency using ABC charts (Antecedent – Behaviour- Consequence) to determine triggers and reinforcement patterns. Hypotheses to explain the behaviour included separation anxiety and lack of appropriate stimulation. A classroom intervention was designed based on provision of a choice of rewards from a visual display following a period in which positive behavioural responses were displayed and negative behaviours were avoided. This was effective in combination with medication change.

TEACCH: Development of Communication Skills
TEACCH, originating in the USA, encompasses a range of systematic interventions with autistic children, focused on developing communication skills, joint attention and social understanding, among other factors (Virues-Ortega et al, 2013). A useful hierarchy of the levels of visual communication is offered. The TEACCH approach is predicated on the notion that individuals with ASD operate better with a visual approach than a verbal one. The levels include:
- Expression of need
- Expression of specific need
- Gestures
- Joint attention (e.g. touch an object/read picture book, point to picture and name)

- Use of visual information to communicate (e.g. use object, picture or written word to communicate "I want a drink")
- Signing (e.g. use of Makaton)
- Use of simple spoken words, when a situation is set up in which what the child needs to communicate is clear.

To make communication easy, simple use of language is stressed supported by concrete information and use of objects as needed. It may be helpful to respond using communication at a range of different levels, producing a positive response as frequently as possible but modelling more advanced communication as well.

TEACCH is widely accepted as useful by practitioners working with younger ASD children with little or no language. The use of a visual timetable with pictures or words symbolising the activities of the day appears to be extremely helpful. Howlin (2005) comments that it provides structure, environmental organisation and clear visual cues, attending to developmental level using individually based teaching and offering cognitive and behavioural approaches.

LEGO Therapy

Owens et al (2008) highlight the difficulty experienced by children with autism in interaction with peers. They state that many social skills interventions exist, yet few have a strong empirical base to support their effectiveness. There is also a well-documented problem with generalisation of skills. They state that social skills groups may be particularly suitable for school age children with high-functioning autism who are at mainstream school or in an inclusion unit within a mainstream school (Owens et al, 2008). They suggest that there are good opportunities within the school setting to include typically developing peers as social role models. They conclude that clinic-based groups can be effective at teaching appropriate social initiations and responses, emotion recognition and group problem-solving, though generalisation is still an issue.

LEGO Therapy is a social skills intervention for school-age children based around collaborative LEGO play. Generalisation of the skills learned has been successfully demonstrated (Huskens et al, 2015). In generating LEGO constructions, groups of children were allocated to one of three roles: the 'engineer' described the instructions; the "supplier" found the correct pieces; and the "builder" put the pieces together. The children swapped roles. The authors state: "*This division of labour with a common purpose allows children to practise joint attention, turn-taking, sharing, joint problem-solving, listening and general communication skills*" (Owens et al, 2008, page 1947). The children attended therapy for 18 one hour weekly appointments. The technique was compared with the Social Use of Language Programme (Owens et al, 2008) which also yielded positive results. Both treatments were helpful in reducing maladaptive behaviour. The authors considered that a helpful feature of LEGO Therapy appeared to be its intrinsic reward value which is a key feature for this client group.

In summary, there is a good evidence base for LEGO Therapy. The technique is useful for school age children who have some language. Young people are motivated to engage socially by being allocated an instrumental role in a process which is intrinsically interesting for them (construction). Similarly, in the context of a residential school for ASD students, young people may be assigned useful social roles which they enjoy, e.g. vacuuming, tidying up

Social Skills Groups
Some success has been reported in the research literature for social skills groups for children and adolescents with autism (Reichow & Vollmer, 2010). High-functioning children and children with Asperger's Syndrome benefit particularly from this approach (Attwood, 2002; Gutman et al 2012). Tuition and practice are typically provided using modelling, role play, video recording and constructive feedback (Bulkeley & Cramer, 1990; 1994). Other techniques used in social skills groups include structured games, analysis of videotaped social behaviour, perspective taking tasks, prompting with cards and "brainstorming". The approach is best for adolescents with some language.

The approach may be used in conjunction with other approaches, e.g. personal skill building based on identified deficits and peer mediation (Kasari et al, 2012). The group setting would provide an additional arena for structured practice of the target skills and strategies. `

Krasny et al (2003) stress that such groups need to break down complex social behaviours into concrete steps and rules that can be memorised and practised in a range of settings. A variety of visual/tangible activities may be used to make abstract concepts concrete. A behaviour plan that specifies individual goals for group members and a specific system for delivering rewards will assist in delivering motivation. Generalisation may be encouraged through community outings, skill practice in naturalistic settings and collaboration with parents and teachers.

Countryman (2008) states that higher functioning individuals can benefit from social skills groups and emphasises the need to improve communication and social competence. He notes, however, that children may become more negative and depressed as they become more aware of the need to improve communication and social competence. Countryman (2008) emphasises the importance of structured teaching of non-verbal communication in early stages of the group process. More advanced topics such as humour, figurative language and sarcasm should be taught as the individuals reach developmental readiness for such topics.
Role-play may be included in the group therapy and target skills and strategies may be tried outside the therapy setting. Social Skills Groupwork may incorporate the following techniques:
- Personal social skill building based on observed deficits: Clients may take turns in rehearsing target behaviours
- Training in recognition of emotion: Clients can review visual material on computer or hard copy photographs
- Training in expression of emotion: Clients can be encouraged through exercises to rehearse behaviours displaying various emotions
- Use of context to interpret social behaviours: Role-plays can be set up around specific situations which set a context for interpreting behaviour
- Use of video: Video modelling and video feedback on behaviour can be delivered within a group context.

- Training in social problem solving: Social problem-solving techniques can be incorporated in role-play.

Social Skills Groupwork has been discussed in detail in Chapter 4. Clearly special modifications need to be made for children and young people with ASD, and it may be helpful to supplement group work with other inputs, e.g. personalised skill building in individual sessions, parent training, and peer-mediated input. Group work may be complemented by an individual approach (personalised social skill building) and peer mentoring. Social Skill Groups offer an opportunity for children and young people with ASD to integrate data on social perception and emotion recognition in a systematic manner by generating realistic context, for example by means of role play.

Clinical Example: A classroom may be used to engage young people in meaningful social interaction by encouraging the students to participate in Hello/Goodbye rituals at the start and end of sessions. The words Hello and Goodbye are accompanied by appropriate musical tunes, songs and gestures with which students are encouraged to contribute at their level. By these means, they are enabled to develop their social language skills and experience positive group inclusion. Students at a more advanced developmental level could be encouraged to develop more complex skills using a similar approach (Reichow & Vollmer, 2010).

Personalised Social Skill Building
Personalised social skill building may be carried out individually if a group context is not appropriate or practical. It is recommended that one of the assessment procedures described above (e.g. the Social Skill Improvement Scales (Gresham et al, 2008) is used to develop a programme. Chapter Three explains individual approaches. These would need to be tailored to the needs of ASD children as described in this chapter. A mirror can be used for training in emotional expression. It may be necessary to desensitise children with ASD for use of a mirror in case they have a negative emotional reaction to this experience. Video modelling and feedback can be used within the context of individual sessions.

Peer Training
The difficulty of children with ASD in forming peer friendships has been highlighted regularly (Attwood, 2002). The importance of peer training for children and young people with ASD cannot be overestimated (Bauminger, 2003). Young people with ASD can be exposed to peers without ASD in natural settings, school clubs or formal social skills groups. The peers without ASD may be given general instructions (e.g. about helping children with social needs generally) or specific instructions in relation to a child with ASD. Only general instructions were given in a study by Kasari et al (2012) in which the effectiveness or peer training for ASD children aged 6-11 was demonstrated within a mainstream school context. In this study, socially skilled typical peers were trained by specialists to identify isolated children and then to teach these children to integrate socially. The outcome was an improvement for the ASD children, which was more effective than direct delivery of social skills to those children through coaching.

Use of Computers

There is a wide application for computers in the field of special education for young people with ASD. Students may be encouraged to participate in a range of activities using the whiteboard which will enhance their social communication skills.

Computer games may be used in treatment programmes, and children with high-functioning autism may benefit from virtual-reality based social interaction training (Fengfeng & Tami, 2013). Computers may be used interactively by therapists to develop social skills. Children and young people with ASD are often more at ease using computers than interacting with people face to face. Some interventions mentioned above for emotion recognition, (e.g. Mind Reading) involve computer use.

Bagatell (2010) notes that computer technology and the internet have played an important role in finally giving a collective voice to individuals with ASD, quoting a member of an ASD self-advocacy group as saying: *"The computer is kind of like what sign language is for the deaf. It's the autistic way of communicating"* (Bagatell, 2010, p 37).

Recent studies have found that virtual-reality software can be beneficial in enabling individuals with autism to practise and improve their social skills (Mitchell et al, 2007; Moore et al, 2005; Fengfeng & Tami 2013)

Clinical Example: In the context of a residential school for students with ASD, video was used to demonstrate appropriate social tasks and reinforce students for performing these tasks (e.g. vacuuming, tidying up).

Other Technologies

There is a rapidly increasing range of other devices which may be used by children and young people with ASD, especially those without language, to enable them to express their needs.

In terms of future potential, the ECHOES project has promise (Bernardini et al, 2014). ECHOES is an interdisciplinary project whose main goal is to develop a technology-enhanced learning (TEL) environment to support young TD (typically developing) and ASD, children between the ages of 5 and 7 years old, in exploring, acquiring and using social and communication skills.

From a technological point of view ECHOES integrates interactive white boards with eye-gaze tracking, facial expression and gesture recognition.

In the design of the learning activities the following six cognitive precursors of social engagement are postulated:
- Imitation
- Dyadic relationships
- Joint attention
- Belief-desire reasoning

- False belief reasoning
- Second-order belief attribution

Children are presented with a set of activities relevant to the precursor in which development is required. It offers a useful innovative approach to the use of technology in enhancing social skills for children and young people with ASD.

Resource List

A number of resources have been described in the previous paragraphs;

- 'MindReading' provides a library of 412 emotions with six video clips for each emotion. Audio clips enable tone of voice to be studied. Access is provided to a learning centre designed with ASD clients in mind. Lessons can be adjusted to suit a wide range of ages and ability levels. The material seeks to assist clients with integration of cross-modal emotional information from faces, voices and contexts, enabling them to understand and predict accurately the emotions and mental states of others.
- A basic but useful Social Skills Programme for use in schools may be found on the website www.educational-psychologist.co.uk
- "TalkTools" (a method of assessing the function of the jaw; Rosenfeld-Johnson, 2017) may be used along with other techniques by Speech and Language Therapists to enhance communication skills and reduce stress caused by problems with articulation and language. The hands-on "TalkTools" approach may enhance sensory integration.
- 'Talkabout' provides an assessment tool which can be used to summarise a young person's non-verbal, verbal and assertiveness skills. The assessment tool can be used subsequently to measure progress. There is a useful social skills assessment tool and a DVD is available. Material suitable for teenagers is also offered. The DVD contains active scenarios for each skill being taught, modelling both poor and good behaviour. Further information can be obtained from the internet: www.alexkelly.biz
- New Social Story Book (Gray, 2015). The book covers a range of social skills such as Giving a Gift, Learning to Help Others, How to Use the Telephone, Smiling and Looking while Listening. These items are typical of what we might teach in a social skills group. Chapter Seven (Time for School) and Chapter Ten (Restaurants and Shopping) will be useful in preparing children for specific social situations. Social Stories are useful for a language level of 3 years and above.

Case Example

Henry (aged 9)

Henry had been diagnosed with ASD. A special school, Hope House, had been set up by his grandmother for Henry and other children and young people with similar difficulties. Henry's behaviour became more settled following the provision of an environment with appropriate facilities for social communication, shared attention and stress reduction, and his learning was greatly enhanced.

The Occupational Therapist found an improvement in terms of anxiety reduction as Henry no longer needed calming activities involving sensory integration and deep pressure. She had noted an improvement in her rapport with him. She considered that he was he was operating at a typical four-year-old level cognitively, but at the level of a much younger child in terms of emotional maturity.

The Speech and Language Therapist found his expressive and receptive language levels to be below four years of age. She advised keeping information short and direct, using the TEACCH approach of, "chunking" pieces of information, with a clear start and end. She felt it was important to give Henry a choice so that he could feel in control, offering two or three activities. She noted that he responded well to a behaviour programme and a visual timetable.

The Speech and Language Therapist reported that Henry took language very literally and was often confused by idioms. He tended to repeat a good deal and "echo" what was said. He needed a good deal of explanation. She found his eye contact could be fleeting and variable. A good deal of work was done using a mirror, which appeared to "desensitise" Henry by reducing his "fear of faces". He tended to avoid looking at faces when he talked to people.

To assist with emotion recognition, the staff had a system of communication with Henry about behaviour and emotion based on the metaphor of traffic lights. If he was rude, he was placed on *Amber* and if he was verbally abusive with swearing and so forth, he was on *Red*. Sanctions such as 'time out in the quiet room' were consistently applied. In terms of emotional empathy, Henry was reported by staff to have some feeling for others and could show sympathy if someone was ill.

Henry was encouraged to learn social rules; he enjoyed playing hide and seek and was able to conform to the rules and count to 20 with assistance. Henry could identify ten school rules for a fellow student, and appeared to have some understanding of agreed codes of behaviour.

To support Henry with exposure to typical peers, social outings were planned and there was a club two nights a week at which Henry met older boys and played football. He also met the children of staff at times

Role-play was used to get Henry involved in a learning activity. He was drawn into a discussion about road safety and a scenario was set up with staff playing the role of cars coming along a road and Henry controlling traffic. This activity helped in the development of his social communication skills, including language and the use of voice tone (prosody).

To support Henry in developing a sense of humour, he was encouraged to participate in a verbal game of "Doctor" jokes. In the educational context, pictures were used to help Henry develop emotional literacy so that he could have words to describe his emotions.

In his Personal Social Health and Citizenship Education programme, Henry was said to be working effectively on a number of objectives related to social skills:

(i) Choose, initiate and follow through a new task

(ii) Make attempts to negotiate with others during a variety of activities

(iii) Behave appropriately e.g. by using a "calming down card" in the quiet room and by using a mood scale".

Henry was fond of animals, therefore stamps in the design of pawprints proved to be useful as tokens in a behaviour programme.

John and George

John and George are 19 year old identical twin boys with severe autism, severe learning difficulties and challenging behaviour. They are low functioning, non-verbal and attend an independent specialist school. They have recently undergone an adult learning disability assessment to determine post 19 provision.

The twins were born prematurely at 35 weeks with bowel blockages and John required immediate surgery for Volvulus resulting in the removal of 50% of his small bowel. Both appeared to develop normally but suffered regression at around 18 months and lost their eye contact, social pleasure and joint attention. They were at the point of being able to point out animals from books and say a few words before their development turned towards autism. John and George suffer with Colitis and are under the care of a consultant gastroenterologist.

During their years in a local special school John and George made one or two friends, children that they seemed to connect with, but sadly these children either moved away or out of their class. By the time the boys were 13 years old they were in a class on their own with no peer group. There was significant regression across all areas of development resulting in some extreme behaviour difficulties including faecal smearing.

John and George have been diagnosed with Irlen Syndrome (Irlen, 1980). Both boys present with motor and vocal tics consistent with Tourette's Syndrome. They have exhibited motor and vocal tics since childhood beginning with slurping sounds when aged three. George's vocal tics include guttural sounds, throat clearing, belching, slurping and coughing; motor tics include jumping, squinting, nose scrunching and grimacing. John has complex and chronic motor and vocal tics - his vocal tics include snorting and grunting; motor tics include body and head jerks, eye rolling, lip smacking, shrugging, squatting and arm flexing. This adds another layer of complexity to them because it can lead to adverse reactions from peers and increased stress for those managing them. John and George are not aggressive children by nature and triggers to outbursts are due to:

- frustration at lack of communication skills,

- inability to complete a task,

- not understanding what is happening or what is asked of them,

- changes in routine,

- transition,

- physical or sensory discomfort/pain,

- hunger/thirst,

- wanting to use the toilet but unable to,

- confusion due to inconsistency of approach and staff working with them.

John pulls down curtains and rips his clothes with his teeth; he will self-injure against his hands, upper arm, knee and fingers and face; he will attack those around him i.e. bite, pull hair and scratch, when distressed or frustrated. George's self-injurious behaviours manifest in head butting his knee and hitting himself; he will pull hair and head butt those around him, when distressed or frustrated, (sudden rapid pacing can be a precursor to this behaviour). Both boys engage in self-stimulatory behaviour and bruxism (grinding teeth) when anxious or under stress. George and John are managed effectively without restraint and medication effectively with an intensive multi-professional therapeutic approach. John has tactile motivators/distracters with him at all times to help regulate his mood and behaviour; he responds well to time out. George is able to moderate his temper through verbal instruction and reduced demands.

The boys present with dyspraxic features affecting both fine and gross motor skills. They have poor bimanual coordination and cannot manage cutlery or routine tasks such as tying shoelaces and manipulating buttons. John has an immature gait on walking and running. Both need individual support in personal care and hygiene tasks. Their auditory and tactile hypersensitivity makes showering, washing hair, brushing teeth and cutting nails difficult.

John and George have progressed and attend a weekly course at a local centre where they take part in gardening activities. They also engage in various forms of work experience e.g. picking up litter, recycling newspapers and cleaning church pews.

Their sensory hypersensitivities impact on all areas of functioning and behaviour. Their responses fluctuate throughout the day.. They do not always respond to redirection and cannot always self-regulate. Any compromise to their well-being affects their sensory perception e.g. making them less tolerant to noise and touch.

Social Understanding and Relating
John and George have poor social awareness and find people unpredictable and they are unable to read social cues, body language or facial expressions and they lack Theory of Mind. They are generally happy boys and can be very affectionate at times. Their sensory processing is delayed and they need time to process instructions. They understand far more than they are able to express and respond positively to praise.
- Sensory hypersensitivities, obsessional and challenging behaviour make social interaction and social situations difficult e.g. eating in the same room as other people. They are very sensitive to what is going on in their

environment e.g. they dislike noise and crowds around them and sudden surprises, preferring quiet and calm environments.

- They have no understanding of social rules and are unaware of personal and social space. They may use inappropriate body language in social situations e.g. George sniffs people and enjoys physical contact under his control. John sits close to preferred adults and occasionally smells them. John needs to be asked first before engaging in contact.

- George will smell and taste a tennis ball; John will continually stroke a soft toy, smelling and biting it.

- They cannot easily relate to their peers or adults, they use peripheral vision when engaging in activities and make fleeting eye contact

- They are very sensitive to each other's moods and relate through non-verbal communication, often staring into each other's eyes. They play apart but use peripheral vision to keep track of each other.

- During leisure time, they will engage in self-stimulatory behaviour e.g. John shreds paper, George paces around the room or sits gently stroking his arm. They need sensory input through pressure to re-focus; George can often be seen clutching pillows or balancing one on his head, John will need his weighted vest, both boys will only settle to sleep under a pile of pillows. John reacts to boredom or over-stimulation by hitting his head, putting his fingers down his throat and gagging; George may shut down or become tearful.

- Their social skills are continually being extended across all social settings through community visits, work experience and play. Opportunities are provided for developing social skills and awareness in real situations, within a context of meaningful inclusion. Familiarity is vital for them and they do not learn or engage unless they are relaxed, at ease and there is considerable input; trust is vital or they will close down.

Social Communication

Initially, at age four, communication was attempted using Makaton symbols and signing but this was unsuccessful. The Picture Exchange Communication System (PECS; Bondy and Frost, 1996), was introduced to the boys when they were 9 years old, mainly at snack times. At this time the boys had no "voice" to express their needs or feelings and communicated their most urgent needs and fears through aggression. They are still dependent on the ability of those who know them well to guess their intentions, however since attending their residential school there has been significant progress in augmented communication and a reduction of self-stimulatory behaviour and aggressive outbursts. They have difficulty differentiating between pictures; therefore, PECS is used in basic format with a combination of gestures and True Object Based Icons. George hands over symbols for what he wants. John requires more guesswork and only selects the nearest item, unless he knows the adult well. They have a small expressive vocabulary to select different snacks and to ask for a drink but neither of the boys can use the system across all contexts. Miming an action, i.e. drink, and auditory clues can also facilitate communication.

Communication is a major challenge for John and George because it reflects their difficulties with cognitive and sensory processing, social impairment and lack of generalisation. They are currently developing non-verbal communication to help express their needs. They need support to communicate their needs, to understand what is required of them and to make themselves understood. John is more obedient and more sensitive than George who is more reluctant to respond to instructions and tends to 'switch off'. Each will giggle when the other is being reprimanded. Requests need to be precise and clear, avoiding unnecessary words. Frustration often results from not understanding what is required of them and sometimes the finished product must be shown first (so that they know what they are aiming for) before asking them to complete a task.

They have no appreciation of the social uses and pleasure of communication; their main concern is to communicate needs and wants. The boys understand simple instructions in both English and Italian. John and George communicate using the following means:

- Motoric (physically manipulating the person e.g. pushing/pulling person by hand towards desired object e.g. to the cupboard for food or to the door to go out).

- Inappropriate behaviours i.e. pulling hair or pinching (the intensity of this behaviour reflects their level of distress or the urgency of their need).

- Proximity (George paces around the person; John stands close to the person. Both will follow parents around the house if they want something or if they sense that they are about to be left).

- Gestural (hand pointing, reaching out, gaze shift).

- Vocalization (crying; sounds to draw attention to themselves).

- Body language (rigid and stiff posture when anxious, relaxed posture when happy).

- True Object Based Icons (TOBIs: Bloomfield, 2000). TOBIs are pictures cut out in the actual shape or outline of the item they represent. These are more meaningful for the boys because they can see and feel the symbol and shape.

- Objects (e.g. hand a packet of crisps to mum indicating 'I want crisps', or bottle of water indicating 'I want water' or door keys 'I want to go out).

John and George sometimes have difficulty filtering a voice from background noises, therefore parents and carers need to be close to them when talking to them and keep speech to a minimum. They respond well when given time to process simple verbal and pictorial information without interruptions i.e. *'kitchen breakfast'*, or if you want them to wash their hands point to the sink and say *'wash hands'*, however they need routine and structure for this to be effective - this is especially crucial because the boys will not respond well if they are not very closely associated and trust the adults involved. They can accept the 'now' and 'next' in context and use some symbols to indicate needs e.g. *toilet, water*.

Their preferred mode of communication is motoric or through objects, which they use spontaneously e.g. George fetches his shoes and coat when he wants to go out; John touches an adult on the chin when he wants a story or gently herds you into the kitchen for food.

The boys often make better meaning out of what they hear or see by looking and listening peripherally (such as out of the corner of their eyes or by looking or listening to something else). In this case, it is a kind of indirectly confrontational approach to communication. To communicate information to them, it is best to be in the same room and mention their name but look at the floor or past them but not at them. They will absorb it and remember it; the information is there and will be triggered later. John and George have a problem with sensory overload; therefore in this way they are less overloaded and more able to understand what is happening.

To move gradually from indirect to more direct confrontational approach to communicate with them, it is best to use minimal speech initially, then speak aloud to yourself and mention their name, then speak in their direction, and finally talk face to face with them.

The boys are learning augmented communication with different methods of improving their communication and social skills. The life skills curriculum is essential for their progress in developing a functional system of communication.

Rigidity of Thought and Behaviour
John and George find it difficult to think or behave flexibly and are resistant to change and the unfamiliar. They have difficulties with abstract thoughts and language and their inability to role play limits many opportunities for language and communication development.

- They thrive on routine and structure responding well to a visual timetable comprising of TOBIs. Both boys will inspect any room or vehicle closely for change and exit routes. They may suffer severe reactions to new situations, e.g.

George did not eat for days when the kitchen cupboards were changed; John became distressed and non-compliant when the minibus colour was changed.

John and George do not like surprises and therefore need to be involved in any changes. They need to have control of their environment e.g. dimmer switches have been installed throughout the house to allow them to control light intensity and they have been made aware of all on/off switches to enable them to turn off any offending appliance. They need to be informed about what is about to happen and what is going on e.g. *'John/George microwave on'*, *'John/George kettle on'* etc., this gives them warning and the opportunity to remove themselves from that environment. They need to be consulted about anything that may make them uncomfortable or upset i.e. *'mummy sit here?'* (pointing to seat next to John/George). This way they have some control over what the other person is doing. They need to be informed about what is going on e.g. *'mummy go kitchen make tea'* – otherwise they become anxious as they are not able to read intentions.

Transition between activities, people, rooms or places is problematic for them. Visual timetables help predict what will happen next and anticipate everyday changes. Favourite activities, routines or objects are strategically sequenced throughout the day. The introduction of a concrete portable schedule reassures when transitions and events will happen and tell them *What? When? Where? How? With whom? For how long? What next?* A sensory diet together with structure and consistency introduced across home and school settings has improved predictability and created positive routines around transitions. Providing opportunities for choice gives them some control over what happens and helps them cope positively with change and transition. They have difficulty learning from mistakes and cannot easily access memories of past experiences or draw on past experiences to solve problems. The curriculum promotes positive choice and changes i.e. learning in a range of different settings, and developing awareness of thinking and learning processes. Consistency makes it easier for them to understand the concept and knowing what the expectations are makes transition easier for them and reduces challenging behaviour.

- **Ritualistic and Obsessive Behaviours** fulfil sensory needs and reflect their need for predictability and order. Both are obsessed with books – George prefers to be in control including arranging seating positions; John will gesture adults to cross their legs before reading a story. These repetitive behaviours are barometers of distress and a reaction against anxiety when faced with transitions and lack of structure and routine.

- Rigidity of thought causes many of problems for them in terms of generalisation e.g. John may not use public toilets; George may not eat his dinner if presented in a different way.

- Both boys present with both hyper and hypo sensitivities in all sensory channels. Fluctuation between hyper and hypo sensitivity can lead to fluctuations between over-reactions and under-reactions to sensory information e.g. lights appear to be too bright one day and dim the next. Both boys will taste everything to identify it along with sniffing. George is prone to pushing small objects up his nostrils, often requiring medical intervention to remove the object; John tends to push objects and his hand to the back of his throat – whether these are sensory stimulatory behaviours or tics is not clear, but they put him at serious risk of self-injury.

A structured, intensive and predictable environment provides a feeling of safety, making understanding of everyday activities easier for them. There is considerable evidence that John and George deteriorate outside a very structured and intensive and predictable environment.

John and George are unable to express their views in conventional ways and every effort is made to see things from their perspective. It is important for them to have many opportunities for making choices and be exposed to a range of positive life experiences within a supported social network.

Appropriate intensive multi-professional intervention optimises their chances of developing useful communication and social skills within a structured environment that promotes a range of augmented communication systems.

References

Attwood T, (2002). The profile of friendship skills in Asperger's syndrome. *Jenison Autism Journal, 14,* 3. [Available via www.tonyattwood.com.au]
Attwood T, (2007). *The Complete Guide to Asperger's Syndrome.* London: Jessica Kingsley
Bagatell N, (2010). From cure to community: Transforming notions of autism. *Journal of the Society for Psychological Anthropology, 38, (1)* 33-35
Baron-Cohen, S., Leslie, A. M., & Frith, U. (1985). Does the autistic child have a "theory of mind"?. *Cognition, 21*(1), 37-46.
Baron-Cohen S, Wheelwright S, Spong S, Scahill V & Lawson J, (2001). Are intuitive physics and intuitive psychology independent? A test with children with Asperger Syndrome. *Journal of Developmental and Learning Disorders,* 5, 47-78
Bauminger N, Shulman C & Agam G, (2003). Peer interaction and loneliness in high-functioning children with autism. *Journal of Autism and Developmental Disorders,*
Bayley N (2005). Bayley-III Screening Test. Pearson.
Beard, C., & Amir, N. (2008). A multi-session interpretation modification program: Changes in interpretation and social anxiety symptoms. *Behaviour research and therapy, 46*(10), 1135-1141.).

Bernardini, S., Porayska-Pomsta, K., & Smith, T. J. (2014). ECHOES: An intelligent serious game for fostering social communication in children with autism. *Information Sciences*, *264*, 41-60.

Bloomfield B, (2000) '*Icon to Ican: A Visual Bridge to Independence*' *TEACCH International Conference*, Chapel Hill, North Carolina.

Bogdashina O, (2003). *Sensory Perceptual Issues in Autism and Asperger Syndrome.* London: Jessica Kingsley

Bondy A & Frost L, (1996) *Picture Exchange Communication System Training Manual.* Cherry Hill, NJ: Pyramid Educational Consultants.

Bowers D, Blonder LX & Heilman KL (1999). The Florida Affect Battery. Centre for Neuropsychological Studies, University of Florida.

Charlop-Christy, M. H., Carpenter, M., Le, L., LeBlanc, L. A., & Kellet, K. (2002). Using the picture exchange communication system (PECS) with children with autism: Assessment of PECS acquisition, speech, social-communicative behavior, and problem behavior. *Journal of Applied Behaviour Analysis*, *35*(3), 213-231.

Countryman J, (2008). Social Skills Groups for Asperger's Disorder and Pervasive Developmental Disorder not otherwise specified. *Psychiatry (Edgemont)*, 5, (1) 42-47.

Crick NR & Dodge KA, (1994). A review and reformulation of social information-processing mechanisms in children and adolescents. *Psychological Bulletin*, 115, (1) 74-101.

Dawson G, Toth K, Abbott R, Osterling J, Munson J, Estes A & Liaw J, (2004). Early social impairments in autism: social orienting, and attention to distress. *Developmental Psychology*, 40, (2) 271-283

Dawson G, Webb S J & McPartland J, (2005). Understanding the nature of face processing in autism: insights from behavioural and electrophysiological studies. *Developmental Neuropsychology*, 27, (3) 403-424.

Fengfeng K & Tami I, (2013). Virtual Reality Based Social Interaction Training for Children with High-Functioning Autism. *Journal of Educational Research,* 106, (6) 2013

Gray C (2010). The new Social Story book; Revised and expanded 10th anniversary edition. Arlington TX: Future Horizons.

Gray C, (2015). *The New Social Story Book*. Future Horizons Incorporated.

Gresham FM & Elliott SN, (2008). *Social Skills Improvement System.* Minneapolis: Pearson

Gresham, F., & Elliott, S. N. (2008). Social skills improvement system (SSIS) rating scales. *Bloomington, MN: Pearson Assessments.*

Gutman SA, Raphael-Greenfield EI & Ashwini KR, (2012). Increasing Social Skill Use in Adolescents with High-Functioning Autism: A Nine-participant Single-Subject Design. *Journal of Occupational Therapy, Schools & Early Intervention, 5, 3-4*

Huskens, B., Palmen, A., Van der Werff, M., Lourens, T., & Barakova, E. (2015). Improving collaborative play between children with autism spectrum disorders and their siblings: The effectiveness of a robot-mediated intervention based on Lego® therapy. *Journal of autism and developmental disorders*, *45*(11), 3746-3755.

Insel TR & Fernald RD, (2004). How the brain processes social information: searching for the social brain. *Annual Review of Neuroscience*, 27, 697-722

Irlen H, (1980) *Irlen Syndrome, Perceptual problems* http://www.irlen.org.uk/

John O, Cooper, Timothy E, Heron, & Heward, W. L. (2014). *Applied Behaviour Analysis*. Pearson educational international.

150

Kasari C, Rotheram-Fuller E, Looke J & Gulsood A, (2012). Making the connection: randomised controlled trials of social skills for children with autistic spectrum disorders. *Journal of Child Psychology and Psychiatry*, 53, (4) 431-439.

Kelly, J. A. (1982). *Social-skills training*. New York: Springer.

Kim JA, Szatmari P, Bryson SE, Streiner DL & Wilson FJ, (2000). The prevalence of anxiety and mood problems among children with autism and Asperger Syndrome. *Autism*, 4, (2) 117-132

Krasny L, Williams BJ, Provencal S & Ozonoff S, (2003). Social skills intervention for the autism spectrum: essential ingredients and a model curriculum. *Child and Adolescent Psychiatry Clinics (North America)*, 12, 107-122

Mancil GR, Haydon T & Whitby P, (2009). Differentiated effects of paper and computer-assisted social stories on inappropriate behaviour in children with autism. *Focus on Autism and other Developmental Disabilities*, 24, (4) 205-215

McCarthy D (1972). McCarthy Scales of Children's Abilities. The Psychological Corporation: San Antonio, TX.

McConachie H, Vandle R, Hammel D & Le Couteur A, (2005). A controlled trial of a training course for parents of children with suspected Autism Spectrum Disorder. *Journal of Paediatrics*, 147, (3) 335-340.

Mitchell P, Parsons S & Leonard A, (2007). Using virtual environments for teaching social understanding to 6 adolescents with autistic spectrum disorders. *Journal of Autism and Developmental Disorders*, 37, 589-600

Moore D, Cheng Y, McGrath P & Powell NJ, (2005). Collaborative virtual environment technology for people with autism. *Focus on Autism and Other Developmental Disabilities*, 20, (4) 231-243

Moree BN & Davis TE, (2010). Cognitive-behaviour therapy for anxiety in children diagnosed with autism spectrum disorders: Modification trends. *Research in Autism Spectrum Disorders*, 4, 346-354

O'Connor E, (2009). The use of social story DVDs to reduce anxiety levels: A case study of a child with autism and learning disabilities. *Support for Learning*, *24*(3), 133-136.

Owens G, Granader Y, Humphrey A & Baron-Cohen S, (2008). LEGO therapy and the Social Use of Language Programme: An evaluation of two social skills interventions for children with High Functioning Autism and Asperger Syndrome. *Journal of Autism and Developmental Disorders*, 38, 1944-1957

Reichow B & Volmar FR, (2010). Social skills interventions for individuals with autism: Evaluation for evidence-based practices within a best evidence synthesis framework. *Journal of Autism and Developmental Disorders*, 40, *(*2) 149-166

Rosenfeld-Johnson, S (2017). *TalkTools*. Retrieved from https://talktools.com/; [01/02/2017]

Sofronoff K, Attwood T & Hinton S, (2005). A randomised controlled trial of a Cognitive Behaviour Therapy intervention for anxiety in children with Asperger's syndrome. *Journal of Child Psychology and Psychiatry and Allied Disciplines*, 46, 1152-1160

Sofronoff K, Attwood T, Hinton S & Levin I, (2007). A randomised controlled trial of a cognitive behavioural intervention for anger management for children diagnosed with Asperger Syndrome. *Journal of Autism and Developmental Disorders*, 37, 1203-1214.

Tonks J, Williams WH, Frampton I, Yates P & Slater A (2007b). The neurological bases of emotional dysregulation arising from brain injury in childhood: A 'When and Where' heuristic. *Brain Impairment,* 8, (2) 143-153.

Tonks J, Williams WH, Frampton I, Yates P & Slater A, (2007a). Assessing emotion recognition in 9-15-years olds: Preliminary analysis of abilities in reading emotion from faces, voices and eyes. *Brain Injury,* 21, (6) 623-629.

Virues-Ortega, J., Julio, F. M., & Pastor-Barriuso, R. (2013). The TEACCH program for children and adults with autism: A meta-analysis of intervention studies. *Clinical psychology review*, *33*(8), 940-953.

Wechsler, D (2016). Wechsler Intelligence Scale for Children ® Fifth Edition UK. Pearson.

White SW, Albano AM, Johnson CR, Kasari C, Ollendick T, Klin A, Oswald D & Scahill L, (2010). Development of a cognitive-behavioural intervention programme to treat anxiety and social deficits in teens with high-functioning autism. *Clinical Child and Family Psychology Review,* 13, (1) 77-90

Zoogman S, Goldberg SB, Hoyt WT & Miller L, (2015). Mindfulness interventions with youth: A meta-analysis. *Mindfulness*, *6*(2), 290-302.

Chapter 6   PROSOCIAL BEHAVIOUR

Section A: YOUNGER CHILDREN

Introduction

In the UK; 6.9% of boys and 2.8% of girls from 5 to 10 years of age exhibit conduct disorder; 40% of 7 to 8 year olds diagnosed with conduct disorder become persistent offenders as teenagers, whilst over 90% of persistent offenders had conduct disorders as children. There are therefore strong arguments for developing effective interventions. Conduct disorder is a psychiatric term describing as an extreme form of disruptive behaviour, so severe that it interferes with a child's ability to learn and develop. It is characterized by persistent aggressive or antisocial behaviour, deliberate damage to property, cruelty to other people and animals, theft, deceit, serious rule violation and bullying. Children presenting frequent but less severe disruptive behaviour are usually classified as experiencing "emotional and behavioural difficulties" (EBD). Conduct disorders frequently co-exist with a range of difficulties such as Attention Deficit Hyperactivity Disorder (ADHD). Challenging behaviour in children and young people is presented in a variety of social settings. In this book "challenging behaviour" is taken to mean "behaviour which is hard to manage". It does not imply a deliberate "challenge".

Systemic issues can be considered in arriving at a formulation. Social skills input may be delivered to this age group in combination with individual therapy, parent training, multi-systemic therapy or social work support. The challenge for the practitioner is to be versatile and resourceful in constructing an appropriate treatment package aimed at modifying the environment as well as providing direct input to the child. Intervention in the home setting is often helpful if the family are interested in receiving external help. Professionals would need to be sensitive to the parents' perception that the problem resides within the child or teenager presenting the challenging behaviour. It is important to provide support with that issue and empathise with this perspective. An additional factor for practitioners to consider is the social context. Smith and Farrington (2004) confirm that there may be continuities in antisocial behaviour and parenting across three generations.

Modifying the Social Environment – Parent Training

There is good evidence that parent training appears to be an effective intervention for childhood conduct problems when delivered across a variety of practice contexts (Michelson & Day, 2010). Parent training approaches are frequently based on the model of social learning theory which is generally found to be effective with this client group. In terms of social skills, this means modifying the social environment so that prosocial skills can be acquired. The parent is supported by the training procedure in the task of socializing the child. Social skills may be taught to the young person directly, but in addition there should always be reinforcement from the social environment. Structural Family Therapy advocated by Salvador Minuchin (2006) is particularly relevant in this context.

To aid in developing these techniques, several books may be considered useful; Parent-Training Programmes for the Management of Young Children with Conduct Disorders (Richardson & Joughin, 2002), Helping Children with Aggression and Conduct Problems (Bloomquist & Schnell, 2002.

What Works

Webster-Stratton et al. (2001) considered that parent training programmes had been the single most effective treatment approach for reducing oppositional defiant disorder and conduct disorder in young children. However, they noted that in their own studies approximately one third of children with conduct problems whose parents received parent training continued to have peer relationship problems and academic and social difficulties at school 2-3 years later. Furthermore, it was difficult to engage some parents for a variety of reasons, and some parents had difficulty in implementing or maintaining the strategies owing to their own interpersonal and family issues. They therefore tested the approach of directly training children in social skills, problem solving and anger management.

The "Dinosaur School" curriculum addresses interpersonal difficulties typically encountered by young children with conduct problems: lack of social and conflict-resolution skills, loneliness and negative attributions, inability to empathise or to understand another perspective, limited use of feeling language, and poor problem solving. Children are encouraged to discuss, model and practice social skills in different situations, using techniques such as videotape modelling. Specific strategies were used to strengthen motivation, hold attention and reinforce key concepts and newly acquired skills. Child-size puppets were used in every session to participate as group members and enlist the children's assistance in solving problems and role-playing situations. A range of techniques were used to enhance generalization and parents and teachers were fully involved in reinforcing skills and monitoring behaviour. The children were divided into groups of five or six and came to the clinic weekly for 18-22 sessions with two therapists.

The results were interpreted as indicating that the Dinosaur Child Social Skills and Problem Solving training programme was successful in producing statistically and clinically significant improvement in child conduct problems and problem-solving strategies. There was good evidence for maintenance and generalization across situations. Negative parenting was found to be the main risk factor for treatment success. The majority of the children classified as ADHD at baseline became non-ADHD at follow-up after one year. These findings are useful for comparison with the NICE guidelines (Version 2 – August 2000) which tend to favour medical management over behavioural intervention as the treatment of choice for HD (hyperactivity).

From the perspective of a practitioner, there are clearly issues about delivering such a comprehensive programme in a health, educational or social services setting. Emotional literacy programmes if included as part of a regular classroom curriculum would help all children – typically developing as well as aggressive, withdrawn and depressed or anxious children – to be socially and emotionally competent, with substantial benefits for society at large.

Assessment of Social Cognition

The Social Cognitive Skills Test (SCST; van Manem et al, 2001) assesses these skills in aggressive children from a developmental perspective. The test consists of six short stories with corresponding pictures. Each story measures eight social cognitive skills. The SCST considers the developmental level of the child and social information processing deficits. It has been found that aggressive children have difficulty verbalizing their thoughts, feelings and intentions and show a lack in non-verbal social understanding.

Skill in Decoding Emotion

Effective social information processing depends both on accurate decoding of non-verbal emotion expressed, and ascertaining the correct emotional tone of a spoken sentence (affective prosody labelling). In assessing affective prosody labelling, a voice recording neutral information (e.g. I am going out of the room now, but I'll be back later) is recorded in different emotional tones (e.g. happy, sad, angry, fearful) and the child is asked to identify the emotion. Deveney et al. (2000) have found that difficulty in ascertaining the correct emotional tone of a spoken sentence may contribute to emotional dysregulation in chronically irritable children, and possibly also to youths with bipolar disorder. Such children are likely to have difficulty with perspective taking, suggesting that deficits in perception of emotional cues may lead to less effective processing of social information. It is therefore particularly important to support children in these client groups in developing skill in decoding emotion.

Problem Solving Skills Development

Problem solving skills development may help children to deal with external problems which trigger antisocial behaviour. The child is first encouraged to generate potential solutions; the child and therapist then decide on the best solution and identify steps towards implementing it. Programmes focus on social cognitions and may be quite intensive. The therapist is active and develops a collaborative relationship. The child is encouraged to develop new interpersonal skills. Useful guidance is provided by Shure et al, (2001); the authors outline their intervention programme "*I Can Problem Solve*" (ICPS), in which children learn a pre-problem solving vocabulary, feeling word concepts, and how to think of solutions to problems and consequences to acts. Step-by-step guidelines are provided to help children think for themselves what and what not to do in a problem situation, and why. The child is offered questions which encourage a proactive approach in combination with perspective-taking.

Social Skills and Anger Coping Skills Development

A range of CBT approaches focus on how children with persistent behaviour problems often have a distorted understanding of social events. The programmes may focus on modifying and expanding the child's understanding of others beliefs, as well as improving the child's own emotional response. In general, the effectiveness of a cognitive-behavioural approach to anger in children and adolescents has been found varied in a meta-analytic study by Sukhodosky et al, (2004).

Kendall (2011) suggests the use of a 'feelings dictionary' to allow children to learn to identify emotional states in themselves and others, thereby acquiring empathy and perspective taking abilities. Cartoon sequences with the thought bubble intentionally left blank can be used to elicit self-talk and identify misattributions and misperceptions of another's intentions. Kendall (2011) reports on the use of self-evaluation exercises to help the child to stop and evaluate recent activities and consider the thoughts and feelings of others in the situation. In role-play, the child is encouraged to talk aloud and consider alternative courses of action. It is suggested that subjects with an internalizing attributional approach are more able to benefit from interpersonal problem solving, whilst those who externalize and demonstrate higher levels of aggression might benefit more from initial emphasis on the behavioural aspects of the intervention with a later shift to self-instructional problem-solving and self-reinforcement.

Kendall (2011) notes that *"Effective cognitive problem-solving requires an understanding of the experience and modification of emotions and effective interventions require recognition of, and therapeutic attention to emotional states… Effective cognitive problem solving requires an understanding of the experience and modification of emotions and effective interventions require recognition of, and therapeutic attention to emotional states"* (Suveg et al, 2007; p4).

Social Skills Development Programmes in Schools
From a review of randomized and non-randomised studies, it appears that the success of a programme targeting aggression in schools depends on its strategy, implementation, format and intensity.

Kamps et al. (2000) offered a 2-year follow-up prevention programme for students with behaviour problems and compared the results to a control group of students. Overall there was evidence of reduced inappropriate behaviour, including aggression, grabbing, out of seat behaviours and negative verbal statements. Compliance with teacher directions increased and more time was spent in positive interaction with peers. Their findings supported the use of screening instruments for young children with behaviour problems and early intervention programmes to promote improved school performance and social interaction skills. It would be useful to employ the Strength and Difficulties Questionnaire (Goodman, 2001) for screening and follow up with an educational intervention, such as this.

Pepler et al (1991) integrated the skill streaming approach (see Chapter 4) with the social information processing model (see Chapter 3) in a programme for aggressive children referred by teachers to a withdrawal group. Basic skills taught included Problem Solving, Knowing Your Feelings, Listening, Following Instructions, Joining In, Using Self-Control, Responding to Teasing, and Keeping out of Fights. "Skill Steps" were generated and opportunities for skill acquisition were offered through role-play and rehearsal, often videotaped. Teacher and parent ratings suggested significant improvements overall as a result of the programme.

Grizenko et al. (2000) developed a that the programme based on the approach described by McGinnnis and Goldstein (1984). The referred children presented disruptive or impulsive behaviour. Skills focused on included "introducing yourself", "joining in", "knowing your feelings", "self-control", "dealing with your anger", "responding to teasing" and "staying out of fights". Techniques used included didactic instruction, rehearsal (practice of a social skill – including role-play and imagining a behavioural performance), feedback, reinforcement, modelling and problem-solving. The authors stated *"The traditional and modified versions of the programme differed only in that the latter specifically explored the concept of the other's perspective, and required the child to verbalise how another might feel during the role-play scenarios. In the modified version, children were also required to play the roles of "the other" (the antagonist) in roleplays, and not just that of the protagonist."* (p504). Grizenko et al (2000) found that the modified social skills program was more effective than a traditional programme in improving behaviour at school, and that some treatment gains were sustained at nine-month follow-up. This approach is certainly interesting in highlighting the value of including explicit work on perspective taking within a more traditional social skills package (see chapter 4 in this book). Grizenko et al., (2000) considered that to generalise treatment effects to the home, parental involvement must be sought. This approach of involving parents has been found useful for children with Attention Deficit Disorder (Pfiffner and McBurnett, 1997).

Research supports the efficacy of a social skills group supported by work with parents for clients presenting challenging behaviour.

Use of Video- Recording of Social Activity

Kern et al (1995) report a study in which a teacher made five-minute video recordings of students playing games with peers. Students were given score sheets and asked to record, *"Yes"* (I got along with my classmates) or *"No"*. Students were encouraged to state what the inappropriate behaviour was and what an acceptable replacement behaviour might be. Students were awarded points for accurate rating and for *"Yes"* agreements with the teacher. Negative peer interactions decreased significantly and appropriate comments increased dramatically.

<u>Case Example</u>

Harry, aged 8

It was felt that Harry would benefit from learning social skills in a group context and that it would be useful to observe his behaviour in a group. Harry said that he would like to learn how to be 'less cheeky'. His main problem was reported to be getting too close to people and being tactile. He also found it difficult to listen. The course covered the following areas:

1. Greetings
2. Compliments
3. Feelings
4. Being bullied
5. Being assertive
6. Generalising skills learnt and coping when nervous

Harry attended five out of six sessions offered. Harry attempted most of his homework assignments. Parents did not attend the parent session. Harry was an enthusiastic member of the group. He fitted in well with the other two group members. It was felt that Harry would have experienced difficulty in a larger group. He quickly became a dominant member of the group and would easily get cross if the other members (including the facilitator) did not behave how he wanted them to. He would be very blunt in telling them, "*You are making me cross because you are not doing what I say*". He would sometimes try to take over the running of the group. Harry was more tolerant of the other group members in the last session he attended and more patient with them when he felt they were not doing well.

Harry had no difficulties understanding the content of the group and reflected this in his role-plays. He was good at telling the others where they were going wrong and at one point wanted to do their role-plays for them because they weren't doing it right. He was good at modifying his behaviour when told, but soon forgot what had been said, e.g., touching strangers. He was impulsive at times. Harry responded well to the reward systems put in place. He responded best to positive reinforcements. He behaved well throughout the group and was a good group member.

Harry appeared to learn the most from the role-plays and enjoyed practising the skills. However, he found it difficult to generalise the skills to different situations and to real life. Harry often needed to be reminded about the different skills he needed in different situations, to help him remember and generalise. It was suggested that people around him should help the generalisation of his skills to different situations and that he should be allowed the space to practise his skills in a safe environment, e.g. with role-plays. Harry was likely to need reminding at times how to act, before entering new to situations, specifically in relation to:

- Getting too close to people and touching others
- Listening to what people are saying
- Responding to what that person has said instead of talking about things of interest to him at inappropriate times
- What he should and shouldn't say to people

Harry worked best with structured activities. When tasks were finished, he enjoyed ticking them off the list. He often referred to the list to see what was happening throughout the time. Often it was easiest to move him on to the next activity when all the objects were moved from the previous activity. To begin with, they were removed from the room and then as weeks progressed, moved to a different part of the room. Harry was able to concentrate during the group if he was given five minutes at the beginning and five minutes at the end of the group to talk about whatever he wanted. Harry was very good at listening to others but often did not agree with what they were saying and would tell them, then discard the information. Where possible, Harry's environment should be structured in order to help him understand what is happening. He should be allowed specific amount of time at points in the day where he can speak about anything he wants. Again, this should be structured.

In conclusion, Harry appeared to have the social skills to make friends and came across as a friendly young man. However, in order to keep friends, Harry needed to learn that he could not control others behaviour and thoughts. People around Harry were advised to be aware of their own social skills and act as a role model.

This case study highlights the need to involve parents, teachers and care staff in promoting the generalisation of skills developed within the group context. It also demonstrates the importance of an individualised approach with in a group context.

References

Bloomquist & Schnell (2002). Helping Children with Aggression and Conduct Problems. New York: Guildford Press, (ISBN: 1-57230-748-X).

Deveney MD, Brotman MA, Decker AM, Pine DS & Leibenluft E, (2012). Affective prosody labelling in youths with bipolar disorder or severe mood dysregulation. *Journal of Child Psychology and Psychiatry*, 53, (3), 262-270.

Goodman R, (2001). Psychometric Properties of the Strengths and Difficulties Questionnaire. *Journal of the American Academy of Child and Adolescent Psychiatry*, 40, (11), 1337-1345.

Grizenko MD, Zappitelli M, Langevin JP, Hrychko S, El-Messidi A, Kaminester D, Pawliuk N & Stepanian MT, (2000) Effectiveness of a Social Skills Training Programme using Self/Other Perspective-taking: A Nine-Month Follow-up. *American Journal of Orthopsychiatry*, 70(4).

Kamps DM, Tankersley M & Ellis C, (2000). Social Skills Intervention for Young At-Risk Students: A 2 Year Follow-up Study. *Behaviour Disorders*, 25(4), 310 – 324.

Kendal PC, (2011). *Child and Adolescent Therapy; Cognitive-Behavioural Procedures.* New York: Guildford.

Kern l, Wacker DP, Mace FC, Falk GD, Dunlap G & Kromney JD, (1995). Improving the peer interactions of students with emotional and behaviour disorders through self-evaluation procedures: A component analysis and group application. *Journal of Applied Behaviour Analysis,* 28, (1), 47-59.

McGinnis E & Goldstein AP, (1984). Skill streaming the elementary school child. Champain, IL: Research Press.

Michelson & Day (2010). Do evidence-based interventions work in the real world? A systematic review of parent training. *Clinical Psychology Forum – Supplement 1,*

Pepler DJ, King G & Byrd W, (1991). A social-cognitively based social skills training program for aggressive children. In, Pepler DJ & Rubin K, (Eds). *The Development and Treatment of Childhood Aggression:* Earlcourt Symposium of Childhood Aggression. (pp 361–379) USA: Erlbaum Associates.

Pfiffner LJ & McBurnett K, (1997) Social Skills Training with Parent Generalisation: Treatment Effects for Children with Attention Deficit Disorder. *Journal of Consulting and Clinical Psychology*, 65, 749-757.

Richardson & Joughin, (2002). Parent-Training Programmes for the Management of Young Children with Conduct Disorders. London, RCP/Gaskell, – ISBN; 1-901242-80-3.)

Shure MB, Aberson A & Fifer E, (2001). I Can Problem Solve (ICPS): A Cognitive Approach to Preventing Early High Risk Behaviours. In: Cohen, J, *Caring classrooms/intelligent schools: the social emotional education of children.* Williston: Teachers College Press.

Smith CA & Farrington DP, (2004). Continuities in Antisocial Behaviour and Parenting across Three Generations. *Journal of Child Psychology and Psychiatry*, 45, (2) pp230-247.

Spence SH, (1995). *Social Skills Training. Enhancing Social Competence with Children and Adolescents.* UK: NFER-Nelson Publishing Company Ltd.

Suveg C, Sood E, Comer J & Kendall PC, (2009). Changes in emotion regulation following cognitive-behavioural therapy for anxious youth. *Journal of Clinical Child and Adolescent Psychology*, 38, 390-401

Minuchin, S., Lee, W. Y., & Simon, G. M. (2006). *Mastering family therapy: Journeys of growth and transformation.* John Wiley & Sons.

Suveg C, Southam-Gerow M, Goodman K & Kendal PC (2007). The role of emotion theory and research in child therapy development. *Clinical Psychology: Science and Practice,* 14, 358-371.

Webster-Stratton C, Reid J & Hammond M, (2001). Social Skills and Problem-solving Training for Children with Early-onset Conduct Problems: Who Benefits? *Journal of Child Psychology and Psychiatry*, 42, (7) 941-952.

Section B: ADOLESCENTS

Theoretical Introduction

Three main theoretical streams are useful in providing help for adolescents to learn prosocial skills and modify negative patterns of social behaviour.

Firstly, social skills approaches within this age group have long been associated with learning theory, social learning, and behaviour therapy. Michael Argyle, the influential British social psychologist, helped to launch the approach in the 1960s with some seminal texts (Argyle, 1985). Bandura's approach to social learning theory was important in the 1970s (Bandura, A., 1986). The contribution of Arnold Goldstein (Goldstein et al. 1980) to helping with this age group in reducing challenging behaviour has been well recognized. Feindler and Ecton (1986) have provided an excellent model for groupwork on anger management with adolescents using a cognitive-behavioural approach. Social skills work with adolescents has been influenced by developments in work with adults. The Australian psychologist Sue Spence has retained an interest in social skills throughout her career (Spence et al, 2000).

Secondly, insights from developmental psychology are useful, notably the model of social information processing presented by Crick and Dodge (1994). This has been reviewed extensively in Chapters 3 and 5.

Thirdly, family therapy insights are becoming increasingly relevant. Pocock (2010) has constructed an eco-systemic theory of emotional expression to give contextual meaning to two contrasting clinical topics in relation to anger: self-harm and conduct 'disorder'. In his review of Family Therapy research, Carr (2009) described multi-systemic therapy as a well-established, empirically supported treatment for adolescent conduct disorder or juvenile delinquency (Henggeler et al, 2009). In a randomized controlled trial involving 127 cases, Letourneau et al (2009) found that at one-year follow-up, multi-systemic therapy was significantly more effective than "treatment as usual" with adolescent sex offenders, in that their offending behaviour was reduced along with substance use and other "acting out" symptoms. Multi-systemic therapy has been found useful in reducing juvenile delinquency in New Zealand (Curtis et al, 2009). Foster et al (2009) found that therapist teaching, focusing on strengths, making reinforcing statements, problem-solving and dealing with practical family needs had a significant effect on parental engagement in multi-systemic therapy and their positive response to therapy. Social skills training has been found effective in reducing delinquency when combined with family work (Alexander & Parsons, 1973).

It is proposed that an integration of the above three approaches would be useful in providing enhanced social skills input to adolescents.

Techniques

Objective Assessment of Social Skills

"Multimodal assessment" (systematic gathering of information from the client and other sources such as the family, school or other relevant carers and professionals) will assist the practitioner in building a useful and reliable profile as a basis for planning an appropriate intervention (Spence, 1995).

Anger Management

Anger management (Goldstein et al, 1980; Feindler & Ecton, 1986) should be an important component of the social skills input with this client group. They need to increase understanding of their own emotions, their effect on others and their self-control. Enhanced understanding of consequences and enhanced empathy should be among the objectives for the intervention. Clients can be encouraged to reflect on the social danger signals which are likely to trigger anger arousal, and the most effective techniques for avoiding confrontation e.g. walk away. The effectiveness of these techniques can be reviewed in subsequent sessions.

Multi-Systemic Therapy

It is important to stress systemic factors (family, peer group, school) and address these factors before planning a detailed social skill assessment and intervention. This is particularly the case with challenging behaviour in adolescents as the practitioner is liable to be perceived by the adolescent as part of the adult world – at best irrelevant, at worst persecutory. Assessment of context and the predicament of the adolescent within that context is an essential preliminary to establishing contact with the adolescent. Where possible, contact with appropriate family members and relevant professionals (e.g. parents, teachers, social workers) should be incorporated as part of the intervention.

Groupwork

Social skills groupwork may be carried with adolescents presenting challenging behaviour. Clear boundaries need to be set. and practitioners running the group need to be experienced and confident with the age group. The groups (as is the case with all social skills groups) need to be well structured and clear boundaries need to be set.

Groupwork involving training in anger management may be particularly useful. Kellner and Bry (1999) report on a study in which seven students scored in the clinical range on the Conduct subscale of the Conners Teacher Rating Scale and took part in an anger management programme. The students, placed in a day school for emotionally disturbed adolescents, attended ten weekly 30-minute sessions. Students were asked to complete daily anger logs; to identify the physical sensations of anger arousal, to reflect on the situations that caused it, provide examples of how they handled anger and to determine the degree to which these behaviours met prosocial criteria. Statistical test indicated that significant reductions were achieved in the Conners Parent and Teacher ratings. These gains were still present at six months follow-up. It was suggested that parents and other caregivers might be encouraged to participate in anger management programmes, as this might enhance the generalization effect for such students.

Self-Control Techniques

Typically, clients will have attracted notice through behaviours carried out on impulse, "*in the heat of the moment*". Within the model of cognitive-behavioural intervention (Feindler & Ecton, 1986; Hay et al, 2017), clients may be encouraged to analyse "triggers" (provoking or "risky" situations), increase awareness of their own arousal processes, and reflect on the likely consequences of inappropriate behaviour. Male adolescents may be overly influenced by the need to present a "*macho*" image to maintain a reputation and can be encouraged to reflect on the social advantage of more positive behaviours.

Social Information Processing

Social information processing (Crick & Dodge, 1994) is an advanced component of social skill training which will enhance the ability of clients to understand their response to others and the response of others to their own social behaviour patterns. This approach will enhance role-play interventions with this client group (e.g. clients may be asked to freeze the role-play at various points and share their internal thoughts and feelings). Empathy also may be developed using these techniques.

Case Example
Joshua (aged 18)

Joshua was residing in a home for young people with learning disabilities and challenging behaviour. He was regularly in need of restraint by carers and was seen for anger management. Rapport was established by seeing him with the manager of the home or senior care workers whom he trusted. He had issues around contact with his family, which created stress for him but were not discussed within the social skills sessions; these were confined to enhancing insight into his own arousal processes (e.g. physical manifestations of anger) and developing techniques to "*keep safe*" (e.g. walk away). The approach to his outbursts was non-judgemental encouraging him to develop his own self-control techniques. Nevertheless, careful discussions with care staff around appropriate handling techniques (backing off, avoiding confrontation) were an important component of the intervention. Detailed social skill assessment procedures were found helpful in gathering information and monitoring the effect of the intervention. A reduction in the need for restraint was attained.

Techniques used with Joshua:
- Anger Management: Education provided to young person to enhance insight into anger process; e.g. identify physical sensations linked to anger and triggers
- Social Information Processing: Staff encouraged and supported in identifying young person's social information processing e.g. perception of staff coming close as a threat
- Objective Assessment of Social Skills: Use of standardised assessment procedure, see SSIS above, to determine client's strengths and weaknesses; e.g. self-control
- Non-Judgemental Counselling: Staff were encouraged and supported in enabling Joshua to download about stressful matters, e.g. family contact, to reduce inner stress. Joshua was encouraged to link stress factors to heightened sensitivity to triggers.
- Self-Control Techniques: Joshua was encouraged to use appropriate self-management strategies (e.g. walk away) having identified triggers.

- Multi-Systemic Therapy: Other elements in the system (carers, care manager, educational staff on different site) were involved in providing appropriate input to support the intervention.

Alexander (aged 17)

Alexander was seen for social skill intervention in the context of a Young Offender Service. The treating psychologist worked within the Young Offender Service as a member of the team and fed back findings to colleagues working with Alexander on a regular basis. He abused alcohol and cannabis and was estranged from his family. He was living in sheltered accommodation away from home He was frequently involved in physical assaults on several peers. Social skill intervention on an individual basis, involving establishment and maintenance of rapport, anger management, and guidance on social information processing, enabled him to increase self-control, avoid further offending and reduce his abuse of alcohol and cannabis. Enhanced confidence in social situations enabled him to reduce his dependence on alcohol and cannabis.

Techniques used with Alexander:
- Anger Management: Support in identifying and responding to triggers, e.g. body sensations and noting situations in which triggers are likely to occur
- Social Information Processing: Eliciting comment on social interaction and supporting a more empathic response to the cues of others
- Objective Assessment of Social Skills: Use of Spence Self-Report Questionnaire supplemented by comment from workers directly involved in assessment of young person
- Non-Judgemental Counselling: Facilitation of expression of inner stress e.g. from family situations or relationships which may lower threshold for aggressive responding.
- Self-control Techniques: Encouragement of client to respond appropriately to triggers, e.g. walk away.
- Multi-systemic Therapy: Support Alexander in dealing with demands of wider social world, e.g. girlfriend, family, sheltered accommodation; intervene where appropriate with workers directly involved.

Harry (aged 17)

Harry has a diagnosis of autistic spectrum disorder and has no spoken language. He is able to use sign language. He attends a residential school for young people with autism. He presents with symptoms of pica; eating large quantities of paper or other material he can obtain when unoccupied.

He was observed in class with two other students. A visual timetable was used to ensure that Harry was aware of the structure of the lesson. The lesson began with a greeting involving Harry in a social communication programme signifying participation in the educational group. Harry was encouraged to sign "Hello".

The teacher used signs to indicate that it would not be a good idea to eat paper and he responded signing that he did not wish to have paper. Instruction proceeded without paper and was rewarding for Harry. He could construct the letter H on the classroom computer screen. He was able to demonstrate his knowledge of sign language, showing that he knew the signs for the numbers 1-20. The teacher emphasized that he himself was learning sign language thereby handing over some control to Harry. This demonstrated an approach that was organized around the need to encourage behaviour change and provide reinforcement to the student for positive behaviour. Harry then attended a highly-focused speech and language therapy session, in which he was rewarded for picture recognition and attempts to say simple words. The speech and language therapist demonstrated appropriate actions of the mouth and use of teeth and tongue to produce the required sounds. He could imitate these movements. He was able to produce appropriate speech sounds but not to say whole words. Subsequently Harry was involved in psychometric assessment using the Bayley Scales. He was reinforced for successful performance (e.g. puzzle completion, picture matching, correct picture identification) by verbal praise, signing and non-verbal reinforcement (high-five).

This positive educational and therapeutic approach engaged Harry in social situations in which he was able to communicate effectively and reduce his sense of frustration and isolation. The structured input provided a "scaffold" to enable Harry to engage in meaningful social communication to enhance his own learning process with the support of staff. This set the scene for a positive programme to produce behaviour change in the less structured care situation. Social communication is central in providing a programme for behaviour change.

Techniques used with Harry:
- Social information processing: Use of a variety of appropriate channels including verbal and non-verbal communication and signing.
- Self-control technique: Encouraging resistance of the impulse to eat paper.

References

Argyle M, (1985). *The psychology of interpersonal behaviour* (4th ed.). New York: Penguin Press.

Bandura A, (1986). Social foundations of thought and action: A social cognitive theory. Englewood Cliffs, New Jersey; Prentice-Hall.

Crick NR & Dodge KA (1994). A review and reformulation of social information-processing mechanisms in children and adolescents. *Psychological Bulletin*, 115, (1) 74-101.

Goldstein AP, Sprafkin RP, Gershaw J & Klein P, (1980). Skill streaming the adolescent: *A structured learning approach to teaching prosocial skills*. Champain, IL: Research Press.

Feindler EL & Ecton RB, (1986). Adolescent Anger Control: Cognitive-Behavioural Techniques. New York: Pergamum.

Hay, C., Widdowson, A., & Young, B. C. (2017). Self-control stability and change for incarcerated juvenile offenders. *Journal of Criminal Justice*.

Kellner MH & Bry BH, (1999). The effects of anger management groups in a day school for emotionally disturbed adolescents. Adolescence, 34, (136), 645-652.

Spence, S. H., Donovan, C., & Brechman-Toussaint, M. (2000). The treatment of childhood social phobia: The effectiveness of a social skills training-based, cognitive-behavioural intervention, with and without parental involvement. *The Journal of Child Psychology and Psychiatry and Allied Disciplines*, 41(6), 713-726.

Chapter 7   SOCIAL ANXIETY

Introduction
This chapter will address the potential value of social skills development for young clients suffering from social anxiety and related conditions. Relevant theoretical points will be discussed, useful lines of intervention indicated and case examples provided.

Anxiety, Social Isolation and Unassertiveness
Social skills development is particularly relevant for young people experiencing difficulties with the peer group. Social anxiety, social isolation and lack of assertiveness are frequently associated with such difficulties. This group of factors may be associated with prior social stress and with problems of identity and self-esteem. In the child development literature, there is a clear contrast between "neglected" children, who are not selected as companions, and "rejected" children who are likely to alienate others by their antisocial behaviour (Kochanska et al, 2017). Adolescents who have been "neglected" children are likely to display social anxiety, isolation and unassertiveness (Kinniburgh et al, 2017). Clearly, such young people require direct help with initiating social contacts and establishing and maintaining friendships. Social skills development is appropriate with such young people and produces excellent results. It is advisable to treat these young clients separately from those who present with antisocial aggression.

School Attendance Difficulty
School attendance difficulty is a problem which causes great concern to parents and education agencies and which tends to deteriorate in adolescence. School attendance difficulty may occur as a result of either truancy or school phobia. It is important to distinguish between truancy and school phobia. In truancy, the child or adolescent is absent without the knowledge of the parent. There may be many reasons for the behaviour and social skill intervention needs to be based on an analysis of the factors involved. It is useful to consider truancy as an aspect of antisocial behaviour, as it frequently accompanies other antisocial behaviours and tends to occur under similar conditions (Lewis et al, 2016).

School phobia is a psychological condition involving both the child and family. The parent or parents are aware of the behaviour and typically the child remains within the home. Usually the parents make repeated efforts to get the child to go to school, but without success. The causes of the difficulty are not fully understood but it is clear that family processes are involved and that separation anxiety is an important factor. The difficulty in family communications experienced in school phobia may be helped by a social skills development approach. Parents can be helped to be assertive and to adopt a firm but friendly approach whilst being alert to their child's real anxiety. If poor peer relationships are a component of the school phobia, these can be remedied by means of individual or group social skills training (Esvelt-Dawson et al., 1982; Havik et al, 2015).

School phobia in which there is a component of separation anxiety is well treated by systematic desensitisation and gradual exposure (Yule et al, 1980). Children and adolescents suffering from separation anxiety can be helped to be become more assertive and self-confident through social skills development, thereby enhancing their positive sense of identity (Erikson, 1965; Leary, 2013).

Social Anxiety

Social anxiety in adolescence may be very acute. Social anxiety is commonly described as shyness, embarrassment, timidity or self-consciousness. It is exacerbated by stressful situations such as having to address an audience, adverse criticism, bullying or name-calling (Leary, 2013). Social anxiety is frequently a result of lack of familiarity with new social roles. Problem–solving approaches are useful with general anxiety (Kleiner et al, 1987). Using a cognitive approach, clients may be taught to identify maladaptive thoughts and generate alternative ways of thinking (Kendall, 1992). This tactic is particularly useful with clients who suffer from depression, social anxiety, and low self-esteem (Coopersmith, 1967). In cognitive restructuring, clients can be taught to challenge unhelpful thoughts ("*I can't cope with being picked on by that lot during break, I'll stay in*") and negative beliefs ("*my personality is no good, I'll never get any friends*") and substitute more positive thoughts, beliefs and attitudes about themselves in their inner dialogue. Children who are prone to social anxiety may be vulnerable to bullying (Olweus, 1994). Heimberg (2002) notes that cognitive-behaviour therapy (CBT) for social anxiety may include exposure, cognitive restructuring, relaxation training, and social skills training, and comments that social skills training may provide benefits because of the training aspects, e.g. repeated practice of feared social behaviours, the exposure aspects, e.g. confrontation of feared situations or the cognitive aspects, e.g. corrective feedback about the adequacy of one's social behaviour. Heimberg's (2002) comment based on work with adults would be appropriate for social skills work with children and young people.

The literature on children and young people would suggest that cognitive and behavioural methods should be used in combination in a similar manner (Kendall, 1992; Kendall, 1994; Kashdan & Herbert, 2001). Kendall (1994) presents the useful model of the "Coping Cat" which is widely used in clinical contexts with socially anxious children and children experiencing other forms of anxiety. Reviewing several studies of parental influence on social anxiety, Kashdan and Herbert (2001) found support for the hypothesis that the developmental shift from a reliance on parental guidance and nurturance to self-regulation and the formation of intimate peer relationships can be delayed or advanced by parental behaviours. The implications for involving parents in treatment are clear. Cartwright-Hatton et al (2005) reported on an experiment in which two groups of children aged 10-11 years who had demonstrated different levels of anxiety on a social anxiety questionnaire. They participated in a conversation with an unfamiliar adult and rated their performance in a number of domains, after which independent observers also rated their performances. Whilst independent observers were unable to distinguish between the low and high social anxiety groups, high socially anxious children rated themselves as appearing significantly less skilled than their low socially anxious counterparts. It was noticeable that the high socially anxious children rated themselves particularly poorly in terms of how nervous they looked. The authors conclude that socially anxious children may not necessarily display social skills deficits, but may perceive that they appear nervous during social encounters. They advise that clinicians should consider using CBT to address these concerns, rather than relying on social skill remediation (Cartwright-Hatton et al, 2005).

However, a number of points should be noted in considering the implications of this study. In defining social skills, the authors appear to be applying a mainly behavioural definition (such as that used by La Greca and Santogrossi, 1980), rather than accepting the more modern concept that social skill development incorporates cognitive as well as behavioural elements. In their study, the child is observed in a one-to-one situation with an adult, whilst children experiencing social skill difficulty frequently do so in group situations with peers. In selecting children for social skill intervention, it is customary to obtain assessment from a variety of sources, rather than relying on self-report (as the authors seem to suggest). The authors in their discussion suggest that socially anxious children may benefit from an intervention that focuses on their maladaptive beliefs about their appearance to others during social encounters, perhaps using video feedback on performance. Such a procedure could be effectively implemented in the context of a social skills group, in which anxiety-provoking situations could be role-played and reassuring video playback could then be provided.

Finally, early treatment of social withdrawal may have a role in preventing later social anxiety (for example in adolescence). Goodwin et al (2004), reporting on a 21-year longitudinal study, note that anxious or withdrawn behaviour in childhood is associated with elevated rates of anxiety disorders and major depression during adolescence and young adulthood.

Depression
Depression is more prevalent in adolescence than in the pre-pubertal stage, particularly in girls (Rutter, 1986). Affect disorders including depression occur in 10-15% of adolescents (Herbert, 1991). There have been recent advances in the epidemiological study of adolescent depression. In a study of 1072 adolescent girls, Cooper and Goodyer (1993) found that 20% had had some symptoms of depression over the last year. The estimated prevalence for major depressive disorder was 6%. Scores on a self-report questionnaire of mood disturbance increased with age, as did the prevalence of depressive disorder. A large proportion of the interviewed girls reported depressive symptoms which did not meet criteria for major depressive disorder. The estimated prevalence of this "partial syndrome group" was 20.7% (Cooper & Goodyer, 1993).

Social difficulty can be a symptom of depression, frequently requiring individual therapy as well as medication (Toolan, 1980; Leary, 2013). Cooper and Goodyear (1993) found that all 20 girls aged 11-14 suffering from major depressive disorder showed symptoms of social withdrawal. Social withdrawal was found to be the best predictor of major depressive disorder. It may therefore be argued that social skill development would be a useful adjunct to other treatments for depression in children and young people.

Adolescence is clearly a key transitional stage in development from the biological, social and psychological point of view (Montemayor, 1990). Forehand et al (1991) report that boys experience more social difficulties and less social competence at pre-adolescence but less problems and more competence by mid-adolescence. Rutter (1986) found that prior to adolescence; depressive findings were twice as common in males, whereas during adolescence girls were twice as likely to manifest such symptoms. Links et al (1989) reported an increase in emotional difficulties (depressive mood, anxiousness) during adolescence for females and a decrease in such problems for males. Forehand et al (1991) state that these findings support the view that "internalizing problems are more likely in boys at pre-adolescence and in girls during adolescence. By "internalizing", we may understand that in depression; aggressive impulses are directed inward towards the self rather outward towards others and the environment. It is likely that children who lack competence in social situations will withdraw and a cycle of "internalisation" will ensue. It is likely that social skill development would be a useful way to intervene in this process and build self-esteem at the same time as promoting assertive behaviour.

Frame et al, (1982) report using behavioural treatment for depression in a ten-year-old boy. Behaviours treated included inappropriate body position, lack of eye contact, poor speech and bland affect. The treatment methods used included instructions, modelling, role-play and feedback. Treatment effects were maintained at twelve-week follow-up. The boy had previously experienced suicidal thoughts and made suicidal gestures, and had violent temper outbursts. Prior to treatment, the boy was frequently uncommunicative in interpersonal situations, with poor eye contact, inaudible speech or one-word answers, bland facial expression, and body postures indicative of social withdrawal, such as turning his head away from a speaker or placing his hands over his face. Treatment was given daily in twenty minute bursts. The youngster was told at the beginning of each session what constituted the inappropriate behaviour to be worked on for that day, and a more appropriate response was then modelled for him by the therapist. The child was asked to perform a role-play scene, praised for appropriate responses and presented with a new scene. Help was given with inappropriate behaviours, and the scene was then re-played till the response was acceptable.

There is therefore research evidence suggesting that social skills development may prove to be helpful in treating some of the symptoms of depression in adolescents, and in reducing the risk of onset of major depression. The literature on anxiety would suggest that cognitive and behavioural methods should be used in combination (Kendall, 1994).

Serious depression may be treated by medication in adolescence, but it is generally advised that psychological support should be offered in addition (Toolan, 1980). Given concerns about the identification, diagnosis and treatment of depression in adolescence, (Murray & Cartwright-Harris, 2006; Iliffe et al, 2009; Dubicka et al, 2010); the notion of revisiting social skills development as a useful intervention for this client group (incorporating cognitive-behavioural components) has considerable validity.

Suicide and Self-Harm

Adolescents frequently express stress through self-harm (e.g. deliberate cutting) and attempts at suicide, which are sometimes successful. Adolescent suicide has increased dramatically in recent decades (Henry et al, 1993; Bradshaw, 2016). There has been an escalation of concern in Britain regarding suicide in young offender prisons (Moore et al, 2015). The most common predictor of adolescent suicide, in relation to peers, is difficulty with personal relationships (Bradshaw, 2016). Social skills development can help adolescents to deal with their social and interpersonal stresses in an effective manner, providing a fresh approach to their difficulties. To help adolescents at risk of suicide, Strother et al (1986) developed programmes designed to increase communication skills, assertiveness, and coping techniques.

Addictive Behaviours

Adolescents under stress are at risk of becoming involved in addictive behaviours, such as smoking or the misuse of alcohol, drugs or other substances (e.g. glue). The psychological factors in these processes are similar. There are elements of stress, peer influence, and physical dependence. Social skills training has a powerful potential to intervene at the stage when these behaviours can be prevented and more adaptive behaviours learned. Through social skills training, clients can learn to reduce stress by assertive interpersonal techniques and to resist peer pressure to indulge in addictive behaviours. Social skills training provides a source of positive peer influence to counteract the peer pressure towards addictive behaviours which occurs in the community.

Social skills training can also reduce behavioural excesses in clients presenting addictive behaviours. Schrader et al (1977) used an anger control package, aimed at reducing aggression, with six adolescents who had a history of using soft drugs. There was a measurable effect on verbal aggression and disruptive classroom behaviour.

Summary of Theoretical Section

Social skills development can help reduce psychological distress in a number of ways for children and adolescents who suffer from "internalising problems". Such difficulties may include social anxiety, social isolation, social withdrawal, poor self-esteem and a poor sense of identity. Such young people who are prone to bullying and social isolation can be helped to be more socially assertive both by cognitive and behavioural approaches. By increasing assertiveness and friendship-making skills, social skills development can improve self-esteem and reduce social withdrawal, one of the main indicators of depression in adolescents. Conceptually, the term "social skill" may be interpreted to include cognitive coping skills and management of emotion where these are applied in relation to social settings. An integrated approach to the treatment of social anxiety and related conditions is proposed.

Techniques for Treating Social Anxiety

Objective Assessment of Social Skills
Miers et al (2009) suggest that: *"with good performers one would wish to focus on cognitive distortions with the help of video feedback, but with poor performing individuals a social skills training would be preferable. If still needed, the cognitive model should then be applied."* (page 1048). This would appear to be consistent with good practice in applying social skills assessment and therapy with children and adolescents. It is generally advisable to use multiple measures, sampling for example teacher and parent opinion, in preference to relying on the young person's subjective response to questionnaires (See Chapter 2). It follows that where social anxiety is identified, an objective social skills assessment should be carried out. If social skill performance deficits are identified, a social skill development approach should be tried first. If there are no identified social skills deficits, a CBT approach could be considered.

Group Social Skills Training
In a quasi-experimental study with adult psychiatric patients diagnosed as having generalised social phobia, it was found that group social skills training (SST) was more effective than CBT (Van Dam-Baggen & Kraaimat, 2000). Patients participating in SST experienced a significantly greater reduction of social anxiety and a greater increase in social skills than those in CBT; furthermore, the social anxiety and social skills cores of the SST group at follow-up reached the level of a normal reference group, whilst the scores of the CBT participants improved only to the level of patients with other anxiety disorders (but not social anxiety) (Van Dam-Baggen & Kraaimat, 2000). Given that social skills groups are particularly helpful for young people in that they provide a ready-made peer group it is likely that such findings might be replicated with children and adolescents. Practical guidance in running social skills groups is provided in Chapter 4.

Involving Parents
Frankel et al (1996) emphasise the need for parental support in helping socially rejected children, demonstrating that this can enhance generalisation. Their paper makes practical suggestions for primary school age boys, but could be adapted for adolescents.

Cognitive Behaviour Therapy (CBT)
Cognitive-behaviour therapy is considered the treatment of choice for social anxiety in the adult literature (Heimberg, 2002). The components are considered to be exposure, cognitive restructuring, relaxation training, and social skills training. A modern approach to social skill development for children and young people would incorporate exposure since clients are encouraged to experiment with new behaviours in social situations which they find problematic. Cognitive restructuring occurs as clients are encouraged to problem-solve and rethink their approaches in social situations. Research has demonstrated the importance of a successful adaptation to the peer group in children and adolescents experiencing difficulty with social skills (White et al, 2007). It is therefore likely that this

contributes to self-esteem and a sense of well-being which would be a useful antidote to social anxiety.

Macdonald et al (2003) demonstrated how the NHS can set up a group to teach social skills to children using a cognitive behavioural framework. Parents were invited to a parallel parents' group. Each group lasted for 90 minutes and ran weekly for 6 weeks. Parents valued the contact with professionals and therapists' contact with teachers ensured full knowledge of children's behaviour transfer of skills to schools. MacDonald et al (2003) suggest that cognitive behavioural techniques with children undergoing groupwork require intensive liaison to facilitate generalization of skills learnt. The themes worked on in the sessions included *feelings, developing friendships* and *communication skills*; techniques used included small group discussions, role-play exercises, art activities and feedback. The parents' group was primarily a support group. Parents were informed of the week's session content and homework, and thereafter set their own agenda. Quantitative and qualitative outcomes are recorded and 3-month follow-up data from parents suggested that some transfer of skills had occurred. Parents and teachers were able to make the therapists aware of individual difficulties, so that the therapists could introduce parents and teaches to relevant social skills techniques for a child's social difficulties. They further suggest future developments could include creating a manual on social skills training to be given to parents and teachers at the end of the course. This procedure was not specifically designed for children suffering from social anxiety, but could no doubt be usefully adapted for such children when social skills intervention is deemed appropriate. The multi-systemic approach states that significant involvement of parents and teachers) is crucial.

Kashdan and Herbert (2001) describe the process of interaction of social anxiety with withdrawal from social situations, which may lead progressively to clinical manifestations of Social Anxiety Disorder (SAD) and delay in progressing through developmental milestones such as dating, employment and independent living. A combination of CBT for social anxiety disorder with behavioural training in social competence is likely to be efficacious for clients who are undergoing this kind of process.

Behavioural Exposure-Based Intervention in School
Masia et al (2001) reported promising results for a behavioural treatment group for six adolescents with social anxiety disorder. They attended 14 group sessions, including psychoeducation, realistic thinking, social skills training, exposure and relapse prevention. It was found useful to run the group in a school setting as this was where impairment was greatest, and realistic exposure exercises could be conducted. On the Social Phobia and Anxiety Inventory for Children (SPAI-C; Beidel et al, 1998) four out of the six participants achieved a lower score. On the Fear and Avoidance Hierarchy (FAH; Elliot & Church, 1997) significant reductions were noted. This study provides a useful pointer for future work in integrating a social skills group approach with exposure-based therapy, which is extremely useful in treating anxiety.

Learning Disabilities

Mishna and Muskat (2004) suggest that children and adolescents with learning disabilities (LD) are vulnerable to psychosocial difficulties. Both the detrimental impact of LD on social adjustment and the significance of peer relations for developmental needs make group therapy a natural intervention. Mishna and Muskat (2004) consider that many students with LD fit the criteria and can benefit from group psychotherapy. They present a model of group therapy for older children and adolescents with LD. The leaders use special techniques to accommodate the LD and to foster the group process.

Summary of Techniques

There appears to be a sound evidence for integrating techniques such as group social skills work, exposure based therapy, cognitive behaviour therapy and social information processing in the treatment of social anxiety and related conditions in children and adolescents. A multi-systemic approach is important both for assessment and therapy.

Case Examples

Jane (aged 15)

Jane was referred to the Child and Adolescent Mental Health Service with a history of shyness, anxiety at school and some school refusal. She also felt uncomfortable in crowds. She lived with her parents and two younger brothers. Although there were no identifiable strains in the family, Jane's mother described a family history (maternal) characterised by mental health problems - depression, agoraphobia.

The parents described a normal developmental history. However, Jane was always very shy. She was the victim of bullying in primary school. When she became increasingly withdrawn in secondary school, the parents went to their GP for a referral to the Child and Adolescent Mental Health service (CAMHS).

Presenting Problems

In addition to experiencing panic symptoms in social situations, Jane worried that she could faint and that people would stare at her. To control for this, Jane would take deep breaths, force herself to talk (e.g. in class) and would go to a quiet spot when in the shopping mall. In addition to meeting criteria for social anxiety, Jane also presented with features of depression. She found the transfer to secondary school difficult, i.e. the bigger school, more difficult subjects and older children.

Case Conceptualisation

Jane's early vulnerabilities, i.e. the interaction of biological and psychological vulnerability, could have predisposed her to the development of social anxiety. In addition to the family history, Jane was described as someone who had always been shy. This perception from her parents could have resulted in them being reluctant to encourage social approach behaviours. Jane further experienced peer rejection from an early age and on entering secondary school, experienced panic.

These experiences have the potential to produce negative feedback loops, involving anxiety and avoidance.

Therapy

The following treatment goals were agreed with Jane:

- To be able to initiate and maintain a conversation
- To visit the local shopping mall without having to go to a quiet corner or taking deep breaths to calm down

The initial steps of treatment included psycho-education on social anxiety. This was followed up by agreeing a fear hierarchy of feared situations which was then used for exposure activities, i.e. starting a conversation with a class mate. These activities were used as an opportunity to challenge unhelpful thoughts, i.e. *'people are staring at me in the shop'* - versus – *'the shop assistant was looking at me as she saw me as a potential customer'*. Negative Automatic Thoughts (NATs) associated with each step on the fear hierarchy were elicited at the beginning of each step - e.g. starting a conversation. This was then followed up with a skill building task using video recording to demonstrate the skills of starting a conversation to Jane. Following the demonstration, Jane was then encouraged to repeat the exercise, i.e. having a conversation with a member of staff (new to her) in the clinic and feedback was offered by playing back the video to her. Jane's unhelpful thought "*I won't know what to say, they will think I'm stupid*" was then challenged and a more balanced alternative was formulated, i.e. "*it is scary, but I can do it, I know what to say*". This was then followed up with a homework exercise, i.e. starting a conversation with a class mate and reporting back on this at the next therapy session.

To summarise, treatment consisted of the following steps:

1. Eliciting NAT
2. Skill building exercise
3. Thought challenging
4. Homework

Parental involvement consisted of feedback to Jane's mother at the end of each session. Although Jane responded positively to this approach, it did not provide the necessary peer-related treatment context and she was referred to an in-service social skills group. Group attendance provided Jane with social opportunities and positive peer interactions. Following this intervention, Jane continued to make good progress and was discharged.

Dave (aged 16)

Dave was referred due to family-related conflict, i.e. him and his father being involved in a physical fight. It became apparent that Dave was refusing to go out with his family during a planned family activity and his father then tried to force him to join the family. The argument turned physical which prompted Dave's mother to seek help via her GP. The case was initially referred to family therapy as it was considered appropriate based on the family/relational conflict.

Presenting Problem

The family therapist considered Dave's difficulties to be in line with social anxiety, i.e. a history of being bullied - both at home (neighbourhood) and school. The bullying at school resulted in Dave dropping out of full time education and at the time of the referral receiving home tuition, avoiding any peer group interaction, refusing to join the home tutor at the local library for tuition and finding it difficult to attend family therapy session due to him feeling overly anxious.

Case Conceptualisation

A behavioural assessment was completed, focusing on avoidance behaviour, safety seeking behaviour, subjective anxiety ratings and associated negative beliefs. Based on his history of bullying, Dave had started to avoid any social situations where there was a potential for him "bumping into" peers. When having to go out and talk to strangers, Dave used the following safety seeking behaviours: avoiding eye contact, believing that if he was not "staring at people" they would not hit him, covering his mouth with his hand when talking, not saying something that could potentially offend others and talking in a very quiet tone of voice. Dave reported feeling very anxious in these situations and experienced associated bodily symptoms - feeling hot, feeling wobbly in his legs and hyperventilating. Associated NATs were: *'they can see I'm feeling weak', 'they will punch me', 'I'm going to struggle to get any words out.'*

Therapy

As a first step, Dave was socialised to the CBT model and was re-assured that therapy would be conducted at his pace. He was also re-assured that there would be no surprises in therapy, i.e. without warning having to talk to a stranger. As part of this collaborative agreement, Dave was requested to attend sessions at the clinic in turn.

To help Dave process his bullying experience and associated trauma, an adjustment of the existing trauma focused CBT approach was introduced. This involved Dave being given the opportunity to share his experiences of being bullied which included a physical assault by some peers in the neighbourhood. A trauma script was compiled based on Dave's account to help him process these experiences. This exercise also allowed Dave to find "his voice" and was used to further the social anxiety work.

Based on the trauma focused work, cognitive reconstruction was introduced, helping Dave to challenge his NATs about all peers being hostile towards him, and the attacks being his fault. Next, the intervention focused on

    i.   Teaching Dave social skills such as eye contact and speaking without covering his mouth

    ii.   Coaching Dave about tone of voice, and starting conversations/introducing himself to others.

As a last step, with the help of the home tutor, Dave started attending classes at the local college. He also started using the bus following a targeted exposure activity teaching him the skills to buy a ticket and board the bus whilst tolerating his panic symptoms. Dave's parents were involved throughout sessions in the form of feedback to ensure their support with sessions, but also to help the relationship between Dave and his father.

Following the above intervention, Dave was discharged.

Patrick (aged 16)

Patrick was referred to Child and Adolescent Mental Health Services for symptoms of anxiety. His mother had a background of social anxiety and depression; she became protective when Patrick had an illness as a young child. He had three older brothers, one of whom had Asperger's Syndrome. Another had social anxiety and a third had no mental health diagnosis.

Presenting Problem
Patrick's anxiety had been long standing; there had been an issue of school refusal since he was seven years old, with accompanying panic attacks. He had been largely out of school since he was 11; recently he had attended secondary school for 2 weeks and had then been in and out for short periods.

Case Conceptualisation
Whilst possible diagnoses included avoidant personality disorder, separation anxiety and panic disorder, he presented primarily as agoraphobic/social phobic, with the social component dominant. He avoided going anywhere on his own. Some negative statements were initiated by Patrick; others were obtained by administering the Social Anxiety Scale for Children-Revised (La Greca & Stone, 1993) and the Liebowitz Social Anxiety Scale (Mennin et al, 2002). Negative thoughts included *"I won't know what to say", "People will stare at me", "I will talk too much" "People won't like me",* and *"Everyone else knows each other".*

Therapy
The parents were given advice and Patrick attended a social skills group. Family therapy was provided. In addition, Patrick was seen for approximately 25 individual sessions with a psychologist to work on his social skills and anxiety. He was able to open up about situations evoking negative feelings and could identify safety behaviours (avoiding stressful situations) and suppression of thoughts by "zoning out" –making his mind go blank.

A hierarchy of stressful situations was generated to support Patrick in attending college, with 10 out of 10 representing the most-anxiety provoking scenario:

- 1 out of 10 – coming to the clinic from the car park on his own.
- 2 out of 10 – going to Sainsbury's with his parents.
- 3 out of 10 – going to Sainsbury's on his own.
- 4 out of 10 – going to the shops for five minutes.
- 5 out of 10 – walking around the shops for ten minutes.
- 6 out of 10 – walking past College at a busy time.
- 7 out of 10 – walking past college
- 8 out of 10 – walking past college at a busy time.

- 9 out of 10 – going up to the door of college and going into reception on his own.
- 10 out of 10 – attending college.

An attempt was made to do exposure work using a diary. This covered situations, emotions, feelings, *'worst thing that could happen'*, *'what actually happened'*, new rating, *'what have you learned?'* It was difficult to secure compliance with this procedure. It was hard to tease out worrying thoughts and specific reactions to peers; he was fearful of negative judgements about his appearance and body image ('hair looks weird', 'looks strange'), and he seemed traumatised and depressed when identifying anxious thoughts. The behavioural part of the exposure was the most effective.

In terms of a cognitive-behavioural approach, the triggers seemed to be waking up alone in a dark room. He had difficulty dropping safety behaviours but he improved in his ability to confront situations; there was a reduction in panic reactions. By 'zoning out' he was able to cope with situations better, but missed out on positive feedback and positive experiences which the situations might offer.

His performance in social situations was enhanced by positive reframing, and exposure to social situations produced some improvement. He was encouraged to rehearse what he might say to his peers on resuming social relationships. Practical problem-solving strategies were suggested – not in terms of specific detail, but rather general lines which he might take. He was encouraged to improve his body language – he tended to hunch up and avoid eye contact.

As therapy progressed he became more talkative and therefore found that people talked more to him. He looked people in the eye and became more confident. In preparation for attending college, he was introduced to adult colleagues in the service and encouraged to chat without feeling under pressure; he was then given positive feedback. The therapist joined in modelling normal social interaction. He was encouraged to undertake a fact-finding survey within the clinic regarding people's anxieties; he believed he was a boring person, but found from the survey that people talk about mundane topics, such as the weather, TV, pets and the bus being late.

Ben (aged 8)

Presenting Problem:
Ben was referred to a social skills group because he was reluctant to try new situations and lacked confidence. He would get very anxious about social situations.

Number of sessions attended: 6/6
Parents did not attend parents group. Ben attempted most of his homework.

Summary of Group Process:
The course covered the following areas:

1. Greetings
2. Compliments
3. Feelings
4. Being bullied
5. Being assertive
6. Generalising skills learnt and coping when nervous

Group Behaviour

Ben was initially a quiet member of the group. He fitted in well with the other two group members but would have struggled in a larger group. He was obviously anxious to begin with but soon settled in to the group. It was difficult to determine his level of understanding. He was reluctant to join in role-plays but managed with a bit of encouragement. He joined in all other activities and was a good group member. He especially enjoyed the group games. However, he learnt more from the discussions than the activities. He became a lot more confident in the group as it progressed.

Ben did not like anything directing at him initially, e.g. questions. He did not like to "*be in the spotlight*". Ben responded well to the structure within the group and appeared to feel more comfortable knowing what was happening throughout the session.

Ben was a lot more accepting when one of the other children did something unexpected than when the facilitator did. For example, he would often not say anything when another group member said something wrong, but would often correct the facilitator if she said something wrong. He coped well when he was asked some difficult personal questions by another group member. He was easily led, at times, by another group member. However, he was easily verbally redirected back on to tasks and his behaviour remained good throughout.

Progress

Ben's social skills improved while in the group. However, it was evident that Ben was unable to generalise his skills to different situations. He appeared to understand the theory behind his social skills and was able to discuss what he should do. However, he was reluctant to practise his skills. Ben's main difficulty was the questions he asked people when trying to get to know them. Instead, of asking personalised questions, e.g. "*What games do you like playing?*", he would ask very specific general knowledge questions, e.g., "*How many moons does the sun have?*" In real life situations, people would probably respond negatively to this and he would get negative feedback from his first encounters with people, thus lowering his confidence and self-esteem. He was encouraged to modify his questions in the group to more acceptable ones but again, he was unable to generalise this idea from one situation to the next.

Conclusions and Recommendations

People around Ben needed to be aware of their own social behaviour and act as a role model.

Ben needed to be helped to generalise his skills to many different situations. This could be done by having conversations with him about how he should act in a specific situation and what skills he needed to use. He needed to be reminded about the skills he required on a regular basis. Ben responded well to being set small aims or goals to complete in social situations. It was stressed that the goals set should be well within his reach and he should be rewarded when completing them. Ben should be gently encouraged where ever possible to integrate himself socially. Any positive experiences should be celebrated.

Ben needed to build his confidence in social situations and the main way this could be done was by exposing himself to social situations. If Ben had a particularly bad time or didn't get a good response from others, he should be given the space to discuss his experience and others should normalise it as much as possible while suggesting how he could do things differently in the future. Ben responded well when this was done in the group.

Ben could correctly say what he should do in social situations; however, in order for him to demonstrate these skills, he required regular, gentle encouragement and reminders to practise whenever possible.

This case highlights the importance of parental input in promoting generalisation and exposure work in treating social anxiety.

References

Bradshaw, J. (Ed.). (2016). *The Wellbeing of Children in the UK.* Policy Press.

Cartwright-Hatton S, Tschernitz N & Gomerersall H, (2005). Social anxiety in children: social skills deficit, or cognitive distortion? *Behaviour Research and Therapy* 43, 131-141.

Cooper PJ & Goodyer I, (1993). A community study of depression in adolescent girls. 1. Estimates of symptom prevalence. *British Journal of Psychiatry, 63, 369-374.*

Coopersmith S, (1967). *The antecedents of self-esteem.* San Francisco. Freeman.

Crick NR & Dodge KA, (1994). A review and reformulation of social information-processing mechanisms in children's social adjustment. *Psychological Bulletin,* 115, 1, 74-101.

Dubicka B, Elvins R, Roberts C, Chick G, Wilkinson P & Goodyer IM. (2010). Combined treatment with cognitive-behavioural therapy in adolescent depression: meta-analysis. *British Journal of Psychiatry, 197, 433-440.*

Elliot, A. J., & Church, M. A. (1997). A hierarchical model of approach and avoidance achievement motivation. *Journal of personality and social psychology, 72*(1), 218.

Erikson E, (1965). *Childhood and Society (Rev. Ed).* Harmondsworth: Penguin.

Esvelt-Dawson K, Wisner K, Unis, AS, Matson, JL & Kazdin AE (1982). treatment of school phobia in a hospitalised child. *Journal of Behaviour Therapy and Experimental Psychiatry, 13, (3) 239-243.*

Forehand R, Neighbours B & Wierson M, (1991). Transition to adolescence: the role of gender and stress in problem behaviour and competence. *Journal of Child Psychology and Psychiatry, 32, (6) 929-937.*

Frame C, Matson JL, Sonis WA, Finikov, MJ & Kazdin AE, (1982). Behavioural treatment of depression in a prepubertal child. *Journal of Behaviour Therapy and Experimental Psychiatry 13, (3) 239-243.*

Frankel F, Cantwell DP & Myatt R, (1996). Helping ostracised children: social skills training and parent support for socially rejected children. In Hibbs ED & Jensen PS, *Psychosocial Treatments for Child and Adolescent Disorders*, APA, Washington.

Goodwin RD, Fergusson DM & Horwood JL, (2004). Early anxious/withdrawn behaviours predict later internalising disorders. *Journal of Child Psychology and Psychiatry 45, 874-883*

Havik, T., Bru, E., & Ertesvåg, S. K. (2015). School factors associated with school refusal-and truancy-related reasons for school non-attendance. *Social Psychology of Education, 18*(2), 221-240.

Heimberg RG, (2002). Cognitive-behaviour therapy for social anxiety disorder: current status and future directions. *Biological Psychiatry*, 51, 101-108.

Henry CS, Stephenson AL, Hanson MF & Hargett W, (1993). Adolescent suicide and families: An ecological approach. *Adolescence 28, (110) 292-308.*

Herbert M (1991). *Clinical Child Psychology: social learning, development and behaviour.* Chichester: Wiley.

Iliffe S, Williams G, Fernandez V, Vila M, Kramer T, Gledhil J & Miller L, (2009). Treading a fine line: is diagnosing depression in young people just medicalising moodiness? *British Journal of General Practice, 59, 156-157.*

Iliffe S, Williams G, Fernandez V, Vila M, Kramer T, Gledhil J & Miller L, (2009). Treading a fine line: is diagnosing depression in young people just medicalising moodiness? *British Journal of General Practice, 59, 156-157.*

Kashdan TB and Herbert J D (2001). Social anxiety disorder in childhood and adolescence: current status and future directions. *Clinical Child and Family Psychology Review, 4, 1.*

Kendall PC, (1992). *Anxiety disorders in youth: Cognitive-behavioural interventions.* London: Allyn & Bacon.

Kendall PC, (1994). Treating anxiety disorders in children: Results of a randomised clinical trial. *Journal of Consulting and Clinical Psychology, 62, 100-110.*

Kinniburgh, K. J., Blaustein, M., Spinazzola, J., & Van der Kolk, B. A. (2017). Attachment, Self-Regulation, and Competency: A comprehensive intervention framework for children with complex trauma. *Psychiatric annals, 35*(5), 424-430.

Kleiner L, Marshal WL & Spivack M, (1987). Training in problem-solving and exposure treatment for agoraphobics with panic attacks. *Journal of Anxiety Disorders, 1, 219.*

Kochanska, G., Brock, R. L., & Boldt, L. J. (2017). A cascade from disregard for rules of conduct at preschool age to parental power assertion at early school age to antisocial behavior in early preadolescence: Interplay with the child's skin conductance level. *Development and psychopathology, 29*(3), 875-885.

La Greca AM & Stone WL (1993). Social anxiety scale for children – revised: Factor structure and concurrent validity. *Journal of Child Clinical Psychology, 22,* (1) 17-27.

La Greca AM and Santogrossi DA, (1980). Social skills training with elementary school students: A behavioural group approach. *Journal of Consulting and Clinical Psychology,* 48, 2, 220-227.

Leary, M. R. (2013). Social Anxiety, Shyness, and. *Measures of Personality and Social Psychological Attitudes: Measures of Social Psychological Attitudes, 1,* 161.

Lewis, S., Crawford, A., & Traynor, P. (2016). Nipping Crime in the Bud? The Use of Antisocial Behaviour Interventions with Young People in England and Wales. *British Journal of Criminology,* azw072.

Links PS, Boyle MH & Offord DR, (1989). The prevention of emotional disorders in children. *Journal of Nervous and Mental Diseases, 177, 85-91.*

Macdonald E, Chowdhury U, Dabney J, Wolpert M and Stein SM, (2003). A social schools group for children: the importance of liaison work with parents and teachers. *Emotional and Behavioural Difficulties,* 8, (1) 43-52.

Masia CL, Klein RG, Storch EA and Corda B, (2001). School-based behavioural treatment for social anxiety disorder in adolescents: results of a pilot study. *Journal of the American Academy of Child and Adolescent Psychiatry,* 40, (7) 780-796.

Mennin DS, Fresco DM, Heimberg RG, Schneier FR, Davies SO & Liebowitz MR, (2002). Screening for social anxiety disorder in the clinical setting: Using the Liebowitz Social Anxiety Scale. *Journal of Anxiety Disorders,* 16, 6, 661-673.

Miers AC, Blote AW, Bokhorst CL and Westenberg PM, (2009). Negative self-evaluations and the relation to performance level in socially anxious children and adolescents. *Behaviour Research and Therapy, 47, 1043-1049.*

Mishna, F & Muskat B, (2004). "I'm not the only one!" Group therapy with older children and adolescents who have learning disabilities. *International Journal of Group Psychotherapy,* 54, (4) 455-476.

Montemayor R, (1990). Continuity and change in the behaviour of non-human primates during the transition to adolescence. In Montemayor R, Adams GR, & Gulotta TP (Eds.) *From childhood to adolescence: A transitional period.* London: Sage.

Moore, E., Gaskin, C., & Indig, D. (2015). Attempted suicide, self-harm, and psychological disorder among young offenders in custody. *Journal of correctional health care, 21*(3), 243-254.

Murray J and Cartwright-Hatton S, (2006). NICE guidelines on treatment of depression in childhood and adolescence: implications from a CBT perspective. *Behavioural and Cognitive Psychotherapy, 34, (2) 129-137.*

Olweus D, (1994). Annotation: bullying at school: basic facts and effects of a school-based intervention programme. *Journal of Child Psychology and Psychiatry, 35, (7) 1171-1190.*

Rutter M, (1986). The developmental psychopathology of depression: issues and perspectives. In Rutter M, Izard CF & Read PB (Eds.) *Depression in young people, 3-30.* New York: Guildford.

Schrader C, Long J, Panzer C, Gillett D & Kornblath R, (1977, December). *An anger control package for adolescent drug abusers.* Paper presented at the 11th Annual Convention of the Association for Advancement of Behaviour Therapy, Atlanta.

Strother DB, (1986). Practical applications of research: Suicide among the young. *Phi Delta Kappan, pp. 756-759.*

Toolan JM, (1980). Depression and suicidal behaviour. In Sholevan GP, Benson RM & Blinder BJ (Eds.) *Treatment of emotional disorders in childhood.* Lancaster: MTP.

Van Dam-Baggen R and Kraaimaat F, (2000). Group Social Skills Training or Cognitive Group Therapy as the Clinical Treatment of Choice for Generalized Social Phobia? *Journal of Anxiety Disorders, 14*, (5) 437-451.

White, S. W., Keonig, K., & Scahill, L. (2007). Social skills development in children with autism spectrum disorders: A review of the intervention research. *Journal of autism and developmental disorders, 37*(10), 1858-1868.

Yule W, Hersov H & Treseder J, (1980). Behavioural treatment of school refusal. In Hersov L & Berg I, (Eds.) *Out of school.* Chichester: Wiley.

Theoretical Introduction

Children and adolescents who are socially anxious, isolated and unassertive are particularly likely to experience bullying either by their immediate peer group or somewhat older and stronger peers. Olweus (1994) defines bullying or victimisation as a situation in which "*A student is being bullied or victimised when he or she is exposed, repeatedly and over time, to negative actions on the part of one or more students*" (p. 1173). Olweus defines a negative action as when someone intentionally inflicts, or attempts to inflict, injury or discomfort on another. In bullying, there is an imbalance of strength or power so that the student who is exposed to the negative actions has difficulty in defending him/herself and is somewhat helpless against the student or students who harass. Olweus distinguishes "direct bullying/victimisation", characterised by relatively open attacks, from "indirect bullying/victimisation" which takes the form of social isolation and intentional exclusion from a group. Olweus (1994) found that boys were more frequently involved than girls as perpetrators of bullying and were more likely to be involved in direct bullying either as perpetrators or victims. Olweus did not find empirical support for the view that victimisation is caused by "external deviations" (unusual appearance, being overweight, being red-haired, wearing glasses etc.). Rather, personality characteristics/typical reaction patterns, in combination with physical strength or weakness in the case of boys, are important for the development of these problems. Nash et al (2001) suggest that for children aged 8-18 years with persisting communication problems associated with cleft palate, learning to be a competent and effective communicator is more pertinent for psychological welfare and quality of life than continuing to pursue improved speech, which may not only be unattainable, but may adversely affect the child's perception of his/her own capabilities.

The typical bullying victim may be characterised as anxious, insecure, cautious, sensitive and quiet (Slonje & Smith,2008). When attacked, they commonly react by withdrawal. They have a negative view of themselves and their situation: they often look upon themselves as failures and feel stupid, shamed and unattractive. They are socially isolated, disinclined to violence. If they are boys, they are often physically weaker. They give a loud and clear message to others that they are insecure individuals who will not retaliate if they are attacked. Such young people are likely to have had some or all personality characteristics from an early age (Wolke & Lereya, 2015). Clearly, such characteristics are likely to be reinforced by repeated peer harassment.

Effective, well targeted social skills training can have a powerful positive effect for such young peoples. By being taught friendship making skills, they can learn to reduce their social isolation. By learning to be appropriately assertive, they can reduce the "victim-type" signals emitted. The feedback received from the peer-group will rapidly improve their self-esteem, which can be further enhanced by cognitive therapy techniques.

"Provocative victims"

Olweus (1994) identifies a smaller group of victims who are characterised by both anxious and aggressive reaction patterns. These students often have problems with concentration, irritate others and are hyperactive. They are likely to provoke negative reactions from large groups of students or an entire class.

It is likely that such young people suffer from a constitutional difficulty such as attention deficit disorder or have difficulty with sensory integration (Sijtsema et al, 2014). They therefore need a careful diagnostic assessment followed up by an individually tailored programme to minimise the effect of their condition on both their study skills and their social life. Such young people may have particular difficulty in listening, conversation skills and "tuning in" to the world of others. As the difficulties are largely behavioural, a behavioural approach in social skills training would be appropriate helpful. In addition, the problem-solving *Stop Think Do*" approach (Beck & Horne, 1992) would be particularly helpful to them in reducing their tendency to offend others through their thoughtless actions. They are also in need of help with friendship making skills and social-perspective taking.

Long-Term Effects of Bullying

Olweus (1994) reports that former victims were more likely than their non-victimised peers, to be depressed and have poor self-esteem in adulthood. His pattern of findings suggested that this was a consequence of early, persistent victimisation. The importance of offering social skills training in adolescence to reverse this trend is therefore underlined. Olweus has also found that self-reported increases or decreases in bullying over time were accompanied by parallel changes in global self-esteem (Olweus & Alsaker, 1991). Kaminski & Fang (2009) have found a link between victimisation by peers and adult suicide. Wolke et al (2012) have carried out a prospective study demonstrating a link between peer victimisation and borderline personality symptoms at 11 years of age. They noted an increased risk of borderline personality disorder symptoms according to self-report and teacher report. Evidence of more severe or chronic exposure to bullying was found to be associated with highly increased odds of developing such symptoms.

Risk Factors

Anxiety and poor social skills are both risk factors for victimisation; Crawford and Manassis (2011) suggest two independent pathways to victimization: firstly anxiety, which independently predicted being victimised and secondly, poor social skills, which predict lower friendship quality and thereby place a child at risk for victimisation.

Fox and Boulton (2005) studied 330 pupils aged between 9 and 11 years from various schools across the UK, who provided self-report, peer and teacher report data. It was concluded that victims were perceived by three different sources to have poor social skills.

Perren and Alsaker (2006) examined social behaviour and peer relationships in 5-7 year old children. The children were classified as victims, bully-victims bullies and non-involved by means of teacher ratings and peer nominations. Compared to non-involved children, victims were more submissive, had fewer leadership skills, were more withdrawn, isolated, less cooperative, less sociable and frequently had no playmates. Bully victims were more aggressive, less cooperative, less sociable and more frequently had no playmates than non-involved children. They suggest that some of these social behaviours may be considered as risk factors; they emphasise the significance of peer relationships and comment that victimised children's lack of friends might make them psychologically and socially vulnerable therefore more prone to becoming easy targets.

In a similar study, Toblin et al (2005) reached comparable conclusions. They examined the social-cognitive and behavioural attributes of children who are concurrently aggressive and victimized by their peers. 240 elementary school children (mean age 9.5 years) completed self-report inventories, a social-cognitive interview and peer nomination inventory. Behavioural adjustment was rated by teachers and school records provided information on academic functioning. Aggressive victims were characterised by impairments in self-regulation, bullies tended to exhibit aggression-related biases in social-cognitive processing, and passive victims were characterised by non-assertive behaviours and low levels of social skill.

Champion et al (2003) suggest that victimised adolescents have subtle difficulties managing confrontation adaptively in a variety of contexts for peer interaction. Pellegrini et al (2010) suggest that in many cases bullying is a form of proactive aggression, used to accomplish goals, such as gaining access to toys or extorting a peer's lunch money.

There is some evidence from the literature that children with Asperger's Syndrome (Sofranoff et al, 2011) and those with autistic traits (Bejerot and Mortberg, 2009) are vulnerable to bullying. There is also evidence that children with Attention-Deficit/Hyperactivity Disorder (ADHD) are vulnerable to peer victimisation (Wiener and Mak, 2009).

Finally, Shakoor et al (2012) in a longitudinal study assessed Theory of Mind in 2232 children at age 5 using eight standardised tasks and identified those that that were involved in bullying as bullies, victims or bully-victims at age 12 using mothers', teachers and children's reports. It was found that poor Theory of Mind at age 5 predicted involvement in bullying in early adolescence. These associations remained for victims and bully-victims when child-specific and family factors were controlled for.

Consequently, there is substantial evidence that enhancing social skills in terms of empathy and perspective taking in early childhood is a useful preventive factor for involvement in bullying at a later stage.

Techniques for Intervention

Behaviour Change

Behaviour change can be achieved by noticing and recording actions or responses, noticing triggers, consequences and setting up a plan to replace less effective actions or responses by more effective behaviours or responses. For example, a victim of bullying may be helped to see that responses which show anxiety make the bullying more likely to recur; a different set of social responses can then be planned.

Friendship Building

The literature clearly indicates that friendship building is a key ingredient to reducing peer victimisation. Erath et al (2010) have found that associations linking social anxiety with loneliness and self-reported victimization were attenuated among early adolescents with more close friendships. Most social skills programmes incorporate elements that support friendship building. Glick and Rose (2011) found that high-quality friendships were linked to emotionally engaged strategies in coping with social stress. Looking at online game-playing, Leung (2011) found that online victimization was negatively related to friendship satisfaction, while online friendship was positively linked to social competence, friendship satisfaction, self-esteem and life satisfaction. Most social skills programmes already incorporate elements that support friendship building and an increased focus on this area would be helpful to support victimised children and adolescents.

Social Skills Programmes

This should be delivered to the victims or those at risk of victimisation. It is proposed that direct intervention with victims or those at risk of victimisation is most appropriate, as there are a number of issues which make intervention directly with the bullies problematical (Pellegrini et al, 2010; Home et al. 2008). Intervention with bullying behaviour is perhaps best undertaken using a systemic approach involving a whole school or institution (Michelson et al, 2013). It is beyond the scope of this book to evaluate such approaches.

DeRosier (2004) tested the efficacy of a generic social skills intervention (S.S.GRIN) for children experiencing peer dislike, bullying or social anxiety. Children were randomly allocated to treatment or no treatment control groups. Results indicated that S.S.GRIN increased peer liking, enhanced self-esteem and self-efficacy, and decreased social anxiety compared to controls. In a well-controlled study, DeRosier and Marcus (2005) tested the long-term effectiveness of a social skills programme for peer-rejected, victimised and socially anxious children, finding positive treatment effects one year after the intervention, including higher social acceptance, increased self-esteem and lower levels of depression and anxiety.

Tierney and Dowd (2000) described the use of social skills groups to help female students with emotional difficulties. Students were identified by their teachers as unhappy and/or friendless. The groups ran for six sessions and covered speaking and listening, friendships, bullying and getting to know themselves and each other.

The authors concluded that while social skills groups can be effective in providing support for young people, schools need continued support to develop the confidence to run them successfully.

Assertiveness Training

Smith et al (2001) affirm that effective programmes should incorporate both assertiveness training and social skills training to assist victimised young people in building and maintaining better quality friendships. Assertiveness training developed initially as an important aspect of behaviour therapy with adults (Liberman, 1975). Assertiveness, involving reasonable self-confidence and a strong sense of self, is an importance aspect of social competence which adolescents need to develop. Lack of assertiveness is frequently a factor in social difficulty.

The assertive individual can stand up for his or her rights in a reasonable manner considering the requirements of the situation, showing an ability to evaluate the various factors involved and generate an appropriate response. The assertive individual possesses the skills which make it possible to enter into new social relationships and to develop and maintain these relationships. Lack of appropriate assertiveness may be shown either by failure to make any response at all in a social situation or by unnecessary aggression which is detrimental to social relationships. Assertive behaviour involves communicating thoughts and feelings clearly in an appropriate tone of voice with firm eye contact. People who are habitually under-assertive often feel angry and frustrated but are prevented by a feeling of anxiety from taking decisive action. Often, as a result of doing this many times, they come to deny that their anger exists. Over-aggressive behaviour would be shown in violent gesture, under-assertive behaviour is denoted by submissive posture; e.g. If someone pushes in front of us in a queue, an assertive approach would involve a polite but firm verbal response, indicating clearly that the offending behaviour is not acceptable and suggesting a change to a more acceptable form of behaviour; going to the back of the queue. An example of unnecessary aggression would be verbal or physical abuse in this context; passive acceptance of the situation would denote under-assertiveness.

Assertiveness training, therefore, is an import part of social skill training and is an effective technique for providing help to adolescents having trouble with a wide range of situations, including bullying.

Cognitive Restructuring

The contents of the mind from moment to moment may be characterised as "thoughts and images" (cognitive products). These thoughts and images provide information to the thinker on internal responses to external events. For example, the victim, seeing the bully in the distance, may think, "Oh Heck here he comes again" experience unpleasant images of the bully's face, or begin to plan an alternative route to avoid the bully.

Correction of Cognitive Distortions

These "thoughts and images" give us a clue to a deeper or more stable layer of cognitive content or subjective thought - beliefs. For example, the victim may believe "*I am no good to anyone and deserve to be bullied*". This determines the thoughts and images which occur in the mind of the victim. These thoughts may be passive and submissive ("*I am going to be bullied*" rather than assertive and proactive "*I can see their game but there is no way I'm going to put up with that!*"

The notion of cognitive process includes a further aspect of the function of mind - the tasks which the mind must carry out. The mind must receive information (e.g. see the bully) and find some appropriate solution, drawing on past experience (e.g. plan an escape or a response to the bully). Hence, faulty cognitive processing may be seen as equivalent to faulty processing of social information.

Using typical CBT approaches, negative attitudes to the self can be adjusted and replaced with positive self-statements. Behavioural experiments in real life will then reinforce changed cognitive operations and build the confidence and self-esteem of the individual.

Baldry and Farrington (2004) evaluated the effect of an intervention programme on the reduction of bullying and victimisation in schools in Rome. The programme consisted of three videos and a booklet that helped students to develop the social cognitive competence skills to understand the negative consequences of aggressive behaviour. Results showed that the programme worked best for older students, but not for younger ones who in some cases reported an increased level of victimisation after the intervention. This finding perhaps highlights the need to supplement social-cognitive input with appropriate assertiveness training to support victims of bullying, particularly in the case of younger children. The option of multi-systemic intervention is discussed further below.

Problem Solving Training

Problem solving skills training may be used to help clients to generate skill in finding solutions to social conflict situations and weigh up consequences of different courses of action. An example is the *Stop Think Do* approach (Peterson, 1992). Traffic lights are used as a metaphor and clients are assisted in talking through a series of stages, such as reviewing options, planning action and monitoring progress. This approach would be helpful in working out useful strategies for coping with bullying. (See Chapter Three for guidance on social information processing.)

Story-Based Social Competence Training

Rahill (2002) compared the effectiveness of story-based and skill-based social competence programmes for the development of social problem-solving and peer relationship skills in children with emotional disabilities. The story-based programme appeared to be beneficial with participants demonstrating increasing levels of social information processing. There are therefore grounds for incorporating a story-based approach in programmes designed to improve social competence in children who are vulnerable to victimisation.

Multi-Systemic Approach

The use of a multi-systemic approach has been demonstrated with children and young people presenting with antisocial behaviour patterns (see Chapter 6). There is scope for the development of such an approach in relation to bullying.

In order to produce change, intervention at the individual level needs to be complemented with work at the level of the family, the school and the social system. Intervention with the bullies as such is problematic. At a clinical level, Kendall et al (1991) have shown how cognitive-behavioural techniques may be used to reduce childhood aggression. However, young people diagnosed with conduct disorder are likely to possess "callous-unemotional (CU) traits" (Kahn et al, 2011) and assessment of such factors using techniques such as the Antisocial Processes Screening Device (APSD; Frick and Hare, 2001) would be important in attempting interventions with bullies who have this characteristic. Such children tend to minimise the extent to which aggression causes victim suffering and openly acknowledge caring less about distress and suffering in others (Pardini and Byrd, 2011). It is suggested that fostering a warm and involved parent-child relationship may help to facilitate the development of empathy for others over time (Kochanska, 1997; Pardini et al, 2007) and that children with CU traits should be rewarded for engaging in prosocial problem-solving during social conflicts with their peers. Interventions should address the tendency of such young people to view aggression as an effective means for dominating others.

It is nevertheless vital to combine preventive approaches at an early stage with problem focused treatment once bullying behaviour patterns have been identified. The possibility of including anger management approaches should be considered. In treating bullying behaviour, relapse prevention and the promotion of generalisation are particularly relevant, because of the high rewards frequently associated with continuance of the inappropriate behaviour pattern.

In terms of larger-scale interventions, The Olweus Bullying Prevention Programme (Limber, 2011) was developed by Olweus in the mid-1980s. Large scale evaluations (Limber, 2011) have provided compelling evidence of the programme's effectiveness in schools. The programme is based on four principles. The programme prescribes specific interventions at the level of individual victims, bullies, classrooms, schools and communities. Adults at school should
   a) Show warmth and interest in their students
   b) Set firm limits to unacceptable behaviour
   c) Use consistent, nonphysical non-hostile negative consequences for violation of rules
   d) Act as authorities and positive role models (Olweus, 1993).

It is essential to have real and effective communication between education, health and social services to intervene both with prevention of bullying and the support of identified victims. Cowie et al (1992) have reviewed research findings and sought to achieve an understanding of the phenomenon of bullying that can be transcribed into practical ways for schools to recognise bullying regimes, the nature of the bullying incident, and how schools might best respond. The problem was tackled as seen through the eyes of the pupils themselves. Interventions included the use of video, drama, story and role-play techniques to develop social skills, assertiveness, ability to participate in group cooperation and sharing.

Schools usually have a bullying policy in place but it is important to see that this is implemented and reinforced. Useful whole-school interventions have been comprehensively described by Rigby (2002) and Suckling and Temple (2002). Educational staff should set up and maintain simple rules of social behaviour and expect these to be observed. All staff involved in supervising through the day should reinforce the same system, emphasising prosocial behaviour and respect for others. Salmivalli et al (2005) have shown that active teacher involvement in implementing an anti-bullying intervention is important for positive outcome. In schools where unruly behaviour is frequent, this is clearly an issue to be addressed. Parents also should be involved via the school system in supporting prosocial behaviour. The partnership of school and parents in this enterprise is vital.

Ttofi and Farrington (2011) carried out a meta-analysis of 44 programme evaluations which showed that in general school-based anti-bullying programmes are effective; bullying decreased by 20-23% and victimisation decreased by 17-20%. More intensive programmes were more effective, as were programmes including parent meetings, firm disciplinary methods and improved playground supervision. Work with peers was associated with an increase in victimization. Parents or carers can be involved in supporting victimised children and adolescents in their social skills programmes and assertiveness development. Anxious children often come from homes with high levels of anxiety and therefore there is scope for family therapy.

Case Examples

Abbie (aged 14)

Abbie was visually impaired and had been diagnosed with moderate learning disabilities, but was currently coping in mainstream school. She was waiting for a place in a residential school for visually impaired children. She had a diagnosis of autism. Her mother had reported that she was experiencing bullying at school.

Abbie was first seen jointly with her mother. The first 20 items of the Social Skills Improvement System (SSIS) parent questionnaire (Gresham & Elliott, 2008) were administered.

Scores of "Seldom" were obtained on three items involving empathy, social communication and assertiveness. This provided the clinician with an up-to-date impression of the client's social skills from the perspective of the parent.

The therapist noted some ideas for future role-plays, e.g. a game involving recognising emotion in others, displaying emotion in frozen "sculpts" and saying "Goodbye" in different tones of voice, taking turns and joining groups, asking for help from a teacher and standing up for a friend.

Therapy

Sessions involved practical work and role-play on greetings, identification of emotion, facial expressions, tone of voice, conversational skills, and responding to the emotions of others. Exercises in "bad listening" were planned. A mirror was used for observation of facial expression. Material incorporating the "bullies" was incorporated after the third session, enabling assertive body language to be practised along with appropriate tone of voice and language. A need for further work on eye contact and gesture was noted.

These interventions enabled the young person to survive in mainstream school until a place at a more suitable residential special school became available. As such they played an important part in the support system for the young person.

References

Baldry AC and Farrington DP (2004). *Aggressive Behaviour*, 30, 1, 1098-2337.

Beck, J. and Horne, D. (1992) 'A whole school implementation of the Stop, Think Do! Social skills training program at Minerva Special School.' In B. Willis and J. Izard (Eds) Student Behavior Problems: Directions, Perspectives and Expectations. Hawthorn, Victoria; Australian Council for Educational Research.

Bejerot S and Mortberg E (2009). Do autistic traits play a role in the bullying of obsessive-compulsive disorder and social phobia sufferers? *Psychopathology*, 42, 3, 170-176.

Champion K, Vernberg E and Shipman K (2003). Nonbullying victims of bullies: Aggression, social skills and friendship characteristics. *Journal of Applied Developmental Psychology*, 24, 5, 535-551.

Cowie H, Boulton MJ & Smith PK, (1992) *Bullying: pupil relationships*. London: Kogan Page.

Crawford AM & Manassis K (2011). Anxiety, social skills, friendship quality and peer victimisation: An integrated model. *Journal of Anxiety Disorders*, 10, 924-931.

Dadds M, Perry Y, Hawes DJ, Merz S, Riddell AC, Haines DJ, Solak E & Abeygunawardane AI, (2006). Attention to the eyes and fear-recognition deficits in child psychopathy. *British Journal of Psychiatry*,189, 280-281.

DeRosier ME & Marcus SR (2005). Building Friendships and Combating Bullying: Effectiveness of SS.GRIN at One-Year Follow-up. *Journal of Clinical Child and Adolescent Psychology*, 34, 1, 140-150.

DeRosier ME, (2004). Building relationships and combating bullying; Effectiveness of a school-based social skills group intervention. *Journal of Clinical Child and Adolescent Psychology*, 33, 1, 196-201.

Erath SA, Flanagan KS, Bierman KL and Tu KM (2010). Friendships moderate psychosocial maladjustment in socially anxious early adolescents. *Journal of Applied Developmental Psychology*, 31, 1, 15-26.

Fox CL & Boulton MJ (2005). The social skills problem of victims of bullying: self, peer and teacher perceptions. *British Journal of Educational Psychology*, June, 313-328.

Frick PJ & Hare RD (2001). *Antisocial process screening device: technical manual*. Toronto, Canada: Multi-Health Systems.

Glick GC & Rose AJ, (2011). Prospective Associations between friendship adjustment and social strategies: Friendship as a context for building social skills. *Developmental Psychology*, 47, 4, 1117-1132.

Goddard SJ & Cross J, (1987). A social skills training approach to dealing with disruptive behaviour in a primary school. *Maladjustment and Therapeutic Education*, 5, 3, 24-29.

Gresham, F., & Elliott, S. N. (2008). Social skills improvement system (SSIS) rating scales. *Bloomington, MN: Pearson Assessments*.

Home AM, Raczynski K, Orpinas P, (2008). A clinical laboratory approach to reducing bullying and aggression in schools and families. In L'Abate LE (Ed):

Toward a science of clinical psychology: laboratory evaluations and interventions. 117-131.

Kahn RE, Frick PF, Youngstrom E, Findling RF & Youngstrom JK, (2011). The effects of including a callous-unemotional specifier for the diagnosis of conduct disorder. *Journal of Child Psychology and Psychiatry*, 53, 3, 227-281.

Kaminski JW & Fang X, (2009). Victimisation by peers and adolescent suicide in three US samples. *Journal of Paediatrics,* 155, 683-688.

Kendall PC, Ronan KR & Epps JJ, (1991). Aggression in children/adolescents: Cognitive –behavioural treatment perspectives. In: Pepler DJ, Rubin KH, Eds. *The development and treatment of childhood aggression.* Hillsdale NJ; Lawrence Elbaum.

Kochanska G, (1997). Multiple pathways to conscience for children with different temperaments. *Developmental Psychology*, 33, 228-240.

Leung NG, (2011). Online game-playing and early adolescents' online friendship and cyber-victimization. *Dissertation Abstracts International*: Section B: The sciences and Engineering. 72/4-b (2467), 0419-4217.

Liberman RP, (1975). *Personal effectiveness: guiding people to assert themselves and improve their social skills.* Research Press.

Limber SP, (2011). Development, evaluation and future directions of the Olweus Bullying Prevention Program. *Journal of School Violence*, 10: 71-87.

Michelson, L., Sugai, D. P., Wood, R. P., & Kazdin, A. E. (2013). *Social skills assessment and training with children: An empirically based handbook.* Springer Science & Business Media.

Nash P, Stengelhofer J, Toombs L, Brown J & Kellow B (2001). National Survey of children aged 8-18 years with persisting communication problems associated with cleft palate. *Child Language Teaching and Therapy,* 17, 1, 19-34.

Olweus D & Alsaker FD, (1991). Assessing change in a cohort longitudinal study with hierarchical data. In Magnusson D, Bergman LR, Rudinger G & Torestad B, (Eds) *Problems and methods in longitudinal research,*107-132. New York, NY: Cambridge University Press.

Olweus D, (1993). *Bullying at school: what we know and what we can do.* Oxford, England: Blackwell.

Olweus D, (1994). Annotation: Bullying at school: Basic facts and effects of a school based intervention programme. *Journal of Child Psychology and Psychiatry, 35*, 7, 1171-1190.

Pardini DA and Byrd AL, (2011). Perception of aggressive conflicts and others' distress in children with callous-unemotional traits: "I'll show you who's boss, even if you suffer and I get in trouble". *Journal of Child Psychology and Psychiatry,* 53,3, 283-291.

Pardini DA, Lochman JE & Powell N, (2007). The development of callous-emotional traits and antisocial behaviour in children: Are there shared and/or unique predictors? *Journal of Clinical Child and Adolescent Psychology, 36*, 319-333.

Pellegrini AD, Long JD, Solberg D, Roseth C, Dupois D, Bohn C and Hickey M, (2010). Bullying and social status during school transitions. In Jimerson SR, Swearer SM & Espelage DL, (Eds): *Handbook of bullying in schools: an international perspective.*

Perren S & Alsaker FD, (2006). Social behaviour and peer relationships of victims, bully-victims, and bullies in kindergarten. *Journal of Child Psychology and Psychiatry*, 47, 1, 45-57.

Peterson L, (1992). Stop-Think-Do: a system based pro-social skills training programme. *Guidance and Counselling, 8*, 2, 24-35.

Rahill SA, (2002). *Dissertation Abstracts International* Section A: Humanities and Social Sciences, 0419-4209.

Rigby K, (2002). *Stop the Bullying: A Handbook for Schools.* Jessica Kingsley.

Salmivalli C, Kaukiainen A and Voeton M, (2005). Antibullying intervention: Implementation and outcome. *British Journal of Educational Psychology, 75,* 465-487.

Shakoor S, Jaffe SR, Bowes L, Ouellet-Morin I, Andreou P, Happe F, Moffitt TE & Arseneault L, (2012). A prospective longitudinal study of children's theory of mind and adolescent involvement in bullying. *Journal of Child Psychology and Psychiatry, 53*, 3, 254-261.

Sijtsema, J. J., Rambaran, J. A., Caravita, S. C. S., & Gini, G. (2014). Peer Selection and Influence in Defending and Bullying: Effects of Moral Disengagement. In *EARA 2014* (pp. N-A). European Association on Research on Adolescence.

Slonje R & Smith PK (2008). Cyberbullying: Another main type of Bullying? Journal of Scandinavian Psychology, 49, 2, 147-154.

Smith PK & Sharp S, (1994). *School bullying: Insights and perspectives.* Routledge.

Smith PK, Shu S and Madsen K, (2001). Characteristics of victims of school bullying. Developmental changes in coping strategies and skills. *Peer harassment in school: the plight of the vulnerable and* victimised, 332-251.

Sofranoff K, Darke E and Stone V, (2011). Social vulnerability and bullying in children with Asperger Syndrome. *Autism,* 15, 3, 355-372.

Suckling A and Temple C, (2002). *Bullying – a Whole-School Approach.* Jessica Kingsley.

Tierney T & Dowd R (2000). The use of social skills groups to support girls with emotional difficulties. *Support Learning,* 15, 2, 82-85.

Tobin R, Schwartz D, Gorman AH & Abou-ezzedine T (2005). Social-cognitive and behavioural attributes of aggressive victims of bullying. *Journal of Applied Developmental Psychology*, 26, 3, 329-346.

Ttofi MM & Farrington DP, (2011). Effectiveness of school-based programs to reduce bullying: a systematic and meta-analytic review. *Journal of Experimental Criminology, 7,* 1, 27-56.

Wiener J and Mak M, (2009) Peer victimisation in children with attention-deficit/hyperactivity disorder. *Psychology in the schools,* 48, 2,116-131.

Wolke D, Schreier A, Zanarini MC & Winsper C, (2012). Bullied by peers in childhood and borderline personality symptoms at 11 years of age: A prospective study. *Journal of Child Psychology and Psychiatry*, 53, 8, 846-855.

Wolke, D., & Lereya, S. T. (2015). Long-term effects of bullying. *Archives of disease in childhood*, archdischild-2014.

Chapter 9   INTERVENTIONS IN EDUCATION

In this chapter, theories of social and emotional competence are reviewed and approaches to educational intervention are described and evaluated.

What is Emotion?

Izard (2009) describes "emotion feeling" (the direct or basic experience of emotion as *"a phase of neurobiological activity, the key component of emotions and emotion-cognition interactions"* (page 1). At a more complex level, Izard refers to "emotion schemas" – *"dynamic emotion-cognition interactions that may consist of momentary/situational responding or enduring traits of personality that emerge over developmental time"* (page 1). In Izard's conception, *"emotion utilization, typically dependent on effective emotion-cognition interactions, is adaptive thought or action that stems, in part, directly from the experience of emotion feeling/motivation and in part from learned cognitive, social and behavioural skills"* (page 3). However, emotion schemas may become maladaptive and may lead to psychopathology when learning results in the development of connections among emotion feelings and maladaptive cognition and action (Leahy, 2015).

In terms of Crick and Dodge's model of social information processing (Crick & Dodge 1995; see Chapter 3), it would be consistent with a response to an immediate social situation, but also with characteristic ways of responding (enduring traits of personality) which might predictably determine a certain type of behavioural response. These could at times be maladaptive, e.g. consistent attribution of negative attitudes to others could result in aggressive behaviour patterns. A tendency to perceive certain social situations as threatening could lead to avoidance and thereby to loss of opportunity to develop appropriate social skills which might deal effectively with those situations.

In terms of cognitive-behavioural therapeutic approaches, these maladaptive schemas could be conceptualised as dysfunctional core beliefs tending to lead to unhelpful emotions and behaviours. This is a slightly different conception from Izard's (2009) presentation which stresses that the maladaptive schema comes as a package, triggered by basic (biological) emotion feeling but enhanced by "learned cognitive, social and behavioural skills". Nevertheless, the faulty beliefs which cognitive behaviour therapy seeks to correct could be an example of learned cognitive skills being applied in a maladaptive fashion. The practice of checking for "automatic thoughts" in cognitive-behaviour therapy suggests that the approach may be tapping into some basic "emotion feeling".

The concept of "traps" in Cognitive Analytic Therapy (Shannon & Pollock, 2017) is consistent with Izard's notion of maladaptive emotion schemas (Izard, 2009). In psychodynamic approaches, response to new situations in terms of past relations with significant others could at times be seen as an example of maladaptive emotion schemas, if maladaptive behaviour results. In systemic work (work with families), shared maladaptive emotion schemas could result in unhelpful shared "narratives."

If emotions are triggered by biological reactions, what causes these reactions and how are they influenced by cultural and social factors? Ekman et al (1969) noted that certain facial expressions of emotion were recognisable across cultures. Elfenbeim and Ambady (2002) carried out a meta-analysis of emotion recognition within and across cultures. They found while emotions were universally recognised at better-than-chance levels, accuracy was higher when emotions were both expressed and recognised by members of the same national, ethnic, or regional group. Mesquita and Frijda (1992) found evidence for both culturally specific and universal emotional processes, concluding that *"global statements about cross-cultural universality of emotion, or about their cultural determination, are inappropriate."* There is evidence, then, for a cultural component in the expression and recognition of emotion.

Ellsworth (1994) notes that while *"human beings belong to the same species; our brains, our bodies, our autonomic nervous systems, our hormones and our sense organs are similarly constructed"*; on the other hand, *"cultures differ in their definitions of novelty, hazard, opportunity, attack gratification and loss, and in their definition of appropriate responses. They differ in their definitions of significant events and in their beliefs about the causes of significant events, and these differences affect their emotional responses"* (p25). Ellsworth (1994) proposes that emotions result from the way in which people interpret or appraise their environment. Thus, she attributes the rarity of anger among the Utku (Briggs, 1970) to a *"failure to appraise negative events as the fault of other people in the first place"* (p 41). The suggestion here is that there is a cognitive component in the culturally toned experience of emotion.

Frijda and Messquita (1994) argue that the stepped approach to appraisal is universal. Both cultural and biological processes would be involved. Frijda and Messquita (1994) propose a sequential model for such an appraisal process, as follows:

1. Event Coding
2. Appraisal
3. Action readiness
4. Physiological changes/Behaviour.

It could be concluded that emotion is the biologically driven but culturally determined response of an individual to events being perceived as relevant by that individual. Children and young people therefore, in the development of social skill, need to ensure that their emotional responses operate in an adaptive and not a maladaptive manner. It is important to learn to reflect on these processes, as emotions can be "raw", intense and disturbing at times.

Social and Emotional Learning

Rhoades et al (2009) note that social and emotional learning is a key developmental task during early childhood. They found that children who demonstrated better inhibitory control were more likely to be rated higher by teachers on social skills and lower on internalising behaviours. They suggest that early identification of inhibitory difficulties may be beneficial for targeting children at risk for maladaptive outcomes. Given the contribution of environmental experience to the development of inhibitory control skills (Rhoades et al, 2009) they conclude that there are many opportunities to intervene during early childhood.

Sollars (2010) has argued against the need to develop preventive programmes on social and emotional competence, if the adults caring for young children can be role models providing a stable and positive effect on children during one the most crucial and vulnerable periods of life. Teachers are accustomed to a directive role and therefore may need specific coaching to adopt a more "therapeutic" approach. It may be helpful to train teachers in in-depth assessment of social skills through questionnaire, direct interviewing and observation enabling them to have deeper understanding of the skills and process to be developed.

Conner & Fraser (2011) evaluated a preschool social-emotional skills training programme, focused on improving the social information processing and emotion-regulation skills of children. A group based parenting education component was included in the programme. Participants were recruited from four preschools in high-risk neighbourhoods within a large metropolitan area. Comparing the intervention group with a wait list control, the gain scores of the intervention group were significantly better in relation to academic competence, social competence, depression and aggressive behaviour. Caregiver gain score were also significantly better in the intervention group, with relation to parental bonding, child supervision, communication and developmental expectations.

Ashdown & Bernard (2012) investigated the effect of a social and emotional learning skills curriculum ('You Can Do It!' Early Child Education Programme) on the social-emotional development, well-being and academic achievement of 99 preparatory and grade 1 students. Structured lessons with explicit direct instruction designed to teach confidence, persistence organisation and resilience were provided thrice weekly over 10 weeks and supplemented by "a variety of additional social and emotional teaching practices". Classes randomly assigned to this programme were compared to a control group. The results indicated a significant positive effect on social and emotional competence, a reduction in problem behaviours and an increase in reading achievement for the lower achieving students.

Cohen and Mendes (2009) examined the stability of pre-schoolers play behaviour and the relations between emotion regulation, receptive vocabulary and trajectory of social competence deficits. They concluded that without effective interventions, at-risk children were likely to exhibit consistently poor social competence over time. Implications for early intervention and prevention targeting specific behavioural and peer problems were discussed. Richardson et al (2009) investigated whether a social skills programme "Connecting with Other: Lessons for Teaching Social and Emotional Competence" would assist students with disabilities in inclusive classrooms. The results indicated reasonable assurance that the students did grow in the skill areas and were able to interact positively with their peers.

Niles et al (2008) reported a longitudinal study to explore whether social or emotional outcomes for high-risk early adolescent youth that attended an established preventive intervention (Chicago Child-Parent Centre Preschool Programme) were moderated by individual, family and programme variations. They concluded that children experiencing a large number of environmental risk factors (e.g. high family risk status and low parental education levels) were more likely to benefit from programme participation was supported.

Pahl and Barrett (2007) examine the importance of developing social-emotional competence during the early years of life and discuss universal intervention approaches within the classroom, advocating the Fun Friends programme. Pahl and Barrett suggested a universal approach, because such interventions have the potential to be of benefit to a wide range of children (Greenberg et al 2001). Their approach seeks to involve children, families, teachers and schools in the intervention process with the aim of promoting wellness and providing children and families with the skills to conquer challenge and adversity. They seek to develop a "resilient mind-set", Goldstein and Brooks, 2005, have noted that such a mind-set may be an outcome of positive clinical interventions. Pahl and Barrett (2007) envisage that in modern social conditions most children will feel pressure at some stage in their life and therefore it is important to provide these children with the effective coping skills needed to "bounce back".

The Fun Friends programme is a downward extension of the Friends for Life programme, which was found useful in providing a cognitive- behavioural approach for children aged 7-18 years (Barrett et al, 1996; Barrett et al, 2001). Noting the work of Arend, Gove & Sroufe (1979), who found that 5-year-olds who can think of more options for interpersonal problems are more likely to display ego-resiliency, Pahl and Barrett (2007) conclude that *"having multiple ways to solve problems provides flexibility that creates an ego-resilient individual"* (p86). Research has demonstrated the importance of developing strong interpersonal cognitive problem-solving skills (ICPS) early in life (Shure & Spivack, 1982; Shure & Aberson, 2005).

The Fun Friends programme includes cognitive-behavioural components such as cognitive restructuring (changing unhelpful thoughts to helpful thoughts and graded exposure to fears). It covers 5 major areas of social-emotional learning: developing a sense of self, social skills, self-regulation, responsibility for self and others, and prosocial behaviour. Each of 10 sessions involves 10-15 minutes learning activities supported by experiential play-based activities (role play, puppets, games, story-telling). Parents attend parent information sessions and a *Family Learning Adventure* workbook is provided for parents and children. Preliminary results indicated children who received the programme had significantly decreased anxiety scores from pre to post intervention (Pahl & Barrett, 2010). At 12 month follow-up improvements were found for anxiety, behavioural inhibition and social-emotional competence. In the absence of a comparison group it was not possible to establish whether the changes could have been due to natural maturation. Teacher report indicated that some positive changes occurred immediately after completion of the programme.

Frey et al (2005) evaluated the effect of a school-based social-emotional competence programme (Second Step), linking children's goals, attributions and behaviour. The study ran for two years with children aged 7-11 randomly allocated to an intervention or control group. Intervention children were more likely to prefer prosocial goals, required less adult intervention and behaved less aggressively. Teacher ratings of social behaviour showed improvement over time. Holsen Smith & Frey (2008) replicated 'Second Step' in a "real world" implementation in Norway, and assessed the effects after one year of intervention. The programme had significant positive effects on social competence for boys and girls in Grades 5 and 6.

Trentacosta and Izard (2007) assessed the relation between emotion and academic competence. Their study focused on two aspects of emotion competence, emotion knowledge and emotion regulation as students entered elementary school. They noted that *the indirect relations between emotion regulation and academic competence through attention to academic tasks supports efforts to enhance emotion regulation in early childhood so that children can pay better attention and become less distracted as they enter elementary school*" (p87).

There is a sound evidence base supporting the practice of using structured and planned interventions to develop social and emotional competence in educational contexts.

Techniques for Intervention

PATHS
Kusche & Greenberg (1994) introduced the PATHS (Promoting Alternative Thinking Strategies) Curriculum. The PATHS Curriculum is founded on Psychoanalytic Developmental Theory and Developmental Neuropsychology. Children are encouraged to identify and express their feelings in a safe manner, whilst experiencing interactive environmental conditions of respect, caring, empathy and knowledge. Using knowledge of how the brain operates based on recent research, children are taught methods of self-control based on their level of development, e.g. young children are taught to "do Turtle" (A wise old Turtle teaches a little Turtle a special way to calm down when angry – stop, take a breath, say what the problem is and how you feel; Kusche and Greenberg, 2001). The complete PATHS curriculum consists of six volumes of lessons, a teacher's instructional manual, several posters, a set of photographs, Feeling Face cards, and all of the pictures needed for each lesson. Kusche & Greenberg, (2001) have conducted three controlled studies with three different populations (deaf children, mainstream children and children with special needs) and noted improvements in terms of increasing protective factors (e.g. recognising and understanding emotions, understanding social problems) and reducing maladaptive outcomes (e.g. decreased symptoms of anxiety and depression, decreased aggressive and disruptive behaviour).

I CAN PROBLEM SOLVE
Spivack and Shure (1974) identified a set of interpersonal thinking skills which appeared to be related positively to social adjustment and interpersonal

competence. These later became known as Interpersonal Cognitive Problem Solving (ICPS) skills. *Alternative Solution Skills* refers to the ability to think of alternative solutions to real life problems. *Consequential Thinking* refers to the ability to think of alternative outcomes (e.g. of an impulsive or aggressive action). *Social Perspective Taking* involves understanding that others might have a different viewpoint. *Means-ends or Sequential Thinking* involves the ability to plan a series of steps towards a stated interpersonal goal. "I Can Problem Solve" was developed as an educational approach, based on developing key words and phrases such as *"may" "might" "is" "is not" "same" "different"* and using problem solving as far as possible as a method for dealing with real life situations. Teachers are encouraged to ask questions, getting children to think, rather than giving commands. ICPS is planned to dovetail with the developmental needs of preschool children (Shure, 1992) such as language development and perceptual development. The *Raising a Thinking Child Workbook* (Shure, 2000) provides an opportunity for parents to get involved. The approach has been used widely in schools and validated in service evaluations, e.g. by reducing maladaptive outcomes (Shure & Glaser, 2001).

Emotional Literacy Development in Educational Contexts

A range of materials are available to promote emotional literacy in the Early Years (Ripley & Simpson, 2007). This reflects an increased awareness of the importance of enabling children to label their own emotions and understand the emotions of others. Social perspective taking will also be enhanced by these exercises. An increasing use of perspective taking could result in dealing with real life issues in schools, and teachers can learn to role-model appropriate expression of feeling. Readers may wish to refer to the appendix to Chapter 4 where there are useful exercises in emotion recognition suggested within the group work.

CASEL

The Collaborative to Advance Social and Emotional Learning (CASEL; Graczyk et al, 2000) provides regular updates on "quality school-based prevention programmes" covering such issues as programme content, opportunities to practise social and emotional skills, tools for monitoring implementation, and evidence of effectiveness.

An example of such a programme is Open Circle (CASEL Guide, 2013). This programme is designed to equip teachers with effective practices for creating a cooperative classroom community, establishing positive relationships, and effective approaches to problem solving within the classroom. Initial training for the Open Circle programme spans 4 training days and two 2-hour on-site training sessions. There are 34 structured sessions covering relationship building, communication skills, understanding and managing emotions, and problem-solving. Each lesson includes new concepts, opportunities to practise and homework. There is a unit on bullying and components provide support for schoolwide implementation and family involvement.

Evaluation in a small study (n=152) provided evidence of increased positive social behaviour and reduced conduct problems. PATHS, I CAN PROBLEM SOLVE, and the Incredible Years series are similarly evaluated (CASEL guide, 2013). The programmes recommended and regularly evaluated by CASEL are very systematic and highly structured.

A Manualised Approach
The Social Skills Handbook (Hutchings, Comins & Offiler, 1991) can be a useful resource book for teaching social and emotional skills to all age groups, especially for practitioners in special needs schools and mainstream secondary schools. This may be useful for practitioners who are not able to invest in a full-length, highly structured programme. This book would be a useful supplement to the materials suggested in Chapter 4.

Effective Implementation
The road to hell, as we know, is said to be "paved with good intentions"; similar comments apply to educational interventions which are planned but not implemented effectively. An antidote to this problem is provided by Rathvon (2008). Interventions need to be planned logistically, with maximum impact but minimum disruption to existing school environments and procedures. Observations of an objective nature need to be made pre and post intervention in order to measure true change. Rathvon offers a wealth of detail on interventions which have been found effective in all educational areas, including behavioural change and improving social competence. Rathvon notes that low-achieving young people from less advantaged backgrounds may identify with a peer group which values aggressive behaviour and rejects conventional school norms. Rathvon (2008) argues that social skills groups and withdrawal situations have not been proven effective with this population and advocates an approach of producing behaviour change and increase in social competence through classroom procedures which reward positive behaviour.

The *Banking Time* intervention (Rathvon, 2008) is designed to promote positive teacher-student relationships. "*Brief sessions of focused, non-directive interaction are designed to convey messages of safety, predictability and support for exploration rather than evaluation of performance*" (p130). The notion of "Banking" implies that time is spent on building up positive relationships which will be useful if stressful situations occur at a later date. Full details of the method are provided by Rathvon (2008). The intervention may be used with individuals or small groups.

In the *Good Behaviour Game* (Rathvon 2008) a class is split into teams; over a specified period, demerits are deducted, and the team with the fewest demerits is rewarded at the end of the period. Rewards may be 'faded' or delayed as the behaviour standards increase. The game may then be introduced without notice. It is important always to specify the time period and ensure the contingencies are provided as specified. Consistency is vital. This is a good example of *group contingency reinforcement*. Again, full details are provided, along with variations. The method is well validated.

In *Positive Peer Reporting* (Rathvon, 2008) students who are either isolated because of poor social skills or rejected because of negative behaviours are selected by an objective procedure (see Chapter 2). The class is trained in giving appropriate specific compliments to peers, reporting "something positive the person did or said during the day". At the beginning of the class period one or two of the "target students" and two or three others (selected randomly) are nominated as "stars for the day". Students are invited to offer compliments to the "stars". The number of compliments is kept as a tally, earning points towards a group reward. This is a good example of individually focused social skill intervention in the classroom context, supported by group contingency reinforcement. The procedure provides anonymity for the targeted individuals, thus avoiding the risk of embarrassment or stigma.

Peer-Monitored Self-Management (Rathvon, 2008) may be used to decrease *"inappropriate verbalisations such as calling out, talking to peers and making noises"* (p346). Students work in groups and individuals who violate class rules are encouraged to move a dot from a green section to a blue section on a good behaviour chart which is provided on each table. For ten seconds a peer may remind the transgressor, after which the teacher places the dot in a red section. At the end of the session the teacher notes which groups have at least one dot remaining in the green section and a preponderance of dots in the blue section as opposed to the red section. Rewards are provided to winning groups. Here group contingency reinforcement is used to promote both peer monitoring and self-management. There is a risk of negative peer-to-peer interaction in this approach and therefore this tendency has to be firmly discouraged from the outset.

In *Loop the Loop* (Rathvon, 2008) group contingency reinforcement is used to reduce problem behaviour in the playground. Staff are collectively involved in developing an appropriate set of rules (such as "Keep your hands and feet to yourself") and social skills (such as "how to join a game"). These rules are explained to the students and taught by modelling and role play. Playground supervisors are given a positive role in organising and supervising group games. Playground supervisors are equipped with brightly coloured wrist-sized elastic loops which are allocated to students for following the behaviour rules and exhibiting the suggested social skills. A specified time-out location is used for seriously offending students. On return to the classroom students place their loops in a can on the teacher's desk and may be praised for earning them. When the can is full a group reward is provided. The whole-system approach to detailed preparation and planning followed by careful implementation is a strong feature of this method.

Happy Face Charts (Rathvon, 2008) may be used to enhance compliance along with precise requests in preschool children. Students' names are placed on a chart and each student has a Happy Face allocated. The Happy Face is retained as long as the student is compliant with the rules which have been explained and presented on a Rules Chart, such as "Do what you are told the first time you are told." The Happy Face is removed if the student fails to comply with a request. The request is then repeated and if the student complies the Happy Face is restored. If a second repetition does not produce compliance the student is sent to a designated time-out chair for 4 minutes. At the end of the activity rewards are delivered to students displaying Happy Face cards. Happy Face cards are restored to all students at the beginning of the next activity. As standards of behaviour increase, the frequency of reinforcement may be reduced.

Case Example

Research (Bulkeley & Cramer, 1994) yielded insight into the skills required for interventions designed to promote social and emotional competence in educational settings. The aim was to develop two slightly differing group interventions, and compare the difference in outcome. In a straight intervention, the process is somewhat simpler but still requires very detailed planning and design.

In the assessment process, a range of measures were used including the Spence Social Situation Questionnaire, sociometry, and measures designed to obtain teacher evaluation (see Chapter 2 of this volume). Measures were also used to obtain family evaluation of the social and emotional skills of students. Outcome measures were used to determine the effectiveness of the model in a given context, so that the school or organisation could benefit from "action research". In times of economic stringency, this may be particularly important, in terms of providing economic justification for the intervention.

Both teachers and members of clinical staff were involved in delivery of social skills groups. It was noted that more coaching would have been beneficial for the teaching staff. The students selected for groupwork were balanced, as far as possible, for gender, and for type of problem, so that students who lacked confidence in social situations were mixed with those who tended to act out unreflectively and thereby alienated others. It is not suggested that this is the only way to compose groups, but it is certainly useful to consider the type of problem carefully in setting up groups (See Chapter 2). In the author's experience, with young adolescent groups it may be useful to have a blend of personalities within the group. The less inhibited students may be more ready to participate in role play and enjoy action games and techniques. The task of the group leaders will be to draw out the quieter students.

Researchers (Bulkeley & Cramer, 1194) facilitated four social skills groups of ten sessions each with 12 year olds who had been selected by the assessment process as in need of such an input. A manualised approach was employed for the intervention to preserve the validity of the research. The groups were structured with motivational games, teaching content, roleplay practice and homework assignments. The typical content of the groups is to be found in the appendix of Chapter 4. Interventions took place within the school timetable in the afternoon. To meet outside school time may have caused more difficulties around attendance, motivation and students experiencing fatigue by the end of the day.

The project did demonstrate that the school as an organisation can usefully host a programme of social skill assessment, intervention and evaluation and respond positively to outside influences. One possible way forward would be for institutions involved in training teachers to develop appropriate interventions and offer expertise to schools in return for placement of student teachers who are training on their courses. A group approach could be enhanced by taking individual needs into account. This is certainly a useful point to bear in mind when planning educational interventions.

References

Arend G Gove FL & Sroufe LA (1979). Continuity of individual adaptation from infancy to kindergarten: A predictive study of ego-resiliency and curiosity in pre-schoolers. *Child Development,* 50, 950-959.

Ashdown, DM & Bernard ME (2012). Can explicit instruction in social and emotional learning skills benefit the social-emotional development, well-being, and academic achievement of young children? *Early Childhood Education Journal,* 39, 6, 397-405.

Barrett PM Duffy a Dadds M & Rapee R (1996). Family treatment of childhood anxiety: A controlled trial. *Journal of Consulting and Clinical Psychology,* 64, 333-342.

Barrett PM Duffy A, Dadds M & Rapee R (2001). Cognitive-behavioural treatment of anxiety disorders in in children: Long term (6 year) follow-up. *Journal of Consulting and Clinical Psychology,* 69, 1, 135-141

Briggs JL (1970). *Never in anger: Portrait of an Eskimo family.* Cambridge, MA: Harvard University Press

Bulkeley R and Cramer D (1994). Social skills training with young adolescent: group and individual approaches in a school setting. *Journal of Adolescence,* 17, 521–531

CASEL. www.casel.org/guide.

Cohen, JS & Mendes JL (2009). Emotion regulation, language ability and the stability of preschool children's peer play behaviour. *Early Education and Development,* 20, 6, 1016-1037

Conner, NW & Fraser MW (2011). Preschool social-emotional skills training: A controlled pilot test of the Making Choices and Strong Families Programmes. *Research on Social Work Practice,* 21, 6, 699-711

Developmental Psychology 30, 3, 310-320

Ekman P Sorenson ER & Friesen WV (1969). Pan-cultural elements in facial displays of emotion. *Science,* 164 86-88

Elfenbein HA & Ambady N (2002). On the universality and cultural specificity of emotion recognition: A meta-analysis. *Psychological Bulletin,* 128, 2, 203-235

Ellsworth PC (1994). Sense, Culture and Sensibility. In S Kitayama (Ed) *Emotion and Culture:* Washington: American Psychological Association

Frey, KS Nolen SB Edstrom LVS & Hirschstein MK (2005). Effects of a school-based social-emotional competence programme: linking children's goals, attributions and behaviour. *Applied Developmental Psychology,* 26, 171-200.

Frijda NH & Mesquita B (1994). The social roles and functions of emotions. In S Kitayama (Ed) *Emotion and Culture:* Washington: American Psychological Association.

Goldstein S & Brooks RB (2005). *Handbook of resilience in children.* New York: Kluwer Academic/Plenum.

Graczyk PA Matjasco JL & Weissberg RP 2000. The role of the collaborative to advance social and emotional learning (CASEL) in supporting the implementation of quality school-based prevention programs. *Journal of Educational and Psychological Consultation,* 11, 1, 3-6

Greenberg MA Domitrovitch C & Bumbarger B (2001). The prevention of mental disorders in school-aged children: Current state of the field. *Prevention and*

Treatment, 4, Article 1. Retrieved from http://journals.apa.org/prevention/volume 4/pre004001a.html

Holsen I Smith B H & Frey KS (2008). Outcomes of the social competence program *Second Step* in Norwegian Elementary Schools. *Schools Psychology International Copyright.* London: Sage.

Hutchings S, Comins J & Offiler J 1991. *The Social Skills Handbook: Practical activities for social communication.* Speechmark Publishing Ltd.

Izard, CE (2009). Emotion theory and research: Highlights, unanswered questions and emerging issues. *Annual Review of Psychology,* 60, 1-25

James, W. (1884). What is emotion. *Mind,* 4, 188-204

Kusche CA & Greenberg MT (1994). *The PATHS (Promoting Alternative Thinking Strategies) Curriculum.* Seattle: Developmental research and programmes.

Kusche CA & Greenberg MT (2001). PATHS in your classroom: Promoting emotional literacy and alleviating emotional distress. In Cohen J (Ed.) *Caring classrooms/Intelligent schools: the social emotional education of young children.* New York: Teachers College Press.

Leahy, R. L. (2015). *Emotional schema therapy.* Guilford Publications.

Mesquita B & Frijda NH (1992). Cultural variations in emotions: A review. *Psychological Bulletin,* 412, 179-204.

Niles, MD Reynolds AJ & Roe-Sepowitz D (2008). Early childhood intervention and early adolescent social and emotional competence: Second–generation evaluation evidence from the Chicago Longitudinal Study. *Educational Research,* 50, 1, 55-73.

Open Circle: see 2013 CASEL Guide; www open-circle.org

Pahl KM & Barrett PM (2007). The development of social-emotional competence in preschool-aged children: An introduction to the Fun FRIENDS Programme. *Australian Journal of Guidance and Counselling* 17,1, 81-90

Rathvon N (2008). *Effective school interventions: Evidence-based strategies for improving student outcomes.* Guildford Press.

Rhoades, BL, Greenberg, MT & Domitrovitch CE (2009). The contribution of inhibitory control to pre-schoolers' social-emotional competence. *Journal of Applied*

Richardson RC Tolson H Huang T-Y Lee Y-H (2009). Character education: Lessons for teaching social and emotional competence. *Children and Schools,* 31,2, 71-78.

Ripley K & Simpson E (2007). *First steps to emotional literacy.* London: Routledge.

Shannon, K., & Pollock, P. (2017). Cognitive Analytic Therapy. *Individual Psychological Therapies in Forensic Settings: Research and Practice,* 41.

Shure MB & Aberson B (2005). In S Goldstein & RB Brooks (Eds), *Handbook of resilience in children* (373-394). New York: Kluwer Academic/Plenum.

Shure MB & Glaser A-L (2001). I Can Problem Solve: a cognitive approach to the prevention of early high-risk behaviours. In J Cohen (Ed) *Caring classrooms/Intelligent schools: the social emotional education of young children.* New York: Teachers College Press.

Shure MB & Spivack G (1982). Interpersonal problem solving in young children: A cognitive approach to prevention. *American Journal of Community Psychology,*10, 341-356.

Shure MB (1992). *I Can Problem Solve (ICPS): An interpersonal cognitive problem-solving programme* [preschool]. Champaign, IL: Research Press.

Shure MB (2000). *Raising a thinking child workbook.* Champaign, IL: Research Press.

Sollars V (2010). Social and emotional competence: Are preventive programmes necessary in early childhood education? *The International Journal of Emotional Education,* 2,1, 49-60.

Spivack G & Shure MB (1974). *Social adjustment of young children.* San Francisco: Jossey-Bass.

Trentacosta CJ & Izard CE (2007). Kindergarten children's emotion competence as a predictor of their academic competence in first grade. *American Psychological Association,* 7, 1, 77-88.

Chapter 10   OVERVIEW

The aim of this chapter is to review key points which have emerged from each of the foregoing chapters, and to provide new insights relevant for the current decade.

Chapter 1
Chapter I looked at a range of social skill development approaches which could be deployed to assist different age groups with different types of social skill difficulty. Theoretical underpinning -incorporating research on non-verbal skills, social learning theory, assertiveness, and friendship-making skills- was briefly summarised. It was suggested that in general, programmes should be comprehensive, carefully designed and geared to individual need.

While video presentation, adult and peer modelling may be best for younger children, comprehensive group programmes can certainly be helpful for adolescents. In addition to behavioural training using role-play and feedback methods, interpersonal problem solving using vignettes can be helpful and there is scope for modernising this approach using up-to-date technology.

Chapter 2
In Chapter 2 a number of assessment procedures were examined. This form can be used with individual children/adolescents, teachers and parents/carers and the results can be collated. Results can be collated and the data can be used both for problem identification and measurement of treatment outcome. Assessment approaches should be multiple; this is particularly true for children and young people.

The same applies in the case of the Social Skills Improvement System (SSIS; Gresham and Elliott, 2008) which is described in detail in Chapter 2. Obtaining data from child, parent/carer and teacher in the same assessment provides a useful profile. The data provide helpful insights for planning specific individual interventions.

Assessment approaches should also be specific. For example, role-play assessment would be useful for a programme in building assertiveness and developing negotiation skills, as role-play (accompanied by detailed feedback and ideally video playback) is a key treatment activity for working on these areas. Clinicians should not be afraid to develop their own subjective checklists to assess role-play for their own teaching purposes; this may be useful in identifying problems and assessing outcome even if more robust data would be required for a formal research paper.

In a clinical context, assessment procedures may be creative. In assessing social skill in autism, it may be useful to observe pairs of clients cooperating in a Lego construction. Of course, standardised measures are useful but it is often hard to enable autistic children and young people to understand the reason for an artificially constructed situation. Observing clients in action whilst informally assessing a range of variables may be preferable.

Assessment should sample a range of behaviours. For example, in the Vineland Adaptive Behaviour Scales (Cicchetti et al, 2013; Sparrow et al, 2005), communication skills are broken down into three categories (Receptive, Expressive and Written) as are socialisation abilities (Interpersonal Relationships, Play and Leisure Time and Coping Skills.) Adaptive levels and age equivalents are provided for each of these Sub-Domains (categories). Consequently, the Vineland Scales, which may be used to elicit information from a parent or carer, enable clients to be assessed in terms of a range of reliable norms for specific social skills; this is also true of the Strengths & Difficulties Questionnaire (Goodman, 1997). While the Vineland Scales rely on adult evaluation (by a parent, carer or teacher), the Strengths and Difficulties Questionnaire enables the young person's own evaluation to be considered. In a comprehensive evaluation, both forms of assessment could be used. If the assessments are carried out interactively, it is possible to note spontaneous comments which give more insight into the child's thought processes.

It may be useful to assess experiences such as peer victimisation and bullying through a semi-structured interview. A qualitative assessment of this nature may provide useful information to supplement quantitative data for planning therapeutic input.

Overall approach to assessment of social skills should be flexible, using both standardised procedures and innovative approaches as the situation demands.

Chapter 3
In Chapter 3 (regarding social skill interventions), it is emphasised that the substance of the evidence base supports three types of useful approach which can complement each other throughout the social skills arena.

Firstly "micro-skills" (the small change of social intercourse, involving both non-verbal behaviour such as eye contact, facial expression and gesture, and conversational skills) may be studied, using video, role-play, and feedback to assess, maintain and enhance skills. Video feedback may be powerful both for demonstration and reinforcement of micro-skills.

Secondly, the focus could shift to specific areas, depending on the client group. Certain skills such as negotiation and assertiveness can be usefully embedded in a group format with a focus on encouraging client skills through role-play. Group members can contribute to the observation and learning process by commenting positively on specific skills noted during role-play. A tightly structured format is useful in helping the group to maintain focus. Again, video playback can be a useful adjunct to this area of skill development.

Thirdly, at a more cognitive level, a problem-solving approach can be used, presenting problems in the form of a vignette and encouraging clients to brainstorm solutions. These can then be tried out either in role-play or real life. This approach can be used either with individuals or groups.

These three approaches can be used in combination in accordance with client need and available resources. It is generally useful to begin a course with some work on micro-skills.

Chapter 4
Chapter 4 provides a basis for the technique of facilitating social skills groups. These approaches have been tried and tested in clinical practice. Setting up groups requires a range of skills, but can be extremely rewarding for practitioners and effective for producing change in clients. Many issues need to be considered, such as assessment, selection and matching treatment goals to client needs. Group-work at its best provides an ideal opportunity for young people to undertake behavioural experiments, as advocated by Cognitive Behaviour Therapists. Role-play enables skills and assertive behaviours to be practised and the group's positive feedback can provide natural reinforcement for social learning. Negative social cognitions and negative self-image can be counteracted by the positive, cooperative approach encouraged in the groups.

Chapter 5
Moving to Part Two, autism spectrum disorder and other communication disorders are addressed in Chapter 5. Bishop et al (2016) have found that subdivisions of social-communication impairment are relevant in planning assessment and treatment of autism spectrum disorder. Their three-factor model differentiates impairments in "Basic Social-Communication" (e.g. eye contact, facial expression, gestures) from impairments in "interaction quality". If this model is adhered to in future research on social skill interventions in autism, it may be more feasible to demonstrate effective social skill interventions with this client group. The distinction between micro-skills and higher-order social skills may be useful in developing a range of approaches which can be assessed separately in terms of their effectiveness.

Chapter 5 demonstrates approaches to social skill development have considerable promise for children and young people with communication difficulties including those found to be on the autistic spectrum. Autism is characterised by difficulties with communication, social interaction and understanding the world of others. Social skill development has great potential for helping clients with autism to progress in these areas. Practitioners are encouraged to be both innovative and enthusiastic in employing the approaches that are described in detail in this chapter. More able and verbal clients can be helped by highly structured groups enabling them to develop listening ability, empathy, sharing behaviour and friendship-making skills. Less able clients may respond well to group process involving sensory input and shared experience of music.

LEGO Therapy (Owens et al, 2008) has been found extremely useful in clinical practice. The task of jointly completing a Lego construction project provides useful motivation. Assigning clients, a specific role in the construction of a model generates a high level of cooperation and shared attention. It has been found useful to use an observational rating scale to record clients' progress in terms of gain social skills with increasing exposure to the Lego Therapy. The dimensions assessed (FengFeng & Tami, 2013) are as follows:

- Responding and Maintaining Interaction
- Leading or Initiating Interaction
- Nonverbal Communication
- Turn-taking
- Ending Conversations
- Understanding Another's Perspective
- Empathising with Others

There is also a good evidence base for appropriate specialised group social skills training delivered by competent therapists. Freitag et al (2016) have reported on SOSTA-FRA, a highly structured, manualised cognitive-behavioural group-based social skills training programme for children and adolescents with high functioning autism. The technique combines operant behavioural and cognitive techniques together with computer-based and social learning methods of teaching and practising social skills in a group context. Due to the defining pervasive social interaction problems in patients with HF-ASD, group-based social skills training has been recommended as the treatment of choice. Previous studies suffered from severe methodological and practical limitations, also little is known about moderating variables. Freitag et al (2016) aimed to overcome these limitations by conducting a large multicentre randomised-controlled trial testing the efficacy of a manualised group-based intervention in HF-ASD in children and adolescents with a large age range, and additionally exploring moderating treatment factors. This study shows post intervention efficacy of short-term ASD-specific add-on group therapy on parent-rated social responsiveness predominantly in male children and adolescents with HF-ASD.

The manual used by Freitag et al (2016) for this research (Social Skills Training – Autism, Frankfurt; SOSTSA –FRA) includes many of the suggestions for good practice contained in this book. An anger management component is included to aid in emotional self-regulation. Specific procedures are used to promote maintenance and generalisation.

With the less able clients, the technique known as Intensive interaction is a useful way of initiating a lively rapport with others. The worker replicates the sounds and behaviours generated by the client, enabling rapport to be established. In social skills terms, if language is not present, it is natural to fall back on non-verbal forms of communication to enable clients to develop as social beings.

A range of techniques in use with non-verbal clients is discussed in Chapter 5. In terms of input to preschool children with severe autism, Pickles et al (2016) have reported on the long-term follow-up of a randomised controlled trial of parent-mediated social communication therapy (PACT). By analysing the outcomes after six years, they have provided evidence to support the potential value of adding the PACT intervention to educational services for young children with autism spectrum disorder. Pickles and his colleagues suggest that their positive long-term outcomes stemmed from optimisation of parent-child social communicative interactions, which then become self-sustaining.

Chapter 6
Progressing to Chapter 6, evidence has been gathered to demonstrate that in helping children to develop prosocial skills (and inhibit antisocial behaviours), it is likely to be useful to combine a traditional social skills approach (to encourage listening skills, friendship-making behaviour and empathy) with anger management skills (which control impulsiveness and help to regulate emotions). Both these areas can be usefully addressed using group treatment formats,

Chapter 6 has also emphasised the importance of systemic issues in responding to challenging behaviour. It is consistent with the social skill development approach to focus on both assessment and therapy at multiple levels, including the individual, family and school. Every level of social experience is important. Research on multi-systemic therapy has demonstrated the efficacy of intervening at a number of levels simultaneously. This model can be usefully deployed to enhance social skill development.

In developing useful strategies to reduce challenging behaviour it is important to look at the development of prosocial skills in tandem with self-control behaviours and emotional self-regulation. The application of a social development approach informed by cognitive behavioural therapy is particularly important in this regard. Social skills training may be helpful for increasing prosocial behaviours and building healthy peer relationships (Klahr & Burt, 2014).

The research on parent training presented by Webster Stratton and colleagues (2001) shows the value of helping parents to plan effective strategies to support children and young people in developing prosocial patterns of behaviour. Webster –Stratton and her colleagues have also reported on direct behavioural work with children with conduct problems (Webster-Stratton et al, 2004) including social skills and problem-solving training.

With reference to ADHD, Klahr & Burt (2014) comment that *"Evidence suggests that youth with comorbid ADHD and conduct disorder (CD) are as responsive to standard behavioural parent training as are youth with conduct disorder alone"* (p 1303). Further, the authors recommend the inclusion of *"intervention strategies such as social skills training and cognitive-behaviour therapy to address mood and/or anxiety problems, and collaboration with teachers in implementing an Individual Education Plan (IEP) along with standard parent-management training"* (page 4). Social skill training is envisaged as part of a package designed to support children and young people to improve management of their emotions, increase self-control and generate more empathic and prosocial behaviour. It is not expected on its own to reduce antisocial behaviour, although an anger anagement component may be particularly effective in that direction.

With respect to conduct disorder, Klahr & Burt (2014) opine that "a *focus on aggressive and rule-breaking symptoms, respectively, seems very likely to provide useful information.*" They draw a distinction between "*physically aggressive (fighting, hitting, bullying, defiance) and non-aggressive rule-breaking (stealing, lying, vandalism) dimensions of CD/antisocial behaviour*" (p1303). Klahr & Burt (2014) note that young people who exhibit high levels of rule-breaking might benefit from interventions focused on self-control and delay of gratification during adolescence, particularly within peer contexts; they suggest that a careful analysis of peer relationships might therefore be useful in planning intervention.

It is evident that recent research supports the notion that, although social skills development is not a solution for challenging behaviour in children and adolescents, it can form a useful ingredient of a suitable integrated programme designed to be helpful for this client group. Assessment of peer friendships, development of skills in social cognition including the decoding and encoding of signs of emotion, development of social problem solving skills and anger management training may all play a part, to name but a few examples.

Chapter 7
Moving to Chapter 7, in relation to anxiety there is now useful evidence indicating that social skill assessment can be deployed as part of an Interpersonal Therapy (IPT) programme with adolescents (Spence et al, 2016). Significant improvements in social skills and social relationships were noted. In future, approaches integrating IPT with traditional CBT-based social skills training may be found useful in treating anxious and depressed adolescents. It is likely that Social Skills Training in the forms described in this book will be a useful adjunct for more "in-depth" approaches.

Recent research has highlighted the importance of early intervention to anticipate and prevent the incidence of Social Anxiety Disorder. Humphries et al (2016) noted that early life stress was associated with poorer social functioning. They found an association between high levels of early life stress with both greater levels of social problems and an attentional bias away from fearful facial expressions. They concluded that attentional avoidance of fearful facial expressions may be a developmental response to early adversity and link the experience of early life stress to poorer social functioning.

Nikolic et al (2016) have researched autonomic arousal in social situations. They found that children of parents with lifetime social anxiety blushed more during socially challenging tasks than children of parents without social anxiety. They conclude that heightened autonomic activity is a characteristic of social anxiety already during early childhood. Referring to Chapter 2, it is likely that the neglected/withdrawn group of children experiencing social skill difficulty may be at risk of developing social anxiety.

Chapter 8
With reference to Chapter 8 recent reports of cyber bullying highlight the importance of developing useful computer-based techniques; those employed by Beaumont and Sofranoff (2008) in the Junior Detective Training programme may be particularly useful in this area.

Chapter 9
Chapter 9 demonstrates the relevance of Social Skill Development approaches in mainstream education, highlighting the importance of emotional literacy and what has been called "emotional intelligence" in the educational process and reporting on various projects developed in different countries to promote this approach. Examples are provided of how individually focused social skill interventions may be applied in the classroom context, supported by group reinforcement.

References

Beaumont R & Sofranoff K (2008). A multi-component social skills intervention for children with Asperger syndrome: The Junior Detective Training Programme. *Journal of Child Psychology and Psychiatry, 49,* 743-753.

Bishop, SL, Havdahl KA, Huerta M & Lord C (2016). Subdimensions of social-communication impairment in autism spectrum disorder. *Journal of Child Psychology and Psychiatry,* 57:8, 909-916.

Cicchetti, D. V., Carter, A. S., & Gray, S. A. (2013). Vineland adaptive behavior scales. In *Encyclopedia of autism spectrum disorders* (pp. 3281-3284). Springer New York.

Fengfeng K & Tami I (2013). Virtual Reality Based Social Interaction Training for Children with High-Functioning Autism. *Journal of Education Research*, 106, 6, 2013.

Freitag, CM, Jensen K, Elsuni L, Sachse M, Herpetz-Dahlmann B, Schulte-Ruther Martin, Hanig S, von Gontard A, Poustka L, Schad-Hansjosten T, Wenzl C, Sinzig J, Taurines R, Geissler J, Kieser M, & Cholemkery H (2016*).* Group-based cognitive behavioural psychotherapy for children and adolescents with ASD: the randomised, multicentre controlled SOSTA – net trial. *Journal of Child Psychology and Psychiatry*, 57:5, 596-605.

Goodman, R. (1997). The Strengths and Difficulties Questionnaire: a research note. *Journal of child psychology and psychiatry*, *38*(5), 581-586.

Gresham, FM, & Elliott SN (2008). Social Skills Improvement System: Rating Scales Manual. Minneapolis: Pearson.

Humphreys KL, Kirkanski K, Colich NL, & Gotlib IH (2016). Attentional avoidance of fearful facial expressions following early life stress is associated with impaired social functioning. *Journal of Child Psychology and Psychiatry, 57:10,* 1174-1182.

Klahr AM & Burt SA (2014). Practitioner Review: Evaluation of the known behavioural heterogeneity in conduct disorder to improve its assessment and treatment. *Journal of Child Psychology and Psychiatry, 55:12,* 1300-1310.

Nikolic M, de Vente W, Colonnesi C & Bogels SM (2016). Autonomic arousal in children of parents with and without social anxiety disorder: a high-risk study. *Journal of Child Psychology and Psychiatry, 57.9,* 1047-1055.

Owens GGY, Humphrey A & Baron-Cohen S (2008). LEGO therapy and the Social Use of Language Programme: An evaluation of two social skill interventions for children with High Functioning Autism and Asperger Syndrome. *Journal of Autism and Developmental Disorders,* 38, 1203-1214.

Pickles A, Le Couteur A, Leadbitter K, Sparrow SS, Cicchetti DV & Balla DA (2005). Long-term symptom reduction following a randomised controlled trial of preschool autism treatment. *The Lancet*, 2016. Vineland-2: Survey Forms Manual. USA: Pearson.

Spence, SH, O'Shea G, & Donavon CL (2016). Improvements in Interpersonal Functioning following Interpersonal Psychotherapy (IPT) with adolescents and their association with change in depression. *Behavioural and Cognitive Psychotherapy, 44,* 257-272.

Webster-Stratton, C, Reid, MJ & Hammond M (2001). Social skills and problem-solving training for children with early-onset conduct problems: Who benefits? *Journal of Child Psychology and Psychiatry, 42,* 943-952.

Webster-Stratton, C, Reid, MJ & Hammond M (2004). Treating Children with early-onset conduct problems: Intervention outcomes for parent, child and teacher training. *Journal of Clinical Child and Adolescent Psychology: The Official Journal for the Society of Clinical Child and Adolescent Psychology, American Psychological Association, Division 53, 33,*105-124.

Printed in Great Britain
by Amazon